WHAT WORKS IN GIRLS' EDUCATION

WHAT WORKS IN GIRLS' EDUCATION

Evidence
for the
World's Best
Investment

GENE B. SPERLING *and* **REBECCA WINTHROP**

With **CHRISTINA KWAUK**

Foreword by MALALA YOUSAFZAI

BROOKINGS INSTITUTION PRESS
Washington, D.C.

Copyright © 2016
THE BROOKINGS INSTITUTION
1775 Massachusetts Avenue, N.W., Washington, D.C. 20036
www.brookings.edu

The Brookings Institution is a private nonprofit organization devoted to research, education, and publication on important issues of domestic and foreign policy. Its principal purpose is to bring the highest quality independent research and analysis to bear on current and emerging policy problems. Interpretations or conclusions in Brookings publications should be understood to be solely those of the authors.

Library of Congress Cataloging-in-Publication data is available.
978-0-8157-2860-3 (pbk. : alk. paper)
978-0-8157-2861-0 (epub)
978-0-8157-2862-7 (pdf)

9 8 7 6 5 4 3 2 1

Design and Composition by Chris Krupinski

To our mothers

Doris Sperling, for 50 years as an education pioneer
for equity and for assessing and teaching every child as
an individual, for founding the Family Learning Institute,
for improving the lives of countless students, and for being
a hero to her children, grandchildren, and husband.

Kathryn Winthrop, for loving, supporting, and empowering
her daughters; for being a role model, showing that it is never
too late to pursue your dreams and that success is possible as
a woman in a man's world; and for making the world a
better place through her preservation of our cultural heritage.

CONTENTS

63 CHAPTER 3. GLASS HALF FULL: THERE HAS
BEEN REAL PROGRESS, BUT A GIRLS' EDUCATION
CRISIS REMAINS

101

CHAPTER 4. WHAT WORKS: A CATALOGUE OF EVIDENCE ON ADDRESSING GIRLS' EDUCATION NEEDS

190

CHAPTER 5. FIVE COMPELLING CHALLENGES FOR THE NEXT DECADE

LIST OF FIGURES

LIST OF BOXES

Voices

Definitions

A Note on the Evidence

A Good Example

ACKNOWLEDGMENTS

Ten years ago, the Center for Universal Education, while based at the Council on Foreign Relations, produced *What Works in Girls' Education: Evidence and Policies from the Developing World,* a compendium of the latest evidence on girls' education coauthored by Barbara Herz and Gene B. Sperling. We start by thanking Barbara Herz not only for the intensive work she did over a decade ago coauthoring that book, but also for her decades of scholarship on girls' education and the degree she inspired so many people—including many top policy officials—to understand the importance of educating all girls everywhere. This book builds on that volume, capturing the learning from the past decade of scholarship, program innovations, policy experimentation, and evaluation on the topic of girls' education. We hope that it will be just as useful as the first volume and serve as a guide to key topics for interested nonexperts and a catalogue of the latest data on what works to advance girls' education for those who are helping to meet this global challenge.

We especially want to thank Malala Yousafzai for her interest in this book and for speaking out on behalf of all the girls in the world who are struggling to get an education. We greatly appreciate the Malala Fund's support in disseminating the results of this book, and we are deeply indebted to Meighan Stone for her ongoing collaboration on issues of girls' education.

Many thanks to all those who provided invaluable guidance and input during the writing of this book. In particular, we are hugely indebted to those who reviewed drafts, shared their experiences and materials, and gave helpful suggestions—including Maria Andrawis, Zama Coursen-Neff, Julia Dicum, Caitlin Fowler, Nora Fyles, Dakmara Georgescu, Dileni Gunewardena, Maki Hayashikawa, Jennifer Hills, Catherine Howgego, Abid Hussain, Khadim Hussain, Maysa Jalbout, Lucy Lake, Cynthia Lloyd, Yolande Miller-Grandvaux, Shirley Miske, Kjersti Okkelmo, Alisa Phillips, Stephanie Psaki, Jamila Razzaq, Nicolas Reuge, Pauline Rose, Rosemary Rugamba-Rwanyange, Suman Sachdeva, Urvashi Sahni, Mioko Saito, Marni Sommer, Lakshmi Sundaram, Frances Vavrus, and Judith-Ann Walker. We are also grateful to our colleagues at the following organizations for providing collective feedback: the Africa Network Campaign on Education for All, FHI 360, the Forum of African Women Educationalists, the Global Partnership for Education, and Plan International.

We owe special thanks to Christina Kwauk, a skilled researcher with a doctorate in comparative and international development education, who throughout the writing of this book has demonstrated incredible professionalism and good humor. When we started the research for this book there was no plan to put her name on the cover, but after the tremendous contribution and insights she made we felt it was both fitting and deserved. We also want to extend our thanks to the very able research assistance we received from Romina da Costa, Elena Losada, Bridget McElroy, Eileen McGivney, and Emily Richardson. We would also like to thank Alfred Imhoff for his strategic advice and excellent assistance in finalizing this book, and to Renee McAlpin and Andrea Holcombe for their assistance in reviewing the final text. We are particularly grateful to our colleages at the Brookings Instititution and the Brookings Institution Press whose guidance and support were instrumental in bringing this book to fruition: Steven Bennett, William Finan, Jenifer Gamble, Valentina Kalk, Neil O'Reilly, and Janet Walker.

Finally, we want to thank our families—(Allison, Miles, Nina, Derick, and Samantha for Gene) and (Santiago, Nico, Jean-Marc, and Anna for Rebecca)—for their support and endless patience with us as we finished this book.

FOREWORD

My story is not of one girl but of many. It is the story of Malala from Pakistan. It is the story of the sisters I have met from Syria and Nigeria who have been denied an education or been targeted for going to school. It is the story of millions of sisters who I do not know by name, but who continue to struggle for what should rightfully be theirs—a safe, free, quality education that allows them to fulfil their dreams and transform the places in which they live.

Every girl, no matter where she lives, no matter what her circumstance, has a right to learn. Every leader, no matter who he or she is or the resources available to him or her, has a duty to fulfil and protect this right. Unfortunately, many leaders are not taking this responsibility seriously. They spend their money in other ways. They identify the problem as too large, or the solutions as unclear, or the girls who miss out as deserving less than their own sons and daughters.

Getting millions of girls into school in the next 15 years may seem impossible but it is not. The challenge is significant but the world does not lack the funds or the knowledge to achieve 12 years of free, safe, quality primary and secondary education for every girl—and every boy.

We have shown how the necessary funding can be found. This book now shows what works to support girls' education and helps us understand why. It also makes it clear that the world cannot achieve a sustainable, peaceful, and prosperous future without investing in girls' education.

The world's leaders have just opened the door on a new future by agreeing to a set of ambitious goals for our people and planet. But these will not be achieved without investment in girls' education. How can we all succeed when half of us are held back?

This is why this book is needed now. To help us meet the ambition set out in the new Sustainable Development Goals. To help us understand how we can overcome the barriers to girls' education which have stood for too long without adequate understanding, challenge, or action to overcome them. To show the world's leaders that girls' education is not only the right thing, but the smart thing to do if we are to meet the new future they have opened to us.

This book shows clearly what girls and women themselves have known across generations: *the world cannot afford to NOT educate its girls.* Girls' education is the key to our new and better future. The key to increased health, prosperity, and security. If the world's leaders truly want to invest in this future then they must deliver on their promises and start investing in books, in education—in hope for girls who have too often been left behind.

Girls are desperate to learn and to lead. I have met many of my brave sisters who every day encounter incredible obstacles to education, including war, poverty, and even personal attacks. Yet their knowledge for learning is never overwhelmed and they continue to show up. It is time that our commitment, determination, and action mirrors and honors theirs. This book helps us understand how it can.

It helps us understand what we must do together to see the last girl forced to marry rather than go to school, to work rather than learn, to be denied an education because her family cannot afford it, or fear for her safety when she leaves for school. It helps us understand how girls who beat the odds and show up for school can receive the education they deserve, the education that will allow them to learn, grow and become leaders in their communities.

This book also reminds us that the world has set its ambition for education too low for too long and shows how we can help girls stay in school for longer. A quality basic education is a first and necessary step but if we are to truly see the power of girls to transform our world we must aim higher and secure a full course of primary *and* secondary education for every girl. As my father always believed for me and as I now believe for every girl, basic education begins to unlock girls' potential but secondary education provides them with the wings to fly: to transform not only their lives but the lives of their families and their communities.

This book shows the world that it must do more for girls' education if it is to secure the future it wants. It also shows how this can be done from primary through secondary school. But the reason I welcome this book above all else is because it shows us that any efforts to get all girls into school will not work unless they address the violence and conflict that can stop girls from learning.

This summer, as I said "goodbye" to my life as a child on my 18th birthday, I stood with girls who had been forced to leave their country and flee to Lebanon, girls who had been forced to leave not just their homes but their schools. But they refused to leave their education. To them the right to an education was just as basic as the right to food or water. Yet the world is failing them by failing to protect this right.

If we are to see our world transformed by educated and empowered girls then we have to end violence against girls whose only crime is wanting an education—not just the violence of conflict but the violence of forced marriage, of child labor, of targeted attacks, of assault or abduction in the classroom. This book helps us understand how we can do so.

I am proud that the Malala Fund is a partner with the Center for Universal Education at the Brookings Institution and with Gene Sperling, its founder, and Rebecca Winthrop, its current director, who are authoring this book. The future of girls globally depends on all of us working together, across cultures and our differences, joining together in this common cause. I'm grateful for their hard work, which they have undertaken for decades.

It is my hope that the evidence this book presents encourages our leaders to match the courage, determination and ambition of girls who struggle daily to realize their right to an education. The challenge is significant but the knowledge and funding are available to meet it. All that is needed is the action. I believe that we can and will educate every girl. I hope that you will join us.

Malala Yousafzai
Student, Nobel Peace Prize Laureate, and Co-Founder of the Malala Fund

CHAPTER 1

Introduction

A s Malala implies in her moving foreword to this book, there should not be a need for a book like this on the evidence for the benefits of girls' education. For many, the idea that any child could be denied an education due to poverty, custom, the law, or terrorist threats is just wrong and unimaginable. Period. End of story. Indeed, those of us who have worked to make the case for girls' education with evidence, statistics, and case studies know well that the millions of people around the world who recoiled at hearing of girls being kidnapped in Nigeria, or shot in Pakistan, or threatened in Afghanistan simply because they wanted an education did not need a book of evidence to know it was wrong. They did not need academic studies or policy analyses to know that little girls should have the same chances as their brothers to learn; to contribute to their families, communities, and nations; and to make good on their dreams.

And yet, we know that a thorough understanding of the evidence on why girls' education matters and of the evidence on what works in educating girls is undeniably essential. We understand that in virtually every nation, resources are scarce and that those arguing for a greater investment in girls' education must come to the table with not only a soft heart but also hard-headed evidence on why the returns from investing in girls are so high that no nation or family can afford *not* to educate their girls. This book is for those who want to understand this evidence. It is designed to provide easy and one-stop access to hundreds of studies on girls' education for any academic, expert, nongovernmental organization (NGO) staff member, policy-maker, or journalist seeking to dive into the evidence and policies on girls' education. But it is also designed and written for the concerned global citizen who simply wants to better understand the issues and do their part in working for high-quality girls' education around the world. (This is the second time that the Center for Universal Education has sponsored the writing of such a book. An earlier version of this book was also produced from the Center in 2004, with the coauthorship of longtime girls' education champion and expert Barbara Herz. Eleven years later, we felt that the proliferation of new studies, new developments, and new issues demanded a second book, which we are proud to roll out, together with Malala and the Malala Fund, along with the documentary on her fight for girls' education.)

The Power of Evidence and Girls' Education

Whether you are an expert or a generalist and concerned citizen, we think you will find that there are two things about the evidence on girls' education that are both striking and profound:

- *First, the evidence is extensive on education for girls in poor nations.* The sheer magnitude of evidence is undeniable. There are few if any policy areas in the world where the evidence is so deep and sweeping as are the findings that support a far greater global commitment to girls' education.

- *Second, girls' education is the world's best investment with the widest-ranging returns.* What the evidence contained in this book makes so clear are the vast, wide-ranging, and multifaceted returns from investing in girls' education. Thus, this second aspect is why we believe that girls' education is the best investment that can be made anywhere in the world. In advanced nations, we are used to hearing the case for why education in general contributes to wages, growth, and upward mobility. These returns from education are just as strong in poorer nations as well. But what makes girls' education in developing nations truly the investment with the highest return in the world is the degree to which it leads to better outcomes in not only the traditional economic areas of growth and incomes but also in its positive impact in areas like reducing rates of infant mortality, maternal mortality, child marriage, and the incidence of HIV/AIDS and malaria, along with its positive impact on agricultural productivity, resilience to natural disasters, and women's empowerment. In chapter 2, this book breaks down the evidence by categories in all these areas.

"Especially Girls": Never Forgetting the Boys

One challenge in writing a book on girls' education is the danger of giving the impression that the crisis in education in many poor nations is just a girls' issue. Nothing could be further from the truth. The percentage of boys completing a high-quality secondary degree program in many developing nations, especially when they are from poor or rural regions, is usually higher than girls but is still disturbingly low. And increasingly, in both developed and some developing nations, we are seeing places and ages where educating boys is becoming more challenging than educating girls. The authors of this book are, respectively, the founder and the current director of the Center for *Universal* Education, where "universal" means everyone—girls and boys, middle class and poor, urban and rural, those with disabilities and those without. No one with whom we have ever worked would be satisfied with achieving "gender equity" if it simply meant that both boys and girls were stuck at an equal level of low and inferior educational completion and learning. It is just as heartbreaking and tragic to witness boys seeing their spirits and often future prospects crushed by being denied the chance for an education or being forced into unacceptable child labor. And we know as well that the subject matter of girls' education will never be solved if it is seen as just a gender issue or a challenge to be addressed only by women. At the national levels, men and women in leadership positions must see this as an economic, health, and moral imperative. And even at the family level, we know that, for example, the miracle of Malala was in part made possible by a father who at every step of the way supported his daughter's education, advocacy, bravery, and leadership.

"Education is the most powerful weapon which you can use to change the world."

Nelson Mandela, Former President of South Africa and Nobel Peace Prize Laureate

So when we call for girls' education, we are essentially calling for high-quality, universal education—but especially for girls. Why "especially"? There are at least three reasons. First, though there are exceptions as mentioned above, in most cases girls are being educated at lower rates and are completing less education than boys—so quite simply, for girls the gap is larger and the problem is greater. Second, while the benefits for a boy child and girl child in terms of their earnings and job prospects may have an equal impact on their education, it is girls' education that produces the exceptional amount of multifaceted gains in areas like health and infant mortality mentioned above. And third, around the world girls and women still face exceptional and disturbing discrimination and subordination that boys and men do not face. This makes a focus on girls' education especially important, both because of the need for additional interventions to overcome those discriminatory barriers and the more serious negative outcomes—like child marriage—that are more likely when girls are not educated, but also because of the need for education to empower women with the tools they need to fight for gender equality within their families, communities, and nations.

Girls' Education: Progress and Crisis

One place we struggled in writing this book was how to portray the subject matter of chapter 3: the state of girls' education. Our struggle had two sources. The first source was the fact of real improvement in girl's education; since the Education for All (EFA) and Millennium Development Goals (MDGs) were set forth—and even since the first edition of this book was published, in 2004—there has been significant and impressive progress. The number of girls out of primary school has been virtually cut in half, and adolescent girls and women are completing more years of school than ever before. This progress over a period of fifteen years has been the result of extraordinary efforts by girls, local and national leaders, dedicated community and international NGOs, foundations, and scholars—and thus of course was not something that should be underplayed.

The second source of our struggle was the fact that this book must make clear that the state of girls' education is still more of a crisis than a situation ready for congratulations. This is especially true of girls who face multiple disadvantages—because they come from a large and poor family; because they live in a rural area; because they face discrimination due to their ethnicity or a disability; or because they are caught up in violence or humanitarian emergencies.

We also share the view expressed by Malala in her Nobel Peace Prize acceptance speech that we cannot claim success simply because a low bar was set for our aspirations. We have always said that the MDG of universal primary education by 2015 was simultaneously the world's most ambitious and pathetic goal. It is ambitious because in 2000, there were 100 million children out of school and progress seemed far away. But it was pathetic because no serious advocate or scholar ever thought that primary education was high enough of a global aspiration for educating girls or boys. Universal primary education should always be viewed as a crucial and necessary step for a high-quality education—*not as the destination*. In chapter 3, we describe the progress made and gaps that remain in the quest for a more important and consequential goal: *universal high-quality secondary education*.

Furthermore, we know that while the MDG aimed at universal completion, the goal has never been about just getting kids into classrooms but about how to help more girls and boys achieve the true learning they need to succeed at all aspects of their lives. *Thus, we make clear in this book that the goal for girls' education can be nothing less than a high-quality secondary education.*

A Commitment to the Evidence on What Works

We also know that even in the most advanced and well-off nations, educators and policymakers struggle to understand which educational methods and policies are most effective and which do not work at all. That is why there must be an evidentiary laser focus on what works for attendance, learning, and female empowerment in developing nations. The reason for the evidence-based focus of this book is not simply to convince policymakers of the wisdom of investing in girls' education; it is equally aimed at ensuring that we are continually learning from and thus reexamining and experimenting with what works best both to get girls into schools and to ensure they are learning in the classroom. In girls' education, as in most human endeavors, this is a dynamic rather than static process. New developments and new studies shed light on older understandings. Many of the initial studies have focused on those interventions that could lower the real and perceived costs, indirect costs, and opportunity costs of parents choosing to educate their girls.

Certainly, we have learned that charging per-pupil fees is particularly harmful to the cause of girls' education. Around the world, parents of large and poor families, when forced to pay a fee for each child, will often choose to educate only their boys. Eliminating fees and reducing additional costs for school uniforms and books, along with hidden fees, can clearly make a major difference in attendance. In recent years, there has been an increasing policy and academic focus on scholarships and cash transfers that are conditioned on school attendance—indeed, both Mexico and Brazil have had national policies in these areas. However, the global community has also learned from experience that simply reducing fees or instituting compulsory education without a commensurate commitment to ensuring a supply of high-quality teachers, classrooms, and books and supplies can lead to severly overcrowded classrooms and a deterioration in quality, making clear the need to design both access and quality strategies together.

Studies continue to show that schools a long distance away from the communities where girls live can be a significant deterrent to both primary and secondary education, and that closer schools with more community engagement can be an important solution. Between the first book in 2004 and this current book in 2015, we have also seen some studies raise questions about the importance of interventions like latrines and other aspects of what were considered girl-friendly schools—showing the need for constant reexamination and reevaluation of the evidence and assumed understandings. Likewise, new evidence has shown new areas where girls' education brings high returns, such as in resilience to natural disasters and the management of the coming effects of climate change.

In chapter 4, we catalogue the evidence on what works by subject matter, giving the reader both the key findings and the exact citations to the authors and publications of the top studies and evaluations of education interventions. We realize that such a cataloging of evidence does not read like a thrilling spy novel. But we heard repeatedly from policymakers, academics, journalists, students, and those seeking to simply learn about girls' education that in the first *What Works in Girls' Education* book, the act of simply bringing together the evidence-based literature into one organized chapter was very useful. For this new book, we kept many of the best studies but sought to add the considerable amount of impressive new research that has taken place during the last decade.

Five Compelling Challenges

Although we want to stress that there is still more work to be done to ensure that the MDG of universal primary education by 2015 is met, we also believe that it is important for the global community to place a special focus on five future challenges: (1) to achieve actual learning and a high-quality education; (2) to enable girls to complete secondary education and to address the learning needs of out-of-school adolescent girls; (3) to help girls overcome violence and conflict; (4) to assist girls make school-to-work transitions; and (5) to empower girls and women through education.

1 Quality Learning

Some who are skeptical about the movement toward universal education have expressed two criticisms—that advocates of universal education have been focused only on attendance and not learning and a high-quality education; and that it might have been better to move more slowly on universal access until there was more certainty that large inflows of children into schools would not strain efforts for high-quality learning. We do not agree with either of these contentions, for two reasons. First, serious education advocates have always sought not to just boost enrollment and attendance but also to ensure completion and effective learning. The reality is that too often it was easier for national policymakers to go without the revenues from fees than to carefully plan and pay for larger percentages of their youth to attend school. Second, no one in the United States or other wealthy countries would ever recommend that we allow half our children to be denied an education so that we can ensure there will be adequate resources for the other half to get a higher-quality education. Likewise, we would never take this position for children in other nations.

However, this does suggest that we must ensure that one of the five major future focuses is learning and a high-quality education. For this one area, we should point out that the same policies and interventions that are best for girls are also best for boys. In other words, well-trained teachers, teaching methods that work for students at all levels, a high-quality and accessible curriculum, and a focus on ensuring early basic reading and mathematics skills help provide a high-quality education to all children.

Nonetheless, considering the obstacles and biases against girls going to school in many parts of the world, ensuring a high-quality education may be even more important for making the case for girls' education. In 2011, the Center for Universal Education called for a transformation of the existing global compact on education—one that has principally focused on governments financing and implementing initiatives to increase primary school enrollment in poor countries—to a global compact on learning. As outlined in the report, *A Global Compact on Learning: Taking Action on Education in Developing Countries*, a global compact on learning would expand the focus and nature of existing bilateral partnerships to include global partners working together—from governments to civil society to philanthropy to the private sector. It would also raise the ambition to ensuring all children are learning the skills they need to succeed in life from early childhood through secondary education. This vision is one whose time has come; it is one with support from multiple partners and reflects discussions around new sets of global goals, including the Sustainable Development Goals. Now, implementing these goals must be a top priority.

2 Reducing Violence Against Girls and Helping Girls Learn, Even in Conflicts and Emergencies

Unfortunately, the issue of violence that is directed against girls simply because they are seeking an education has become worse and worse in recent years. Although the near assassination of Malala and three of her fellow students and the kidnapping of nearly 300 schoolgirls in Nigeria have grabbed headlines and our hearts, there are more and more incidents of violence that never make the news but increasingly create a choice that no parent should ever face: Provide an education for your girl, or keep her out of harm's way.

To make this one of the five major global focuses, we first need to understand the four different categories of violence and emergencies that girls face and to understand the interventions that work best in each case:

- *Girls affected by humanitarian emergencies*: Ensuring education for girls affected by humanitarian emergencies—whether they be from war, natural disasters, or epidemics—has too often been ignored by the global community. Frequently, global responses focus on life saving measures like food and water without recognizing that education can be life saving and life-sustaining for girls and boys, particularly for their psychological and social wellbeing. We cannot give up on these children simply because they have the misfortune to be living in places where often poor governance, unrest, and disaster combine to overwhelm the coping capacity of families, communities, and governments.

- *Refugee girls*: Girls and boys who have been forced to flee their homes and nations are often among the worst-off children in the world. They face the traumas of humanitarian emergencies but do so in a foreign land with a foreign language and, at times, hostile host communities and governments. For many refugee girls and boys, education becomes a crucial intervention to sustain hope for a better life and to find ways to support their development, especially since they are frequently refugees for a significant portion of their childhoods.

- *Girls threatened and attacked because they go to school, even outside of war and conflict*: These are the girls like Malala and the girls kidnapped by Boko Haram who face attacks—from kidnapping to rape to dismemberment to murder—simply because they are seeking an education. These attacks on girls and girls' schooling, often employed as a tactic of terrorist groups, occur across a wide range of contexts, including in places that are not engulfed in war.

- *Girls subject to sexual violence in and around schools*: Aside from the dramatic cases of war, attacks on girls' education, and other violence, too many girls still face sexual abuse and exploitation in and around schools. Although the overwhelming majority of teachers and adults involved in schools are honorable and committed, there must be zero tolerance for sexual abuse and exploitation in and around schools and there must be a focus on specific policies to prevent such occurrences.

3 Secondary Education and Adolescent Girls

As mentioned above, the global community must now be clearly and unequivocally focused on enabling adolescents—especially girls—to complete secondary education. This is not to suggest that we should de-emphasize primary education; you cannot walk before you run, or reach secondary school if you have not attended and completed primary school. But future national education plans should be devised with universal secondary education in mind and should be judged by their strategies' effectiveness in reaching such goals. One cannot overestimate the importance or the challenge of this goal. There is no question that meeting it will require innovation, resources, and a commitment to teaching. Even in developing nations that have moved to free primary education, fees are still frequently charged for secondary school. And it will require more investment in teaching and teachers to ensure that they have the capacity to teach at higher levels to older students. In this section, we also add "adolescent girls," because in the push for secondary education for girls, we do not want to forget or leave behind those girls who have dropped out or never had the chance to start education along with the rest of those in their age group—especially because of the increasing evidence base showing that alternative education paths for these girls are important.

4 Transitions from School to Work

Many poor parents who choose not to send their girls to school simply do not believe that education can provide an alternative economic path for their daughters. Thus, a greater focus on connecting secondary education to jobs not only provides the existing supply of educated girls with economic opportunities, but will inevitably create a positive cycle of demand for more and better education for girls. This must be one of the new major focuses for education for girls in the post-2015 era.

5 Empowering Girls to Lead

Today, even in 2015, one of the world's great moral crises is that so many women around the world, including in many developed nations, face discriminatory laws, domestic violence, economic barriers, and a lack of equal pay, job opportunities, and political representation. The push for girls' education must have a special emphasis and focus on empowering girls to overcome such barriers and to lead change for women. Yet, even when girls are successfully going to school and mastering their core subjects, they may be learning—from the stories in their textbooks or the statements of their teachers—that their place in the family and society is not in leadership roles. Too often, we see curricula that portray women in a passive and discriminatory manner, a dearth of mentors, and an education system that places too little focus on the soft skills, sports participation, and leadership skills that are critical to success in jobs, to a more dignified family life, and to promoting political change. Education is empowering, but it will be more so if we start focusing on teaching empowerment and leadership skills to girls.

"What we are learning around the world is that if women are healthy and educated, their families will flourish. If women are free from violence, their families will flourish. If women have a chance to work and earn as full and equal partners in society, their families will flourish."

Hillary Rodham Clinton, Fourth World
Conference on Women, Beijing, 1995

The Positive Generational Cycle of Girls' Education

Although this book includes hundreds of studies that document the high returns generated by educating girls, none of them truly captures the full returns from girls' education on a generational basis. As documented in chapter 2, we know that when girls are educated, they become educated mothers who are far more likely to encourage both their daughters and sons to go to school and to become more dedicated students. And this is perhaps the greatest return from girls' education: the belief that when a single girl who would have been denied an education receives a high-quality education, it starts a positive cycle of education and empowerment from mother to daughter, generation after generation. Perhaps no specific study of the hundreds cited in this book can ever precisely calculate the generational impact of the positive ripple created by a single girl overcoming barrier after barrier to get a high-quality education—and yet, even in a book on evidence, this inter-generational impact we take on faith is one more reason that there is no greater investment in the world than educating girls.

CHAPTER 2

The World's Best Investment:
Girls' Education

Educating girls may be the investment for developing countries with the highest return when one considers the exceptionally wide range of crucial areas where educating girls and women brings positive results. Although, as in developed nations, girls' education brings positive returns for income and economic growth, what has brought girls' education to the top of developing nations' policy agendas has been the evidence of high returns in other crucial areas—including improving children's and women's survival rates and health, reducing population growth, protecting children's rights and delaying child marriage, empowering women in the home and in the workplace, and improving climate change adaptation. Indeed, evidence from a diversity of contexts and across generations shows the enormous benefits that girls' education has not only for girls themselves but also for their children, families, communities, and countries. It is one of the smartest investments a country can make and an important step in breaking the cycle of intergenerational poverty. We have reviewed evidence on the economic, social, and political benefits of girls' education, and though one could break down these effects into a considerable number of areas, we have sought to organize the evidence to focus on the *top ten reasons* why girls' education may be the smartest investment the world:

1. **It increases economic growth.** Education for girls and boys increases productivity, including in agricultural production, and is an important contributor to economic growth. Globally, women participate less in the formal economy; but multiple studies have estimated the economic benefits that would accrue from giving women the education and skills they need to join the labor force.

2. **It improves women's wages and jobs.** Better-educated women have higher earnings and are able to get and keep better jobs. Particularly in areas where women are not as well represented in the formal economy as men, girls' education can help reduce the gender gap in the labor force,

and increased levels of education can increase women's wages more than men's.

3. **It saves the lives of children and mothers.** Increasing levels of girls' education has been shown to dramatically reduce the incidence of infant and maternal mortality. Better-educated adolescents and women are better able to seek and negotiate life-saving health care for themselves and their young children. Rigorous analyses over the last several decades have demonstrated that increasing girls' education can literally save the lives of millions of young children and pregnant mothers.

4. **It leads to smaller and more sustainable families.** Girls' education also helps reduce population growth. Women with higher levels of education have fewer children and more frequently employ sound reproductive health practices.

5. **It results in healthier and better-educated children.** Better-educated mothers have healthier and better-educated children who are more likely to benefit from adequate nutrition and immunizations, attend school more regularly and longer, and study more frequently.

6. **It reduces rates of HIV/AIDS and malaria.** Girls' education is often called the *social vaccine* against HIV/AIDS because of the dramatic reduction in the incidence of the disease among better-educated girls and women. This also holds for malaria because better-educated girls and women are less likely to contract malaria and are more likely to use prevention techniques, such as bed nets.

7. **It reduces rates of child marriage.** Girls who are better educated are less likely to be married off as children and are more likely to have opportunities to build a healthier and more prosperous life for themselves and their families.

8. **It empowers women.** Better-educated women are more empowered women. When girls go to school, they develop into women who have more say over their lives, are less likely to be subject to domestic violence, participate more in decisionmaking in households, and have an increased sense of their own worth and efficacy.

9. **It increases women's political leadership.** From community councils to national office, girls' education helps give women the skills they need to play leadership roles in public life. Better-educated women are more likely to participate in volunteer and elected decisionmaking bodies at all levels. In these roles, some country studies suggest, they are much more

likely to serve as advocates for decisions and policies that benefit family and community life, such as improved social services.

10. **It reduces harm to families from natural disasters and climate change.** Higher levels of education generally help prepare families for coping with shocks. Girls' education in particular is associated with reduced injury and death and increased family and community resilience from the hazards of natural disasters and extreme weather that results from climate change.

The rest of this chapter considers, in detail, each of these top ten reasons why girls' education may be the smartest investment the world.

1 Increases Economic Growth

Education for girls and boys increases productivity, including in agricultural production, and is an important contributor to economic growth. Female education, in particular, appears to substantially improve agricultural output and productivity. For the past two decades, economists have shown that, controlling for other factors, increasing girls' and boys' years in school has a significant and positive effect on economic growth. Recently, however, a new analysis has shown that the skills students learn while at school constitute the major driver of education's effect on economic growth. This analysis takes advantage of the increasing number of countries who have participated in international student assessment programs during the last ten years. This analysis has profound implications for the importance of the quality of the education that girls and boys are accessing. After all, we now know that "a big portion of the benefits of girls' education come from not just being in school but learning well while there" (King and Winthrop 2015).

"Investment in girls' education may well be the highest return investment available in the developing world."

Lawrence Summers,
As the World Bank Chief Economist, 1992

Evidence Continues to Mount That Increases in Girls' Education Have a Positive Impact on a Developing Nation's Growth

In the 2004 version of "What Works in Girls' Education" (Herz and Sperling 2004) classic studies were cited by Robert Barro, David Dollar, and Roberta Gatti, showing the linkage between education for girls and overall economic growth. The last decade has only seen more studies confirming this basic linkage:

- **In a study of 146 nations from 1950 to 2010, Barro and Lee find that schooling has a significant positive effect on output, with the rate of return being a 5 to 12 percent increase in economic growth for each additional year of schooling in the average population.** In a large study of educational attainment levels for 146 countries from 1950 to 2010 published in 2013, the authors improved on their previous studies, which also found that education levels were strong determinants of differing growth rates across countries. In 1994, they found that female schooling levels played an important role in increasing growth directly and also through its impact on increased life expectancy and lower fertility rates.

  Barro, Robert J. and Jong-Wha Lee. 2013. 2013. "A New Data Set of Educational Attainment in the World, 1950–2010." *Journal of Development Economics* 104: 184–98.

  Barro, Robert J., and Jong-Wha Lee. 1994. "Sources of Economic Growth." *Carnegie-Rochester Series on Public Policy* 40: 1–46.

  Barro, Robert J. 1991. "Economic Growth in a Cross Section of Countries." *Quarterly Journal of Economics* 106, no. 2: 407–43. doi:10.1016/0167-2231(94)90002-7.

- **"The increase in educational attainment accounted for around 50 percent of economic growth (2.1 percent per annum on average, for the 30 countries from 1960 to 2008), of which over half was due to increased female educational attainment."** The study, by the Organization for Economic Cooperation and Development (OECD), accounted for changes in population, technology, and other factors that have helped increase economic growth over nearly 50 years, and still found that increasing the average educational attainment of the whole population by one year leads to a 10 percent increase in per capita output per annum. Also, narrowing gender gaps in educational attainment had an additional impact on increasing economic growth during the period.

  OECD. 2012. *Closing the Gender Gap: Act Now.* Paris: OECD.

- In a study of 100 countries, Dollar and Gatti found that increasing the share of women completing secondary education by 1 percent increases economic growth by 0.3 percent, a significant amount.

    Dollar, David, and Roberta Gatti. 1999. *Gender Inequality, Income, and Growth: Are Good Times Good for Women?* Working Paper 1 for *Policy Research Report on Gender and Development*. Washington: World Bank.

- A study that looked at 13 countries that were not expected to meet the MDG on gender parity in education found that they would have grown 0.1 to 0.3 percent faster each year from 1995 to 2005, and 0.4 percent faster from 2005 to 2015, if they met the goal by 2005. The authors point out that though these might sound like small gains, in fact, as they compound over time, it would translate into as much as 10 percent higher income in 2015.

    Abu-Ghaida, Dina, and Stephan Klasen. 2004. "The Economic and Human Development Costs of Missing the Millennium Development Goal on Gender Equity." *World Development* 32, no. 7:1075–1107.

- Gender education inequality explains 0.9 to 1.7 percent slower growth in East Asia, the Middle East, and North Africa, and 0.1 to 1.6 percentage points in South Asia. Taking into account the fact that gender gaps in education affect economic growth through both direct and indirect effects, Klasen and Lamanna estimate the combined cost of gender inequality in education and employment.

    Klasen, Stephan, and Francesca Lamanna. 2009. "The Impact of Gender Inequality in Education and Employment on Economic Growth: New Evidence for a Panel of Countries." *Feminist Economics* 15, no. 3: 91–132.

The Quality of Schooling Is Closely Associated with Economic Growth

- Although studies showing the correlation between years of education and economic growth are critical, new studies emphasize that "it is the quality of schooling across countries (albeit measured simply by average student test scores) that is more strongly associated with economic growth—and also with sustained increase in demand for schooling." More years of schooling without clear improvements in learning and the skills of students will not translate into the same degree of higher productivity or real advances in the lives of young people. The recent literature has further explored the relationship between economic growth and education to find that in fact it is the quality of school and its ability to improve students' cognitive skills that actually increase gross domestic product (GDP).

King, Elizabeth, and Rebecca Winthrop. 2015. *Today's Challenges for Girls' Education*. Washington: Brookings Institution.

- **A twenty-nation study over a forty-year period found that models that include direct measures of cognitive skills can account for about three times the variation in economic growth as models that include only years of schooling:** The amount that students learn in the classroom varies widely between countries, and a study by the economists Hanushek and Woessman found that across more than twenty developing and developed countries, "cognitive skills have a strong and robust influence on economic growth." Using student mathematics and science test scores in addition to the number of years of schooling and income levels in countries, Hanushek and Woessman find that "test scores that are larger by one standard deviation (measured at the student level across all OECD countries in PISA) are associated with an average annual growth rate in GDP that is 2 percentage points higher over the whole forty-year period [1960–2000]."

Hanushek, Eric A., and Ludgar Woessman. 2008. "The Role of Cognitive Skills in Development." *Journal of Economic Literature*. 46, no. 3: 607–68.

Increased Female Education Increases Agricultural Productivity

- **A study of Kenya, Tanzania, and Uganda found that educational opportunities through farmer field schools increased the value of crops and livestock, as well as resulting in a 61 percent increase in income.** The education program was particularly effective for women and illiterate farmers across the three countries, which shows that targeted education programs toward female farmers can have a large impact on agricultural productivity.

Davis, K., et al. 2012. "Impact of Farmer Field Schools on Agricultural Productivity and Poverty in East Africa." *World Development* 40, no. 2: 402–13.

- **The International Food Policy Research Institute (IFPRI) has found that increasing educational attainment for women in Kenya could increase their agricultural output by 25 percent.**

IFPRI. 2005. Women: *Still the Key to Food and Nutrition Security*. Washington: IFPRI.

- **Another sixty-three-country study by IFPRI found that more productive farming due to increased female education accounted for 43 percent of the decline in malnutrition achieved between 1970 and 1995.**

  Smith, Lisa C., and Lawrence Haddad. 1999. *Explaining Child Malnutrition in Developing Countries: A Cross-Country Analysis.* IFPRI Food Consumption and Nutrition Division Discussion Paper 60. Washington: IFPRI.

- **Even in rural economies, education makes a difference in productivity. In Kenya, for example, more education (and more inputs) for female farmers, relative to male farmers, increases farm yields by as much as 22 percent.**

  Quisumbing, Agnes. 1996. "Male–Female Differences in Agricultural Productivity: Methodological Issues and Empirical Evidence." *World Development* 24, no. 10: 1579–95.

- **Education of female farmers was found to increase agricultural production in households, particularly in households with a female head.** A study of farm households in fourteen Ethiopian villages found that education had an important role to play in agricultural production in rural Ethiopia.

  Weir, Sharada. 1999. *The Effects of Education on Farmer Productivity in Rural Ethiopia.* Working Paper 99-7. Oxford: Centre for the Study of the African Economies.

- **Apart from basic skills, education affects agricultural productivity through a number of channels, such as the adoption of improved technology.** Knight, Weir, and Woldehanna used data from rural Ethiopia to show that schooling increases agricultural productivity because educated farmers are less risk averse and more likely to adopt farming technologies. Another study of Kenya by Saito, Mekonnen, and Spurling shows much lower adoption rates for improved seeds and fertilizers for females than for males, in part due to lower education levels.

  Knight, John, Sharada Weir, and Tassew Woldehanna. 2003. "The Role of Education in Facilitating Risk-Taking and Innovation in Agriculture." *Journal of Development Studies* 39, no. 6: 1–22.

  Saito, Katrine, Hailu Mekonnen, and Daphne Spurling, 1994. *Raising the Productivity of Women Farmers in Sub-Saharan Africa.* World Bank Discussion Paper 230. Washington: World Bank.

- **Female farmers have been identified as a key lever for improving agricultural productivity through education, due to their impact on productivity and access to credit.** A study of four African countries conducted by the World Bank found that because women farmers have such low levels of education, improving their educational attainment would potentially have a very large impact on their productivity. Access to credit is another channel through which education may help female farmers be especially more productive. Using data from Kenya, this study concludes that education is a significant determinant of female farmers' access to formal credit, though it was not a significant determinant for male farmers.

- **This same study of African countries also found that women farmers are a critical target group; their generally low levels of education mean higher potential productivity gains from giving them access to education and other endowments.** Women account for three-fourths of all food produced in Sub-Saharan Africa, yet women who head farm households have not only lower educational attainment than men but also lower educational attainment than other women. In Nigeria, women who head farm households had, on average, 1.6 years of education, compared with 3.0 years for men and 2.5 years for all the women surveyed. Therefore, women farmers represent an especially important target group for increased education to raise overall agricultural productivity.

    Saito, Katrine, Hailu Mekonnen, and Daphne Spurling, 1994. *Raising the Productivity of Women Farmers in Sub-Saharan Africa*. World Bank Discussion Paper 230. Washington: World Bank.

2 Leads to Better Wages and Jobs for Women

For several decades, rigorous economic analysis has shown the high returns from education in the labor market. Better-educated women and men earn more. Primary education has long been thought to produce the highest return. However, recent analyses by multiple economists have shown that secondary and tertiary education actually have higher returns in increased individual earnings. Additionally, these returns are slightly higher for women than men. This does not take away from the need to invest in primary education, both because to reach higher levels of education, girls and boys must first complete primary school, and because of the range of social benefits beyond the individual benefits of higher wages that accrue with increased primary education. Questions about the wage return on skills (e.g., literacy and numeracy levels) versus the years in school have also emerged in recent years due to increasing data from international student assessments. Similar to the analysis on education and economic growth above, the wage return on skills learned in school appears to be even higher than the wage return on years in school. Attending school helps increase individual earnings, but learning well while there and having strong skills to deploy in the labor market help boost earnings even more. In addition to higher earnings, increased education also has the added benefit of helping women get and keep better jobs. In the developing world, many women are engaged in vulnerable employment (e.g., informal economy, unpaid work for their families). Women who have an education are able to access better and more secure jobs in the formal economy.

Education Increases Women's Wages

- **The rate of return on an additional year of schooling has been consistently estimated to be a 10 percent increase in wages. The latest data find returns to be slightly higher for women, especially for secondary and tertiary education.** For decades, rates of return on education have been calculated by George Psacharopoulos across more than 100 countries in the world, and the average is typically about 10 percent for each additional year of schooling, with primary schooling typically receiving the highest return.

- **The latest estimates calculated by Patrinos and Montenegro for the World Bank find that for women, returns are slightly higher than for men, at 11.7 percent, compared with 9.6 percent.** Additionally, this new analysis shows that higher levels of education now have the greatest returns. For women, tertiary education has a return of 16.8 percent.

    Patrinos, Harry, and Claudio E. Montenegro. 2014. *Comparable Estimates of Returns to Schooling Around the World*. World Bank Policy Research Working Paper 7020. Washington: World Bank.

- **These new studies of the returns on education confirm pioneering work by the Yale economist Paul Schultz, who found that returns from secondary education for women were in the range of 15 to 25 percent**. "Increasing investments in women's human capital, especially education, should be a priority for governments seeking both economic growth and human welfare."

Schultz, Paul. 2002. "Why Governments Should Invest More to Educate Girls." *World Development* 30, no. 2: 207–25.

- **An analysis of numeracy skills of adults in OECD countries found that having above-average numeracy skills is associated with 18 percent higher earnings.** Getting girls into school is important for increasing wages; but more important, getting them learning helps improve their prospects in the labor market. A new analysis shows that the wage return on skills is even higher than those for years of schooling.

Hanushek, et al. 2015. "Returns to Skills Around the World: Evidence from PIAAC." European Economic Review 73: 103-130.

- **"Returns to education in *wage* employment in Bangladesh and Pakistan are about twice as high for women as for men.** Among wage workers, it is clear that returns from education are significantly and substantially *greater* for women than men in India, Bangladesh, and Pakistan. This could reflect the scarcity of educated women combined with the existence of jobs that require (or which are largely reserved for) educated women."

Aslam, Monazza. 2013. *Empowering Women: Education and the Pathways of Change.* Background paper for *EFA Global Monitoring Report* 2013/4. Paris: UNESCO.

- **In Pakistan, "women who complete middle and high school, for instance, live in households that enjoy nearly 14 and 29 percent (equivalent to $5.30 and $10.80) higher monthly consumption per capita, respectively, relative to women with less than middle school education."** A study looking at cash transfer programs found that higher levels of education reaped rewards in terms of both higher earnings and more marriage opportunities that increased household wealth.

Alam, Andaleeb, Javier E. Baez, and Ximena V. Del Carpio. 2011. *Does Cash for School Influence Young Women's Behavior in the Longer Term? Evidence from Pakistan.* Policy Research Working Paper 5669. Washington: World Bank.

- **A seven-country analysis showed that in Sub-Saharan Africa, education has a strong effect on closing the earnings gap.** The higher the education level, the lower the gender wage inequality. According to this study, "what is indeed remarkable is that gender disparities in earnings varied with the level of education, and the higher the education level, the lower the extent of inequalities in labor income per hours worked."

- **In Ghana, men with no education earn 57 percent more than women with no education. But as women's education levels increase, the earnings gap narrows.** Men who have completed primary school earn 24 percent more than women with the same completion level, and the gap narrows to 16 percent for those with a secondary education. In this sense, education can promote gender equality in the labor market.

  Kolev, Alexandre, and Nicolas Sirven. 2010. "Gender Disparities in Africa's Labor Market: A Cross-Country Comparison Using Standardized Survey Data." *In Gender Disparities in Africa's Labor Market*, edited by Jorge Saba Arbache, Alexandre Kolev, and Ewa Filipiak. Washington: World Bank.

- **In Pakistan, working women with a high level of literacy skills earned 95 percent more than women with weak or no literacy skills, whereas the differential was only 33 percent among men**.

  Aslam, Monazza, et al. 2010. *Economic Returns to Schooling and Skills: An Analysis of India and Pakistan*. RECOUP Working Paper 38. London: UK Department for International Development.

Education Helps Women Get Better Jobs and Reduce Rates of Vulnerable Employment

- **Education increases women's access to jobs in the formal sector, which is crucial because women in low-income countries are largely employed in vulnerable, informal employment that does not provide wages, stability, or benefits.** According to the International Labor Organization (ILO), "educating girls has proven to be one of the most important ways of breaking poverty cycles and is likely to have significant impacts on access to formal jobs in the longer term." According to the ILO, in Sub-Saharan Africa 84 percent, and in South Asia 83 percent of all working women work in "vulnerable" employment, meaning they work in the informal sector, are self-employed, or work unpaid for their families. Other developing regions also have high rates—in Southeast Asia and the Asia-Pacific region, two-thirds; and in the Middle East, 56 percent—in stark contrast to the developed economies, where just 8 percent of women work in these conditions.

ILO. 2012. *Global Employment Trends for Women*. Geneva: ILO.

ILO. 2014. *Promoting Equality and Addressing Discrimination*. ILO Policy Brief. Geneva: ILO.

- **"In middle-income countries in Latin America—such as Argentina, Brazil, El Salvador, and Mexico—the proportion of women in paid employment increases sharply as women's education level rises,** according to analysis of labor force survey data for the *2013/4 EFA Global Monitoring Report*. In Mexico, while 39 percent of women with primary education are employed, the proportion rises to 48 percent for those with a secondary education. Education plays a much stronger role in determining women's engagement in the labor force than it does for men in these Latin American countries."

  UNESCO. 2014a. *Gender Summary: Teaching and Learning—Achieving Quality for All—EFA Global Monitoring Report 2013/4*. Paris: UNESCO.

- **In a study of Brazil and Guinea, women with higher schooling levels were less likely to work in the informal and domestic sectors with low wages or subsistence pay.** Education gave them the opportunity to earn higher wages in formal employment.

  Malhotra, Anju, Caren Grown, and Rohini Pande. 2003. *Impact of Investments in Female Education on Gender Inequality*. Washington: International Center for Research on Women.

- **Higher levels of education reduce the probability of women in India and Pakistan being stuck in unpaid, informal labor: In a study of labor market trends in India and Pakistan, Aslam and colleagues found that in India women who have little or no education have a high probability of working in unpaid family labor or casual work, but this probability decreases rapidly with education level.** In Pakistan, an education of ten or more years has a strong influence on the probability of women gaining employment as a wage earner, and all levels of education help to increase the probability that women will enter the labor force.

  Aslam, Monazza, et al. 2010. *Economic Returns to Schooling and Skills: An Analysis of India and Pakistan*. RECOUP Working Paper 38. London: UK Department for International Development.

3 Saves the Lives of Children and Mothers

Studies from more than two decades ago have demonstrated that increasing girls' education can increase the chances a child survives past their fifth birthday. Child mortality is a serious and tragic problem in many parts of the developing world. However, a recent rigorous analysis has shed light on just how dramatically effective girls' education can be. We now know from a seminal study published in 2010 that over the past forty years, increasing levels of girls' education have been responsible for more than half the reduction in infant mortality, saving the lives of an estimated 4.2 million children. Better-educated girls and women are better able to seek and negotiate life-saving health care for their young children and for themselves. Similarly, increasing girls' education can help reduce maternal deaths. Like child mortality, maternal mortality, or when women die during childbirth, is a sad reality in many parts of the developing world. Here, too, it was recently estimated that increasing levels of girls' education have been responsible for half the reductions in maternal mortality, meaning, by some accounts, that girls' education has been more effective than typical health interventions. Interestingly, though every additional year a girl goes to school brings an added benefit in terms of a reduction in child and maternal mortality rates, girls who reach secondary school are more likely than their peers who just reach primary school to survive childbirth and have children who survive past age five.

Children's Lives Are Saved When Mothers Have a Better Education

- **A seminal study of child mortality in 175 countries from 1970 to 2009 found that increases in women's education are responsible for more than half the reduction in under-five child mortality.** Of the 8.2 million more children who survived past age five, increases in women's educational attainment led to 4.2 million of them. This accounts for half the decrease in child mortality over forty years, meaning schooling of women of reproductive age makes a very large contribution to the health of their children.

  Gakidou, Emmanuela, et al. 2010. "Increased Educational Attainment and Its Effect on Child Mortality in 175 Countries Between 1970 and 2009: A Systematic Analysis." *The Lancet* 376, no. 9745: 959–74.

- **A fifty-eight-country study commissioned by UNESCO shows that universal primary education for girls would reduce child mortality by 15 percent and universal secondary education would reduce child**

mortality by 49 percent. In Sub-Saharan Africa, the under-five mortality rate is nearly twice as high for mothers with no education as for those who have completed secondary school.

UNESCO. 2014c. *Teaching and Learning: Achieving Quality for All—EFA Global Monitoring Report 2013/4.* Paris: UNESCO.

UNICEF (United Nations Children's Fund). 2010. *Progress for Children: Achieving the MDGs with Equity.* New York: UNICEF.

- **The same study of fifty-eight low- and middle-income countries found that a literate mother is 23 percent more likely to have a skilled attendant present during birth, which significantly increases the chances of a child living past the age of five.** In Mali, maternal literacy almost tripled this likelihood of child survival. The first day is critical for newborns to survive. According to the UN Interagency Group for Child Mortality Estimation (UNIGCME), 36 percent of newborns' deaths occur on the same day as their birth, which in 2013 meant that almost 1 million of these children died. Though access to a professional to assist with delivery can prevent newborn deaths, more than half of all births in Sub-Saharan Africa do not have a skilled attendant present, or over 35 million births per year. Educating mothers would help make the delivery process safer and save lives.

UNESCO. 2014c. *Teaching and Learning: Achieving Quality for All—EFA Global Monitoring Report 2013/4.* Paris: UNESCO.

UNIGME. 2014. *Levels and Trends in Child Mortality Report 2014: Estimates Developed by the UNIGME.* New York: UNICEF.

Lawn, Joy, et al. 2014. "Every Newborn: Progress, Priorities, and Potential beyond Survival." *The Lancet* 384, no. 9938: 189–205.

- **In Burkina Faso, if all women completed primary school, under-five mortality would fall 46 percent, and would fall 76 percent if all women completed secondary school.** Considering that the country's enrollment ratio is one of the lowest in the world, with just 25 percent of girls in secondary school in 2012, investing in girls' education could have a big impact on the high child mortality rate, especially as Burkino Faso has a significantly higher child mortality rate than even other low-income nations.

Gakidou, Emmanuela. 2013. *Education, Literacy and Health Outcomes Findings.* Background paper commissioned for *EFA Global Monitoring Report 2013/4.* Paris: UNESCO.

- **Using household demographic surveys for twenty-six countries in Sub-Saharan Africa, UNESCO found that 1.8 million fewer children would have died before age five in 2008 if all women had a secondary education.** "If the average child mortality rate for the region were to fall to the level for children born to mothers with some secondary education, there would be 1.8 million fewer deaths—a 41 percent reduction."

  UNESCO. 2011. *The Hidden Crisis: Armed Conflict and Education: EFA Global Monitoring Report 2011*. Paris: UNESCO.

- **The Yale economist Paul Schultz found that an extra year of girls' education cuts infant mortality by 5 to 10 percent.** His review of many country studies found that each additional year of a mother's schooling cuts the expected infant mortality rate by an average of 5 to 10 percent. This link "is especially striking in low-income countries. The pattern has been widely replicated across comparative data bases . . . and through repeated censuses."

  Schultz, T. Paul. 1993. "Returns to Women's Schooling." In *Women's Education in Developing Countries: Barriers, Benefits, and Policy*, edited by Elizabeth King and M. Anne Hill. Baltimore: Johns Hopkins University Press.

- **A study by Hill and King found that increasing girls' enrollment in primary school reduced infant deaths by 4.1 per 1,000, and increasing girls' enrollment in secondary school reduced infant deaths by 5.6 per 1,000.**

  Hill, M. Anne, and Elizabeth King. 1995. "Women's Education and Economic Well-Being." *Feminist Economics* 1, no. 2: 21–46. doi: 10.1080/714042230.

- **According to a study based on 139 Demographic and Health Surveys for fifty-eight countries from 2005 to 2011, if all women completed secondary education in low- and lower-middle-income countries, the incidence of diarrhea would fall 30 percent because they are more likely to purify their water.** Educated women are more likely to provide proper sanitation that prevents diarrhea and also are more likely to apply proper treatment when their child shows symptoms.

  UNESCO. 2014c. *Teaching and Learning: Achieving Quality for All—EFA Global Monitoring Report 2013/4*. Paris: UNESCO.

  Gakidou, Emmanuela. 2013. *Education, Literacy and Health Outcomes Findings*. Background paper commissioned for *EFA Global Monitoring Report 2013/4*. Paris: UNESCO.

- **Mothers in low-income countries who completed primary school were 12 percent more likely than those with no education to seek health care and apply treatment.** This can have a huge impact because, though easily preventable, diarrhea still accounts for 9 percent of all under-five deaths, according to the UNIGME.

> UNIGME. 2014. *Levels and Trends in Child Mortality Report 2014: Estimates Developed by the UNIGME.* New York: UNICEF.

- **Advances in infrastructure that should improve children's health and sanitation are less capable of reaching children whose mothers are uneducated.** Another study in India found that improving infrastructure through piped water helped improve sanitation, lessen cases of diarrhea, and in turn reduce child mortality. However, for the poorest households where mothers had low levels of education, the health gains by-passed children in these households. When mothers do not have the knowledge to properly use new systems, the improvements are lost on their children.

> Jalan, Jyotsna, and Martin Ravallion. 2003. "Does Piped Water Reduce Diarrhea for Children in Rural India?" *Journal of Econometrics* 112, no. 1: 153–73.

- **"As little as one extra year of maternal education can lead to a 14 percent decrease in the pneumonia death rate—equivalent to 160,000 child lives saved per year,"** according to the global health expert Emmanuela Gakidou in her study using estimates from the Global Burden of Disease study in 137 countries between 1980 and 2010 for under-five mortality rates.

> UNIGME. 2014. *Levels and Trends in Child Mortality Report 2014: Estimates Developed by the UNIGME.* New York: UNICEF.
>
> Gakidou, Emmanuela. 2013. *Education, Literacy and Health Outcomes Findings.* Background paper commissioned for *EFA Global Monitoring Report 2013/4.* Paris: UNESCO.
>
> UNESCO. 2014c. *Teaching and Learning: Achieving Quality for All—EFA Global Monitoring Report 2013/4.* Paris: UNESCO.

- **Mothers' schooling increases her child's chances of survival.** Reviewing studies of women's literacy in five countries, the education experts LeVine and Rowe explore the pathways between schooling and child survival, stating that "the evidence shows definitively that a mother's schooling—at high and low levels of education, in cities and villages, under diverse economic conditions—is related to the chances of her child's survival." Furthermore, they conclude from these studies that it is the literacy skills mothers gain in school that make them "more effective at communication not only in clinics and hospitals but also in other bureaucratic settings they may turn to for help in advancing their children's interests. The more we learn about maternal literacy, the more it looks like an indispensable passport to life-saving services for mothers and children in [less-developed countries]."

LeVine, Robert, and Meredith Rowe. 2009. "Maternal Literacy and Child Health in Less-Developed Countries: Evidence, Processes, and Limitations." *Journal of Development and Behavioral Pediatrics*. 30, no. 4: 340–49.

Increased Women's Education Lowers Maternal Mortality

Better-educated women are less likely to die due to complications during childbirth.

- **Data from 108 countries over twenty years show that if every woman in the world had a primary education, maternal deaths could fall 66 percent and save an estimated 189,000 lives per year.**

- **In Sub-Saharan Africa, maternal mortality could fall by 70 percent, from 500 to 150 deaths per 100,000 births.**

- **Half or possibly more of the maternal death reduction from 1990 to 2010 can be attributed to increases in women's education.**

- **The effect of girls' education is higher than the effect of some of the typical health interventions.** This study also shows that the reason education reduces maternal deaths is that educated mothers have fewer pregnancies and are less likely to give birth as teenagers.

Bhalotra, Sonia, and Damian Clarke. 2013. *Educational Attainment and Maternal Mortality*. Paper commissioned for *EFA Global Monitoring Report 2013/4*. Paris: UNESCO.

UNESCO. 2014a. *Gender Summary: Teaching and Learning: Achieving Quality for All—EFA Global Monitoring Report 2013/4*. Paris: UNESCO.

- **In a study of twenty-four countries across Africa, Asia, and Latin America, Karlsen and colleagues found that women with six or fewer** years of schooling had 2 to 2.7 times the risk of dying during child-birth than women with twelve years of education. The authors conclude that improvements to mothers' education levels are a key strategy to eliminate maternal mortality because "lower levels of maternal education were associated with higher maternal mortality even amongst women able to access facilities providing intrapartum care. More attention should be given to the wider social determinants of health when devising strategies to reduce maternal mortality."

Karlsen, Saffron, et al. 2011. "The Relationship Between Maternal Education and Mortality Among Women Giving Birth in Health Care Institutions: Analysis of the Cross-Sectional WHO Global Survey on Maternal and Perinatal Health." *BMC Public Health* **11**: 606.

- Using data from 148 countries, McAlister and Baskett found gender inequality in education enrollment and literacy rates to be significant and moderately powerful predictors of maternal mortality rates, explaining about 50 percent of variance. These results show that in countries where women have fewer education opportunities than men, they are less likely to survive childbirth.

McAlister, Chryssa, and Thomas Baskett. 2006. "Female Education and Maternal Mortality: A Worldwide Survey." *Journal of Obstetrics and Gynaecology Canada* 28, no. 11:983–90.

- In Chile, a recent study identified women's education as the most important factor in reducing maternal mortality, reducing maternal deaths 29.3 per 100,000 live births for every additional year of mothers' schooling.

- Over a fifty-year period, the maternal mortality rate in Chile declined 93.8 percent, largely due to increases in women's education that helped lower fertility rates, increase incomes, improve hygiene, and increase the use of skilled attendants at birth.

Koch, Elard, et al. 2012. "Women's Education Level, Maternal Health Facilities, Abortion Legislation and Maternal Deaths: A Natural Experiment in Chile from 1957 to 2007." *PLoS One* 7, no. 5: e36613.

- "As the risk of dying in childbirth declines, educational investments increase (and more so for girls). In Sri Lanka, reductions in the maternal mortality ratio increased female literacy by 1 percentage point. And because reductions in maternal mortality ratios also reduce maternal morbidity (in the United States in 1920, one of every six women suffered from a long-term disability stemming from giving birth), improvements in the conditions of childbirth can drive increases in the labor force participation rate of married women."

> World Bank. 2012. *World Development Report 2012: Gender Equality and Development.* Washington: World Bank.

4 Leads to Smaller and More Sustainable Families

Girls' education leads to smaller, healthier, and more sustainable families. A recent 2011 study by two demographers estimated that if all countries expanded to 100 percent enrollment of girls and boys at the primary and secondary levels, there would be 843 million fewer people in the world by 2050. For those worried about the burden that the world's 7 billion people place on the natural environment, this is welcome news. Smaller family size is also welcome news to those working to support healthier mothers and families. Women with higher levels of education have fewer children, particularly once they reach secondary education. Women with higher levels of education are also more likely to give birth for the first time later in life and to have children more than two years apart, both of which are important characteristics because health complications increase when children are born to young mothers and when they are born less than two years apart.

- **"Women with more education tend to have fewer children, which benefits them, their families, and society in general.** In some parts of the world, education has already been a key factor in bringing forward the transition from high rates of birth and mortality to lower rates. Other parts of the world are lagging, however, particularly Sub-Saharan Africa, where women still have an average of 5.4 live births."

  > UNESCO. 2014c. *Teaching and Learning: Achieving Quality for All—EFA Global Monitoring Report 2013/4.* Paris: UNESCO.

- **"The potential contribution of education to stabilizing global population growth should not be underestimated," states UNESCO in the *EFA Global Monitoring Report*.** In a global study using Demographic and Health Surveys, two demographers projected the world's population if all countries shifted gears and took the "fast track," the most rapid educational expansion possible, which would be similar to South Korea's climb in the twentieth century from one of the least-educated to most highly educated populations in the world. In this case, there would be 843 million fewer people in the world by 2050 than if countries kept enrollment increases at current rates.

UNESCO. 2014c. *Teaching and Learning: Achieving Quality for All—EFA Global Monitoring Report 2013/4*. Paris: UNESCO.

Lutz, Wolfgang, and K. C. Samir. 2011. "Global Human Capital: Integrating Education and Population." *Science* 333, no. 6042: 587–92.

- **There would be 2 million fewer early births in Sub-Saharan Africa and South and West Asia if all women had both a primary and secondary education.** Using Demographic Health Surveys for 139 countries worldwide, Gakidou estimated based on current birthrates that in Sub-Saharan Africa and South and West Asia, if all women had a primary education, early births could fall by 10 percent. If all women had a secondary education, early births could fall by 59 percent.

- **According to Demographic and Health Survey data, women with no education in Sub-Saharan Africa have 6.7 births, on average, while the number falls to 5.8 for those with primary education and to 3.9 for those with secondary education.**

UNESCO. 2014c. *Teaching and Learning: Achieving Quality for All—EFA Global Monitoring Report 2013/4*. Paris: UNESCO.

UNPD (United Nations Population Division). 2011. *World Population Prospects: The 2010 Revision*. New York: UNPD. http://esa.un.org/wpp/Documentation/ WPP%202010%20publications.htm.

ICF International. 2012. *STATcompiler: Building Tables with DHS Data*. Calverton, Md.: ICF International. Available at www.statcompiler.com.

- Numerous country studies from Africa, Asia, and Latin America show that educated women have fewer children. The evidence from these studies shows that educated women begin to have children later in life and leave more time between births:

In Nigeria, an evaluation of the universal primary education program implemented in the 1970s showed that four years of schooling reduced fertility of women under twenty-five years old by one child per woman.

Osili, Una Okonkwo, and Bridget Terry Long. 2008. "Does Female Schooling Reduce Fertility? Evidence from Nigeria." *Journal of Development Economics* 87, no. 1: 57–75.

In Angola, the fertility rate of a woman with no education is 7.8 children, compared with 5.9 children for a woman with primary education and 2.5 children for a woman with secondary education or more.

UNESCO. 2014c. *Teaching and Learning: Achieving Quality for All—EFA Global Monitoring Report 2013/4*. Paris: UNESCO.

In Brazil, a study found that illiterate women have an average of 6 children each, whereas literate women have an average of 2.5 children.

World Bank. 2001. *Engendering Development through Gender Equality in Rights, Resources, and Voice*. World Bank Policy Research Report. New York: Oxford University Press.

In Punjab, Pakistan, women "with middle and high school education have around 1.8 fewer children than those with lower than middle school education by the end of their reproductive life. Simple extrapolations also indicate that the 1.4 year delay in marriage of beneficiaries associated with the program could lead to 0.4 fewer births by the end of their childbearing years. Furthermore, better-educated women are expected to not only have fewer children but also invest more in their human capital, which may lead to positive intergenerational effects."

Alam, Andaleeb, Javier E. Baez, and Ximena V. Del Carpio. 2011. *Does Cash for School Influence Young Women's Behavior in the Longer Term? Evidence from Pakistan*. Policy Research Working Paper 5669. Washington: World Bank.

In Pakistan, women with primary schooling are 18 percent more likely to report feeling that they have a say in the number of children they have, compared with women with no education. Women with postprimary education are even more likely to feel they are included in decisions about family size. As compared to women with no schooling, women that attended middle school are 27 percent more likely to feel their preferences are being met; women that attended secondary school are 36 percent more likely to feel this way.

Aslam, Monazza. 2013. *Empowering Women: Education and the Pathways of Change.* Background paper for *EFA Global Monitoring Report 2013/4.* Paris: UNESCO.

The Demographic Health Surveys cited by UNESCO show that "in Nigeria, for example, women with no education gave birth for the first time at age 18, on average, compared with age 25 for those with at least secondary education."

And also, "in Kenya, the probability that a woman with no education would have another child within two years of the second birth was 27 percent, compared with 17 percent among women with secondary education. A period of less than two years between births tends to increase health risks for mothers and their children."

UNESCO. 2014c. *Teaching and Learning: Achieving Quality for All—EFA Global Monitoring Report 2013/4*. Paris: UNESCO.

ICF International. 2012. *STATcompiler: Building Tables with DHS Data*. Calverton, Md.: ICF International. Available at www.statcompiler.com.

- Following the implementation of the Free Primary Education policy in Sierra Leone, which rapidly increased access to primary school, one study found that each additional year of schooling increased women's propensity to use modern contraceptives by 12 percentage points, using data from the 2008 Demographic and Health Survey. Additionally, women who complete primary school (a total of six years of education) desire an average of 2 less children than the sample average.

Mocan, Naci H., and Colin Cannonier. 2012. *Empowering Women through Education: Evidence from Sierra Leone*. NBER Working Paper w18016. Cambridge, Mass.: National Bureau of Economic Research. doi: 10.3386/w18016.

5 Results in Healthier and Better-Educated Children

Better-educated mothers have healthier and better-educated children, who are more likely to benefit from adequate nutrition and immunizations, attend school more regularly and longer, and study more frequently. And evidence is clear that educating women leads to a positive generational cycle, as they are more likely to see that their girls are educated.

Mothers' Education Reduces Malnutrition and Stunting

A mother's education improves children's nutrition and prevents stunting. Malnutrition is the underlying cause of 45 percent of child deaths globally, according to the

UNIGCME. Child stunting, when children are short for their age, is typically a result of malnutrition. And in fact, one global study published in the medical journal *The Lancet* finds that severely stunted children are four times more likely to die before age five than those who have sufficient nutrition.

- **If all women completed secondary education, 26 percent fewer children, or 11.9 million, would suffer from stunting,** according to an analysis of Demographic and Health survey data from 2005 to 2011 by the *EFA Global Monitoring Report* team.

  UNESCO. 2014c. *Teaching and Learning: Achieving Quality for All—EFA Global Monitoring Report 2013/4.* Paris: UNESCO.

- **A study using data from 100 countries shows that if the share of women enrolling in secondary education increased from 50 to 60 percent, there would be a decline in the stunting rate by 1.3 percent.** This study is based on estimations made from cross-country comparisons with data from approximately 100 countries and controls for other factors such as fertility rate, wealth and GDP level, household assets, and access to health services.

  Heady, Derek D. 2013. "Developmental Drivers of Nutritional Change: A Cross-Country Analysis." *World Development* 42: 76–88. doi:10.1016/j.worlddev.2012.07.002.

- **Maternal education was found to be associated with a higher probability of children age 6 to 23 months consuming food rich in micronutrients.** This finding is from an analysis of twelve countries using Demographic and Health Surveys for 2009 to 2011.

  UNIGME. 2014. *Levels and Trends in Child Mortality Report 2014: Estimates Developed by the UNIGME.* New York: UNICEF.

  UNESCO. 2014c. *Teaching and Learning: Achieving Quality for All—EFA Global Monitoring Report 2013/4.* Paris: UNESCO.

  Black, R. E., L. H. Allen, Z. A. Bhutta, L. E. Caulfield, M. De Onis, M. Ezzati, C. Mathers, and J. Rivera. 2008. "Maternal and Child Undernutrition: Global and Regional Exposures and Health Consequences." *The Lancet* 371, no. 9608: 243–60.

- **"In Ethiopia, one-year-olds whose mothers had a primary school education along with access to antenatal care were 39 percent less likely to have stunted growth."**

- "In Vietnam, infants whose mothers had attained a lower-secondary education were 67 percent less likely to have stunted growth." The authors found that "a mother's education improves child nutrition, even after taking into account other factors linked to better nutrition, such as household wealth, mother's height, breast-feeding practices, water, and sanitation."

   Klugman, Jeni, et al. 2014. *Voice and Agency: Empowering Women and Girls for Shared Prosperity.* Washington: World Bank.

- A study of child nutrition in the slums of Nairobi found that the odds of child stunting are 29 percent higher for mothers with no education or lower than secondary education, relative to mothers who have at least secondary education.

   Abuya, Benta A., James Ciera, and Elizabeth Kimani-Murage. 2012. "Effect of Mother's Education on Child's Nutritional Status in the Slums of Nairobi." *BMC Pediatrics* 12: 80.

Mothers' Education Improves Children's Health and Immunization Rate

- In Guatemala, "mothers with more intellectual human capital may be more likely to seek health and childcare information, and may be more aware of and likely to adopt behaviors that result in better-educated and healthier children. These behaviors could be related to nutrition and the care of children, such as breastfeeding, a proper diet, better hygiene, and illness management, as well as behaviors that enhance their children's intellectual development and school performance."

   Quisumbing, Agnes R., et al. 2010. *Mothers' Human Capital and the Intergenerational Transmission of Poverty: The Impact of Mothers' Intellectual Human Capital and Long-Run Nutritional Status on Children's Human Capital in Guatemala.* Chronic Poverty Research Centre Working Paper 160 and IFPRI Discussion Paper 12-4. Washington: International Food Policy Research Institute. http://dx.doi.org/10.2139/ssrn.1719646.

- If all women completed primary school, the number of children receiving an immunization against diphtheria, tetanus, and whooping cough (DPT3) would increase 10 percent, and it would increase 43 percent if all girls completed secondary school. A better-educated mother is more knowledgeable about the benefits of vaccination and more likely to have her children immunized against a range of diseases.

- **A twenty-two-nation study found that a mother's education had the strongest impact on the likelihood of immunizations.** Using Demographic and Health Surveys, the health and demography researchers Desai and Alva found that a mother's education level had the strongest impact on the likelihood of their children getting immunizations, compared with other indicators of their children's health, even after controlling for a variety of family and community characteristics like fathers' education and the presence of sanitation facilities. The authors point to the spillovers and potentially large benefits of higher maternal education levels due to the fact that immunized children also help lessen the risk of infection for the entire community.

  Desai, Sonalde, and Soumya Alva. 1998. "Maternal Education and Child Health: Is There a Strong Causal Relationship?" *Demography* 35, no. 1: 71–81.

- **In rural Uganda, a survey study found that mothers' education is the most "robust predictor of child health and nutrition inequalities."** The study, which collected and analyzed data on mothers and their children in order to identify which socioeconomic factors are most predictive of child stunting, found that other factors such as fathers' education, household assets, and landownership were all weak predictors compared with mothers' education.

  Wamani, Henry, et al. 2004. "Mothers' Education but Not Fathers' Education, Household Assets or Land Ownership Is the Best Predictor of Child Health Inequalities in Rural Uganda." *International Journal for Equity in Health* 3: 9.

- **In India, a large study of more than 5,000 households in the Human Development Survey of 2004–5 studied the pathways through which maternal education improves health outcomes and found that a mother's education has "a substantial estimated impact on children's immunization," even after controlling for regional and household characteristics.** In addition, it found that educating mothers improves children's health through their increased health knowledge and communication ability.

  Vikram, Kriti, Reeve Vanneman, and Sonalde Desai. 2012. "Linkages between Maternal Education and Childhood Immunization in India." *Social Science and Medicine* 75, no. 2: 331–39.

- **In India, when women do not have an education, their knowledge of health suffers, and so their children are less likely to be treated.**

Almost a third of mothers said that they had not immunized their children because they were not aware of the benefits, and a further 30 percent claimed not to know where to go to get their child vaccinated.

O'Donnell, Owen. 2007. "Access to Health Care in Developing Countries: Breaking Down Demand Side Barriers." *Cadernos de Saúde Pública* 23, no. 12: 2820–34. http://dx.doi.org/10.1590/S0102-311X2007001200003.

Pande, Rohini, and A. Yazbeck. 2003. "What's in a Country Average? Wealth, Gender, and Regional Inequalities in Immunization in India." *Social Science Medicine* 57: 2075–88.

Das, Jinshu, and S. Das. 2003. "Trust, Learning and Vaccination: A Case Study of a North Indian Village." *Social Science Medicine* 57: 97–112.

- **In a study in Mozambique, the mother's education level was identified as the strongest determinant of child health, measured as accessing maternity services, getting immunized, and having low levels of malnutrition, even when looking at the impact of the education levels of the other members of the household.**

Lindelow, Magnus. 2008. "Health as a Family Matter: Do Intra-Household Education Externalities Matter for Maternal and Child Health?" *Journal of Development Studies* 44, no. 4: 562–85.

Mothers' Education Increases Children's Schooling

- **A fifty-six-country study of adolescents age fifteen to eighteen years from 1990 to 2009 found that additional years of a mother's education increases her children's average years of schooling.** "The estimated coefficients show that relative to women with education, children of women with six years of education have an additional 2.8 years of education and children of women with twelve years of education have an additional 4.1 years." On average, one additional year of school attained by the mother was associated with approximately 0.32 more year of schooling attained by her children.

Bhalotra, Sonia, Kenneth Harttgen, and Stephan Klasen. 2013. *The Impact of School Fees on the Intergenerational Transmission of Education*. Background paper commissioned for *EFA Global Monitoring Report 2013/4*. Paris: UNESCO.

- **A thirty-five year study in Guatemala found a mother's education and cognitive skills have a greater impact on her children's schooling levels than previously thought.** Using a rich data set from Guatemala that followed the same cohort over thirty-five years, researchers from the International Food Policy Research Institute and the Chronic Poverty Centre estimated that a mother's education and cognitive skills have a greater impact on her children's schooling levels than previously calculated. Additionally, maternal education has a significant impact on a child's health and nutritional status, which in turn improves his or her educational outcomes.

Quisumbing, Agnes R., et al. 2010. *Mothers' Human Capital and the Intergenerational Transmission of Poverty: The Impact of Mothers' Intellectual Human Capital and Long-Run Nutritional Status on Children's Human Capital in Guatemala*. Chronic Poverty Research Centre Working Paper 160 and IFPRI Discussion Paper 12-4. Washington: International Food Policy Research Institute. http://dx.doi.org/10.2139/ssrn.1719646.

- **Multiple studies have found that a mother's level of education has a strong positive effect on her daughters' enrollment—more than on son's and significantly more than the effect of fathers' education on daughters.** Studies from Ghana, Egypt, Kenya, Peru, and Malaysia all find that mothers with a basic education are substantially more likely to educate their children, and especially their daughters, even controlling for other influences. Paternal education also promotes children's enrollment, more for girls than for boys, but the effects of maternal education are stronger.

Lavy, Victor. 1996. "School Supply Constraints and Children's Educational Outcomes in Rural Ghana." *Journal of Development Economics* 51, no. 2: 291–314.

Ridker, Ronald G., ed. 1997. *Determinants of Educational Achievement and Attainment in Africa: Findings from Nine Case Studies*. SD Publication Series, Technical Paper 62. Washington: USAID.

King, Elizabeth, and Rosemary Bellew. 1991. "Gains in the Education of Peruvian Women, 1940–1980." In *Women's Work, Education, and Family Welfare in Peru*, edited by Barbara Herz and Shahidur Khandkher. World Bank Discussion Paper 116. Washington: World Bank.

Alderman, Harold, and Elizabeth M. King. 1998. "Gender Differences in Parental Investment in Education." *Structural Change and Economic Dynamics* 9, no. 4: 453–68.

- **In Pakistan, a rigorous study on children's education found that even when controlling for a wide range of factors, children whose mothers have even a single year of education spend one extra hour studying at home every day and report higher test scores.**

Andrabi, Tahir, Jishnu Das, and Asim Ijaz Khwaja. 2011. *Students Today, Teachers Tomorrow: Identifying Constraints on the Provision of Education*. Policy Research Working Paper 5674. Washington: World Bank.

- **Mothers in India who are literate have children who study over one more hour per day than children of the same age, sex, and prior schooling than children of mothers who are illiterate.** These findings come from a study in India, which uses Rural Economic Development Survey (REDS) data and looks at the allocation of time for all women and children during the crop year 1981–82.

  Behrman, Jere, et al. 1999. "Women's Schooling, Home Teaching, and Economic Growth." *Journal of Political Economy* 107, no. 4: 682–714.

6 Reduces Rates of HIV/AIDS and Malaria

Girls' education is often called the *social vaccine* against HIV/AIDS because of the significant reduction in the incidence of that disease among better-educated girls and women. Increasing girls' and women's education reduces their risk of contracting HIV or transmitting HIV to their babies. Better-educated women have more knowledge about how HIV is contracted and are better prepared to prevent transmission. This also holds for malaria because better-educated girls and women are less likely to contract malaria, have children who are less likely to contract malaria, and are more likely to use prevention techniques, such as bed nets.

- **A study of seventy-two countries has found that HIV prevalence reaches the outbreak level of 5 percent in countries where the literacy gap exceeds 25 percentage points between boys and girls.** By contrast, HIV prevalence rates fall to 3 percent where the literacy gap between boys and girls is below 5 percent. The study analyzed low-risk urban adults in seventy-two countries and controlled for other influences.

  Over, Mead. 1998. "The Effects of Societal Variables on Urban Rates of HIV Infection in Developing Countries: An Exploratory Analysis." In *Confronting AIDS: Evidence from the Developing World*, edited by Martha Ainsworth, Lieve Fransen, and Mead Over. Brussels and Washington: European Commission and World Bank.

- **In Sub-Saharan Africa, just 72 percent of illiterate women know that HIV is not transmitted by sharing food, and only 52 percent know where to seek treatment, compared with 91 and 85 percent of literate**

women, respectively. Analysis of the Demographic and Health Surveys for twenty-six countries in Sub-Saharan Africa and five countries in South and West Asia demonstrates the importance of literacy skills in improving knowledge about HIV transmission. Improving female literacy helps stop the spread of HIV and AIDS. Literate women are more knowledgeable about HIV/AIDS and better equipped to prevent transmission.

- **Women with a postprimary education were five times as likely to know basic facts about HIV/AIDS than illiterate women in thirty-two countries.** Additionally, in South and West Asia as well as Sub-Saharan Africa, a literate woman is 30 percent more likely to be aware of her right to negotiate safer sex if her partner has a sexually transmitted disease.

  UNESCO. 2014a. *Gender Summary: Teaching and Learning—Achieving Quality for All—EFA Global Monitoring Report 2013/4.* Paris: UNESCO.

  Vandemoortele, Jan, and Enrique Delamonica. 2000. "Education 'Vaccine' against HIV/AIDS." *Current Issues in Comparative Education* 3, no. 1.

- **Secondary education completion helps to reduce infection rates.** Analyzing the forces behind the dramatic decline of HIV/AIDS in Zimbabwe, Halperin and colleagues find that high levels of secondary education completion were an important factor in making awareness campaigns and partner reduction efforts more effective, which helps explain a declining infection rate from 29 percent of the population to 16 percent from 1997 to 2007.

  Halperin, Daniel, et al. 2011. "A Surprising Prevention Success: Why Did the HIV Epidemic Decline in Zimbabwe?" *Plos Medicine* 8, no. 2: e1000414.

- **A study looking at the link between increases in women's secondary education and HIV decline in Uganda found that a policy change encouraging girls to attend secondary school could account for as much as half the reduction in the 13 percent decline in HIV prevalence between 1990 and 1995.** Their "results support the view that encouraging girls to stay in school delays their sexual debut and reduces their lifetime risk of acquiring HIV."

  Aslan, Marcella, and David Cutler. 2013. "Girls' Education and HIV Risk: Evidence from Uganda." *Journal of Health Economics* 32, no. 5: 863–72.

- **If all young adults completed primary education, we could expect 700,000 fewer new cases of HIV infection each year, or 7 million in a**

decade. The researchers Bruns, Mingar, and Rakotomalala made broad estimations for a Global Campaign for Education Report on how many cases of HIV/AIDS could be prevented using World Bank global data on the number of new HIV infections contracted by those with a primary school education and those without.

Bruns, Barbara, Alain Mingar, and Ramahatra Rakotomalala. 2003. *Achieving Universal Primary Education by 2015: A Chance for Every Child.* Washington: World Bank.

Global Campaign for Education. 2004. *Learning to Survive: How Education for All Would Save Millions of Young People from HIV/AIDS.* Oxford: Oxfam International.

- **In Malawi, providing small incentives to keep young women in school can reduce the rate of HIV by up to 60 percent.** A randomized control trial of a cash transfer program for thirteen- to twenty-two-year-old women in Malawi showed that not only do small cash incentives keep girls in school, they also help lower the risk of HIV infection. For women receiving cash transfers, 18 months after the program began HIV prevalence was 64 percent lower than for those not in the program. The authors conclude that "interventions that do not directly target sexual behaviour change can be important components of HIV prevention strategies."

Baird, Sarah, Richard Garfein, C. McIntosh, and Berk Ozler. 2012. "Effect of a Cash Transfer Programme for Schooling on Prevalence of HIV and Herpes Simplex Type 2 in Malawi: A Cluster Randomised Trial." *The Lancet* 379, no. 9823: 1320–29.

- **Evaluations of programs incentivizing girls to stay in school in Pakistan, Kenya, and Zimbabwe found an impact in helping to reduce HIV**, including "delayed sexual debut, lowered dropout rates, reduced teen marriage and childbearing, increased bonding and gender equity attitudes, better future expectations and more concerns over the consequences of sex."

UNDP (United Nations Development Program). 2014. *Discussion Paper: Cash Transfers and HIV Prevention.* New York: UNDP.

- **In a South Africa study, young women who had not completed high school had 3.75 greater odds of being HIV infected compared with those young women who had completed high school.** This was found to be true even after controlling for a variety of personal characteristics and sexual activity.

Pettifor, Audrey E., Brooke A. Levandowski, Catherine MacPhail, Nancy S. Padian, Myron S. Cohen, and Helen V. Rees. 2008. "Keep Them in School: The Importance of Education as a Protective Factor Against HIV Infection Among Young South African Women." *International Journal of Epidemiology* 37, no. 6: 1266–73.

- **Out-of-school women in Zambia age fifteen to nineteen were more than twice as likely to contract HIV than those young women who remained in school.** An analysis of trends for HIV infection in Zambia showed that more highly educated young women saw a great decline in HIV prevalence from 1995 to 2003, which was not true for those with lower education levels. In urban areas, 21.2 percent of fifteen- to twenty-four-year-old women with ten or more years of education had HIV in 1995, versus 8.5 percent in 2003; in rural areas, the change was from 28.1 to 5.6 percent. The effect of education was stronger for young women than men, and particularly strong at younger ages than in the entire population.

  Michelo, Chris, Ingvild Sandoy, and Knut Fylkesnes. 2006. "Marked HIV Prevalence Declines in Higher Educated Young People: Evidence from Population-Based Surveys (1995–2003) in Zambia." *AIDS* 20: 1031–38.

- **Young rural Ugandans with secondary-level education are three times less likely to be HIV positive than young rural Ugandans with no education.** A study found that during the 1990s, young people in Uganda who had some secondary schooling were three times less likely to be HIV positive: those who had some primary schooling were about half as likely as those who received no schooling to be HIV positive.

- **Each additional year of education decreases the probability of contracting HIV by 6.7 percent.**

  De Walque, Damien. 2004. *How Does Educational Attainment Affect the Risk of Being Infected by HIV/AIDS? Evidence from a General Population Cohort in Rural Uganda.* World Bank Development Research Group Working Paper. Washington: World Bank.

- **Education helps to protect women against the risk of HIV infection by reducing risky behaviors and increasing a woman's ability to discuss sex with a partner and to negotiate behaviors, such as condom use, that reduce risk.** According to a recent review of research that examined several studies of HIV/AIDS in Africa and Latin America, education's impact is stronger in urban areas and where violence against women is less prevalent.

Malhotra, Anju, Caren Grown, and Rohini Pande. 2003. *Impact of Investments in Female Education on Gender Inequality*. Washington: International Center for Research on Women.

- **The odds of children carrying malaria parasites is 22 percent lower if their mothers have a primary education and 36 percent lower if their mothers have a secondary education, compared with women who have no education.** These findings are based on estimates from Demographic and Health Survey data in areas of high transmission.

- **In Cameroon, estimates indicate that if all women had a secondary school education, malaria incidence would drop from 28 to 11 percent.**

UNESCO. 2014a. *Gender Summary: Teaching and Learning—Achieving Quality for All—EFA Global Monitoring Report 2013/4*. Paris: UNESCO.

- **In the Democratic Republic of Congo, a study interviewing 351 pregnant women found that they were three times as likely to report sleeping under a bed net if they had completed secondary school or higher.**

Pettifor, Audrey, et al. 2008. "Bed Net Ownership, Use and Perceptions Among Women Seeking Antenatal Care in Kinshasa, Democratic Republic of the Congo (DRC): Opportunities for Improved Maternal and Child Health." *BMC Public Health* 8: 331.

- **A study of nine countries in Sub-Saharan Africa showed that "controlling for other factors, completion of six years of primary school by the mother was associated with a reduction in the odds of malaria infection in her child of about 27 percent."** This effect was true even when controlling for household income, urban and rural location of the household, and other socioeconomic characteristics.

Siri, Jose G. 2014. "Independent Associations of Maternal Education and Household Wealth with Malaria Risk in Children." *Ecology and Society* 19, no. 1: 33.

7 Reduces Rates of Child Marriage

A high-quality education for girls is a critical strategy for preventing child marriage and mitigating the harmful consequences for girls who are already married. Child marriage is a global issue with millions of girls married every year around the world. Marriage frequently means an end to a girl's schooling either in the run up to her marriage, or shortly afterward when a girl's domestic duties increase as a result of her new role as a wife and mother. Child marriage not only curtails girls' education but also puts girls at a higher risk of early pregnancy and complications during childbirth.

In the last several years, new advocacy and analysis have emerged on child marriage and we have much better data on how long girls need to stay in school to see the biggest reductions in child marriage. Secondary education, as with other social benefits such as child and maternal survival, is emerging to be much more beneficial than just a primary education. We also have emerging insights on the role of education quality in the relationship between child marriage and girls' education. The dominant thinking has been that if girls are in school, they are at much less risk of child marriage. *Although this is true, findings from various country studies show that girls who are doing poorly in school, not learning well, and falling behind are sometimes being pulled out of school by their parents in order to marry.* Again, like other important benefits of girls' education, the quality of education has important implications here.

- **"A shocking 2.9 million girls are married by the age of fifteen in Sub-Saharan Africa and South and West Asia**, equivalent to one in eight girls in each region." This study goes on to find that "ensuring that girls stay in school is one of the most effective ways to avert child marriage. Being in school builds a girls knowledge and skills so she is better able to delay marriage and can help support the perception that girls are still children and are therefore not of marriageable age."

- **If all girls had a secondary education in Sub-Saharan Africa and South and West Asia, 64 percent fewer girls would get married as children, which would mean a decline of almost 2 million child brides.**

- **"In Ethiopia, while almost one in three young women with no education was married by the age of fifteen in 2011, among women with a secondary education, the share was just 9 percent."**

  UNESCO. 2014c. *Teaching and Learning: Achieving Quality for All—EFA Global Monitoring Report 2013/4*. Paris: UNESCO.

- **"Girls with a primary education are twice as likely to marry or enter into a union as those with a secondary or higher education. However, those with no education are three times more likely to marry or enter into a union before age eighteen as those with a secondary or higher education."**

These findings come from the United Nations Population Fund database for seventy-eight developing countries over the period 2000 to 2011.

- **In Ethiopia, "women 20 to 29 years old with secondary or higher education marry at an average age that is 3.2 years higher than that of women of the same age with no education.** They also have an average of 1.7 fewer children than their counterparts with no education."

- **"In Sub-Saharan Africa, two-thirds (66 percent) of women with no education became child brides, versus 13 percent of those with secondary or higher education—a rate over five times higher."**

    UNFPA (United Nations Population Fund). 2012. *Marrying Too Young: End Child Marriage*. New York: UNFPA.

- **"Only 4 percent of literate girls in Sub-Saharan Africa and 8 percent of literate girls in South and West Asia are married as children. In comparison, over 20 percent of illiterate girls in Sub-Saharan Africa and almost 25 percent of girls in South and West Asia are married as children."** This study from the United Nations Children's Fund goes on to say that "education is preventative for child marriage not only because it keeps girls in a formal system, but also because it gives them a purpose and goals: literacy in itself is strongly correlated with reducing child marriage prevalence. . . . One reason for this may be that literate girls have stayed in education for longer and thus have married later, but there is also strong evidence to suggest that a high-quality education can empower girls to make decisions about whether, when and whom they will marry."

    UNICEF (United Nations Children's Fund). 2014c. *State of the World's Children 2015: Reimagine the Future—Innovation for Every Child*. New York: UNICEF.

- **Across eighteen of the twenty countries with the highest prevalence of child marriage, girls with no education are up to six times more likely to marry as children than girls with a secondary education.**

    ICRW (International Center for Research on Women). 2006. *Too Young to Wed: Education and Action toward Ending Child Marriage, Brief on Child Marriage and Domestic Violence*. Washington: ICRW.

- **In Nepal, evidence shows that getting married at an age below twenty years significantly decreases girls' opportunities in terms of access to** education, with more than three out of ten girls who have married below twenty years having had no access to education. Furthermore, the evidence is clear that Nepalese women with higher educational attainment have higher wages. For instance, an employed female with a tertiary education enjoys a wage that is more than ten times that for a female worker with little or no education.

Scheuermann, A.-K. 2013. *Equity in Education in Nepal: Spotlight on Access, Attainment and Retention*. Kathmandu: UNICEF Nepal Country Office.

World Bank. 2013. *Nepal Human Development Note: Access, Equity, and Quality in the Education, Health and Social Protection Sectors*. Report from Human Development Unit of South Asia Region. Washington: World Bank.

- **A Ghana country study using pooled data from 1988, 1993, 1998, and 2003 found that women with a secondary education or higher have a risk of early marriage that is 41 percent lower than women with primary school or no education, even when controlling for factors such as ethnicity, religion, region, and birth cohort.**

Gyimah, Stephen Obeng. 2009. "Cohort Differences in Women's Educational Attainment and the Transition to First Marriage in Ghana." *Population Research Policy Review* 28: 455–71.

- **Each year married before eighteen increases the probability of illiteracy:** "Across Africa, each additional year a girl is married before age eighteen reduces her probability of literacy by about 6 percentage points, the probability of having at least some secondary schooling by 8 percentage points, and the probability of secondary school completion by almost 7 percentage points."

Wodon, Quentin. Forthcoming. *Child Marriage and Education*. Washington: World Bank—referenced by Klugman, Jeni, et al. 2014. *Voice and Agency: Empowering Women and Girls for Shared Prosperity*. Washington: World Bank.

- **Good academic performance can be a strong disincentive to marry early, according to evidence from fourteen focus group discussions with a total of 106 participants from Jordan, Syria, Iraq, and Palestine.** Conversely, it was also clear that girls that did not do well in school would be married as soon as was appropriate, often after age fifteen.

- **For example, "men participating in Za'atari refugee camp reported that for girls who dropped out of formal education in Syria, marriage**

might follow at ages as low as thirteen. Girls who continued their education, particularly higher education, were considered more likely to marry between the ages of twenty and twenty-seven."

UNICEF Jordan Country Office. 2014. *A Study on Early Marriage in Jordan*. New York: UNICEF.

8 Empowers Women

Girls' education and women's empowerment have an obvious connection. Girls who are able to attend school, and thus to develop important skills such as literacy and numeracy and greater analytical skills, are better able to navigate the world around them. And from that comes a sense of control and an ability to exercise their voice. Recent studies on the relationship between education and women's empowerment in the developing world in particular have been able to identify specific ways in which education empowers women. Women with higher levels of education are less likely to accept domestic violence, have greater control over household resource decisions, and have greater freedom of movement. These insights come from multiple country studies as well as recent rigorous cross-country analyses, such as one led by the World Bank researcher Jeni Klugman, who ultimately concludes that "education is particularly powerful in helping women overcome unequal and oppressive social limits and expectations so they can make choices about their lives."

Klugman's comprehensive World Bank report, titled *Voice and Agency: Empowering Women and Girls for Shared Prosperity*, distills thousands of surveys and finds that education plays a major role for women and girls: "Around the world, we see that better educated women are often better able to make and implement decisions and choices, even where gender norms are restrictive. In all regions, women with more education also tend to marry later and have fewer children. Enhanced agency is a key reason why children of better educated women are less likely to be stunted: educated mothers have greater autonomy in making decisions and more power to act for their children's benefit" (Klugman et al. 2014).

- **Analysis of 2001–12 Demographic and Health Surveys from fifty-four countries shows that a woman's education is strongly linked to measures of agency.** According to the study, "agency is the ability to make decisions about one's own life and act on them to achieve a desired outcome, free of violence, retribution, or fear." As women become more educated, they are less likely to experience one or more of the following "deprivations of agency": a lack of control over household resources, condoning wife beating, and child marriage. Although 65 percent of women with a secondary education or higher experience one of these deprivations, 90 percent of those with primary school or less do. For women who experience all three deprivations, it is just one in twenty for those with a secondary and one in five for women with only a primary education.

- **Using Demographic and Health Survey data from 2001 to 2012, the report finds that "in Cameroon, Côte d'Ivoire, and Mozambique, for example, between 61 and 80 percent of women with no education lack sexual autonomy, compared with fewer than 20 percent of women with higher education."** Sexual autonomy is measured by a woman's ability to refuse sex, to ask her partner to use a condom, or both.

- **"In South Asia, the Middle East, and North Africa, women with more education are less likely to have to ask their husband's or family's permission to seek medical care."**

- **Analyzing data from fifty-two developing countries, the study shows that 43 percent of women without an education have no say in decisions about visits to friends and family, compared with 17 percent of those with a higher education.** On average, women report greater freedom of movement if they are educated, identify themselves as the head of the household, or belong to a richer household.

    Klugman, Jeni, et al. 2014. *Voice and Agency: Empowering Women and Girls for Shared Prosperity.* Washington: World Bank.

- **In a study using national data from Sierra Leone, one additional year of schooling for females made them less tolerant of domestic abuse and more likely to refuse sex when the husband has a sexually transmitted disease (STD).** "An increase in education by one year increases a woman's propensity by 11 percentage points to declare that a wife is justified to refuse sex when the husband has an STD. . . . One additional year of schooling also reduces women's propensity to approve of wife beating by about 10 percentage points," from 36 to 26 percent.

Mocan, Naci H., and Colin Cannonier. 2012. *Empowering Women through Education: Evidence from Sierra Leone*. NBER Working Paper w18016. Cambridge, Mass.: National Bureau of Economic Research. doi: 10.3386/w18016.

• **In Pakistan, compared with women with no education, women with secondary schooling or more are 15 percent more likely to report having a say in who they marry.** Aslam finds that higher schooling for Pakistani girls is related to their perceived role in spouse choice.

Aslam, Monazza. 2013. *Empowering Women: Education and the Pathways of Change*. Background paper for *EFA Global Monitoring Report 2013/4*. Paris: UNESCO.

• **In a study of an innovative secondary education program in Honduras, Erin Murphy-Graham finds that the program improved women's empowerment in their marital relationships, increasing their ability to "negotiate a more equitable domestic division of labor."** The program improved women's gender consciousness, everyday communication, change-directed negotiation skills, and ability to express feelings and demonstrate love and care.

Murphy-Graham, Erin. 2010. "And When She Comes Home? Education and Women' Empowerment in Intimate Relationships." *International Journal of Educational Development* 30, no. 2010: 320–31.

• **"Although reducing domestic violence involves complicated social change, some research suggests that when women gain education, earning capacity, and standing in society, this neglect gives way.** Girls are allowed more equal access to food and health care. The age of marriage rises beyond early teen years and pregnancies are more widely spaced. And women can better seek health care for themselves, and are better able to protect themselves from threats such as HIV/AIDS. In general, female education is more effective in reducing violence against women where social norms already allow women more voice and choice in their own lives, and education can help change those norms."

Sen, Amartya. 2000. *Development as Freedom*. New York: Anchor Books.

9 Increases Women's Political Leadership

From community councils to national office, girls' education helps give women the skills they need to take on leadership roles in public life. Better-educated women are more likely to participate in volunteer and elected decisionmaking bodies across all levels. In those roles, some country studies suggest that they are much more likely to advocate for decisions and policy that benefit family and community life, such as improved social services.

"Breaking patriarchal structures and enabling girls to go to school multiplies their economic choices, and increases their voice and influence in society."

Graça Machel, First Lady of Mozambique and of South Africa, and Erna Solerg, Prime Minister of Norway

---

- **In a review of the literature on girls' education, King and Winthrop find that "one of the pernicious features of gender inequality is that it feeds on itself: parents may have lower aspirations for their daughters than for their sons, and so their daughters too have lower aspirations for themselves.** As they become educated, girls can acquire the skills and confidence to be able to influence their country's legislative agenda and entrepreneurial success. Education gives girls the chance to become policymakers, entrepreneurs, or leaders in their community."

  King, Elizabeth, and Rebecca Winthrop. 2015. *Today's Challenges for Girls' Education*. Washington: Brookings Institution.

- **Case studies of women in an eight-country study concluded that education was crucial to both accessing power and moving up in leadership.** Drawing on life histories of women leaders at different levels of government in eight countries, Tadros found that, among other factors, the profile of women leaders often included education, with a correlation between the level of education and the level of government office. The study finds: "If women are to make the transition from being informal political leaders to assuming formal political office to move from contesting at the local to the meso or national levels, meeting the minimum education attainment that is socially expected is a prerequisite. . . . It is clear that if policies and programmes are serious about expanding the pool of women leaders who are able to nominate themselves for political office beyond the elite cohort, they will have to address the education factor."

Tadros, Mariz. 2014. "Engaging Politically: Rethinking Women's Pathways to Power." In *Women in Politics: Gender, Power and Development*, edited by Mariz Tadros. London: Zed Books.

- A recent analytical review of fifty-four studies about support for women's and girls' leadership in low- and middle-income countries across all geographic regions finds that girls' education and early development are critical to their leadership potential:

"Support to girls' leadership is essential to foster effective women leaders. The evidence points to a strong relationship between girls' experience and opportunities in childhood and adolescence and their leadership capabilities. Girls from disadvantaged households do not have a family life that can provide the foundation for the development and exercise of leadership and political capabilities in adult life. External interventions and positive role models, both in and out of school, can help level the playing field by building girls' self-belief, skills, and networks. As family attitudes and behavior have a strong influence on girls' success, support to families as well as girls is essential."

"Education for all girls is critical to their leadership potential. The evidence shows that women leaders are educated women, and particularly so beyond the community level. Women need an education to access power, but they also need further education and professional training to be credible and have influence once they are in leadership positions, within civic associations, business, and formal political positions."

O'Neil, T., G. Plank, and P. Domingo. 2015. *Support to Women and Girls' Leadership: A Rapid Review of the Evidence*. London: Overseas Development Institute.

- **A study in India using data on electoral outcomes matched with census data on literacy rates shows that narrowing the gender literacy gap raises women's participation as voters, candidacies, and competitiveness in politics.** The study combined information on state assembly elections between 1980 and 2007 with information on literacy rates across 287 districts in India. Average literacy over the period was 34 percent for women and 55 percent for men. It is estimated that raising the female literacy rate to 42 percent would increase the share of female candidates by 16 percent, the share of votes obtained by women candidates by 13 percent, and female voter turnout by 4 percent.

Bhalotra, Sonia, Irma Clots-Figueras, and Lakshmi Iyer. 2013. *Women's Political Participation and the Female–Male Literacy Differential in India*. Background paper commissioned for *EFA Global Monitoring Report 2013/4*. Paris: UNESCO.

- **Education is linked to more democratic, less corrupt institutions**. Research suggests that governments and other institutions function better and with less corruption as women gain education and approach parity with men.

  Basu, Ananya, and Elizabeth M. King. 2001. *Does Education Promote Growth and Democracy? Some Evidence from East Asia and Latin America*. Washington: World Bank.

- **Repeated exposure to female leaders can positively influence both teenage girls' educational attainment and their career aspirations**. This rigorous 459-village study by several researchers, including Esther Duflo, looks at the effects of a 1993 law in India that reserved leadership positions for women in randomly selected villages. A village council could have reserved positions for women in two election cycles, one election cycle, or never. In villages where leadership positions on village councils were reserved for women, adolescent girls were more likely to want a job that required an education, to want to marry after age eighteen, and to want to be something other than a housewife. Furthermore, in villages where council leadership was not reserved for women, boys were 6 percent more likely to attend school than girls, and were 4 percent more likely to know how to read and write. In villages where leadership was reserved for women for two consecutive election cycles, that gap between boys and girls in these education measures was nonexistent.

- **In villages where councils were reserved for women, the proportion of parents who believed that their daughter's occupation should be determined by her in-laws declined from 76 to 65 percent**. This shows how parents' mindsets about their daughters improved with more female leadership in rural councils.

  Beaman, Lori, Esther Duflo, Rohindi Pande, and Petra Topalova. 2012. "Female Leadership Raises Aspirations and Educational Attainment for Girls: A Policy Experiment in India." *Science* 335, no. 6068: 582–86.

- **A study across 265 village councils in India showed that villages where leadership positions were reserved for women invested more in the development priorities expressed by women, such as investments in water and education.** Many cases indicate that women's greater political participation has made a difference for both them and their constituencies.

  Chattopadhyay, Raghabendra, and Esther Duflo. 2004. "Women as Policy Makers: Evidence from a Randomized Policy Experiment in India." *Econometrica* 72, no. 5: 1409–43.

- **In Nepal, women members of community committees were able to influence decisions affecting women's lives**—for example, by lobbying for pumps to operate around mealtimes, when water is most needed and for better access to maternal health care.

  Oxfam. 2014. *Programming on the Right to be Heard: A Learning Companion.* Oxford: Oxfam.

- **In the United States, findings on high profile female leaders indicate that their mothers' education levels were central to the influences they received as young girls about the importance of continuing their education.** The influence of mother's education on their children is evident at all schooling levels, and in all parts of the world. These research studies trace the development of current US governors and university presidents.

  Madsen, Susan R. 2008a. *Developing Leadership: Learning from the Experiences of Women Governors.* Lanham, Md.: University Press of America.

  Madsen, Susan R. 2008b. *On Becoming a Woman Leader: Learning from the Experiences of University Presidents.* San Francisco: Jossey-Bass.

10 Reduces Harm to Families from Natural Disasters and Climate Change

Around the world, women with higher levels of education appear to be more resilient in the face of crisis. They are able to better prepare for, adapt to, and bounce back from disasters. This resilience extends to her children and families. With the increasing attention to climate change, extreme weather, and natural disasters, a number of recent studies have examined the social and economic factors that are associated with reducing vulnerability, especially for adolescent girls (Swarup et al. 2011; Van der Gaag 2013). Female education has emerged, in the words of one rigorous study, as "the single most important social and economic factor associated with a reduction in vulnerability to natural disasters."

"If you want to change a nation, to change our planet, educate a girl."

Julia Gillard, Former Prime Minister of Australia and Board Chair of the Global Partnership for Education

- **A recent study reviewing existing literature on girls' education found that "more educated women are better able to protect themselves and their families from the effects of economic and environmental shocks. . . .** Even when shocks do not have differential gender effects, the absolute welfare losses for both men (and boys) and women (and girls) can be substantial. More educated mothers are able to protect their children's welfare through a higher quality of care and their greater ability to mitigate adverse shocks, such as food price changes, that might reduce food intake."

  King, Elizabeth, and Rebecca Winthrop. 2015. *Today's Challenges for Girls' Education.* Washington: Brookings Institution.

- **A study of developing countries from 1960 to 2003 found that countries with higher levels of female schooling were less likely to suffer high rates of death, injury, and displacement due to weather disasters.** "Educating young women may be one of the best climate change disaster prevention investments in addition to high social rates of return in overall sustainable development goals." For example, they estimate that if countries had invested more in educating women, 465 million people could have been saved from injury, requiring temporary assistance or losing their homes from floods, and 667 million from drought. Education of women would also lower the death toll by over 60,000 from floods. Adopting progressive but feasible policies to educate girls can make countries significantly less vulnerable to natural disasters.

Blankespoor, Brian, Susmita Dasgupta, Benoit Laplante, and David Wheeler. 2010. *Adaptation to Climate Extremes in Developing Countries: The Role of Education*. Policy Research Working Paper 5342. Washington: World Bank.

- **Female education "is the single most important social and economic factor associated with a reduction in vulnerability to natural disasters," finds a study of 130 countries between 1980 and 2010, even when controlling for many other aspects of human development like income and life expectancy.** Although, previously, the Human Development Index was used to study the impact of a country's development level on its vulnerability to climate change, this study looked at education levels and the proportion of women attaining lower secondary schooling and found that women's education is the best investment to improve a country's ability to cope with disasters.

- **This study estimates that deaths due to disaster could be reduced 60 percent by 2050 if 70 percent of all twenty- to thirty-nine-year-old women were to complete lower secondary school.**

  Streissnig, Erich, Wolfgang Lutz, and Anthony Patt. 2013. *Effects of Educational Attainment on Climate Risk Vulnerability Ecology and Society* 18, no. 1: 16. http://dx.doi.org/10.5751/ES-05252-180116.

- **A study of 151 countries found that education levels were significantly correlated with fewer deaths and less damage due to disaster.** In general, societies with higher levels of education have fewer disaster-related deaths, even after controlling for income levels. A study of 151 countries over time found that the income or wealth levels of a country are not always the largest determining factor in its ability to cope with natural disasters. Education levels were significantly correlated with fewer deaths and less damage due to disaster.

  Toya, Hideki, and Mark Sidmore. 2007. "Economic Development and the Impacts of Natural Disasters." *Economics Letters* 94, no. 1: 20–25.

- **In Bangladesh, better-educated households were less likely to experience shocks, meaning adverse events leading to a loss of income or assets due to events like crop damage, a loss of employment, theft, or the illness of a family member.** Based on a study of 2000 households in 2009, households with a head who had secondary education had fewer shocks.

  Santos, Indira, et al. 2011. *How Do the Poor Cope with Shocks in Bangladesh? Evidence from Survey Data*. Policy Research Working Paper 1810. Washington: World Bank.

- **Recent research conducted at the Center for Global Development finds girls' education to be one of the most cost-effective strategies to carbon-emissions mitigation.** "Our research suggests that female education is a major determinant of resilience in the face of weather-related shocks that are likely to increase with global warming. Using an econometric analysis of historical losses from weather-related shocks, we find that expanding women's education faster than currently-projected trends would prevent many thousands of deaths from floods and droughts, and hundreds of millions of cases of weather-related losses related to injuries, homelessness, and other forms of deprivation."

    Wheeler, David, and Dan Hammer. 2010. *The Economics of Population Policy for Carbon Emissions Reduction in Developing Countries.* Working Paper 229. Washington: Center for Global Development. http://ssrn.com/abstract=1824442.

CHAPTER 3

Glass Half Full: There Has Been Real Progress, But A Girls' Education Crisis Remains

The state of girls' education today can be summarized as much progress made, but with a burning crisis still remaining. Here, we review how far we have come over the past several decades and the nature of the girls' education challenge that remains. In closing, we offer insights on the momentum that is building for girls' education, ranging from grassroots advocacy and civil society engagement to an emerging network within the international community.

The Progress Made

The story of girls' education in 2015—the aspirational year of the Education for All initiative and the Millennium Development Goals (MDGs)—is a story of both immense progress and a still-devastating crisis. On the positive side, since the first version of this book was written in 2004, there has been true progress:

- **The number of girls out of primary school has been virtually cut in half.**

- **In 2000, 109.9 million girls of primary and lower-secondary school age were not in school. This means that since 2000, the number of out-of-school girls has nearly halved, and enrollment has increased by 8 percent.**

    UNESCO Institute for Statistics. "UIS StatCentre: Education Statistics." Retrieved July 21, 2015.

- **From 1990 to 2012, the number of countries closing the gender gap in enrollment in primary school rose from 86 to 124, and in secondary school from 40 to 69.**

    Winthrop, Rebecca. December 12, 2014. "Mobilizing Children's Rights, Supporting Local Leaders and Improving Girls' Education." PowerPoint presentation. Center for Universal Education, The Brookings Institution.

United Nations Statistics Division. 2015. "Millennium Development Goals Indicators Database." http://mdgs.un.org/unsd/mdg/.

- **Women and adolescent girls are completing more years of school than ever before. Today, women and girls more than fifteen years old spend, on average, seven years in school, compared with five years in 1990.**

Clinton Foundation, Bill & Melinda Gates Foundation, Economist Intelligence Unit, and WORLD Policy Analysis Center. 2015. *The Full Participation Report: No Ceilings*. Full Participation Project. New York: Clinton Foundation.

The progress made during the last twenty years is in many ways a testament to the effectiveness of having many actors work collaboratively to solve global problems, ranging from dedicated NGOs in both the South and North on both the global and local levels, to farsighted national leaders, to the scholars whose work we cite in this book and who have made the rigorous case for girls' education, to the countless parents and girls and local community leaders whose names will never appear in the history books but who together have made history.

The Crisis Remaining

And yet, amid this progress, there remain tens of millions of lost dreams, wasted potential, and denied opportunity because tens of millions of girls are still being deprived of their basic right to an education. Thus, even with the enormous progress that has been achieved, the state of girls' education remains nothing less than an educational, economic, health, and moral crisis:

"If only I can get educated, I will surely be the president."

A teenage girl in rural Malawi

- **A total of 62 million girls are denied the right to attend primary and lower-secondary school.**

UNESCO. 2015b. *Education for All 2000–2015: Achievements and Challenges—Education for All Global Monitoring Report 2015*. Paris: UNESCO.

- **Girls who seek to attend school face violence and even death in countries ranging from Nigeria to Pakistan—and too many face sexual abuse even when they are at school.**

  Global Coalition to Protect Education from Attack. 2014. *Education under Attack: 2014*. New York: Global Coalition to Protect Education from Attack.

- **Less than one in three girls in Sub-Saharan Africa and fewer than half in South Asia are enrolled in secondary school.**

  Clinton Foundation, Bill & Melinda Gates Foundation, Economist Intelligence Unit, and WORLD Policy Analysis Center. 2015. *The Full Participation Report: No Ceilings*. Full Participation Project. New York: Clinton Foundation.

- **A total of 75 percent of girls start school in Sub-Saharan Africa, but only 8 percent finish.**

  Winthrop, Rebecca and Eileen McGivney. 2014a. "Raising the Global Ambition for Girls Education." Global Views Policy Paper 2014-05. Washington, D.C.: Brookings Institution

- **Poor, rural girls still face a triple disadvantage. In 2010, the poorest women in rural areas in both low- and lower-middle-income countries had spent *less than three years in school.***

  Clinton Foundation, Bill & Melinda Gates Foundation, Economist Intelligence Unit, and WORLD Policy Analysis Center. 2015. *The Full Participation Report: No Ceilings*. Full Participation Project. New York: Clinton Foundation.

- **Armed conflict and humanitarian crises devastate children's chance at an education. In the thirty-five countries that are affected by crises today, there are at least 14 million refugees and internally displaced children between the ages of three and fifteen.** Only half these children go to primary school, and only a quarter attend lower secondary school, with girls being especially hard hit.

  Nicolai, Susan, S. Hine, and J Wales. 2015. *Education in Emergencies and Protracted Crises: Towards a Strengthened Response*. Background paper for the Oslo Summit on Education for Development. London: Overseas Development Institute.

Six Lenses for Viewing the Progress and Crisis in Girls' Education

To understand the progress made and the problems remaining in girls' education, it is important to consider six main areas:

1. **Getting into school.** Enrollment in primary school: How many girls start?

2. **Staying in school.** Completing their education: How many girls make it through secondary school?

3. **Learning in school.** Are girls learning and receiving a high-quality education?

4. **Hotspot countries.** How are girls doing in the "hot spots," the countries still lagging behind?

5. **Humanitarian crises.** How do war and humanitarian crises affect girls' and boys' education?

6. **Most marginalized.** How are the most disadvantaged and most marginalized girls progressing?

The remainder of this chapter walks through the state of girls' education in each of these areas.

1 Enrollment in Primary School: How Many Girls Start?

Today, though the vast majority of children in many countries are in school, millions of girls in the developing world are not. UNESCO's Institute of Statistics compiles the latest education data that governments share, including the number of girls and boys enrolled in primary and lower-secondary school, and every year these data are reported in UNESCO's *Global Education Monitoring Report*. From these data, we know that, globally, **there are more than 62 million girls who should be in primary and lower secondary school but are not**. This number grows significantly if early education is included, which applies to girls who should be enrolled in preprimary school but are not, and similarly for upper secondary.

- **Primary school: 30.6 million girls of primary school age are not in school.**

- **Lower secondary school: 31.6 million girls of lower secondary school age are not in school.**

  UNESCO. 2015a. *Education for All 2000–2015: Achievements and Challenges—Education for All Global Monitoring Report 2015*. Paris: UNESCO.

- **Among "out-of-school children, girls are more likely than boys never to enroll in school (48 percent, compared with 37 percent),** while boys are more likely to leave school (26 percent, compared with 20 percent). Once enrolled, girls are more likely to reach the upper grades."

  UNESCO. 2015a. *Education for All 2000–2015: Achievements and Challenges—Education for All Global Monitoring Report 2015*. Paris: UNESCO.

- **"Twenty years after [the declaration of women's rights in] Beijing, less than one in three girls in Sub-Saharan Africa and fewer than half in South Asia are enrolled in secondary school."**

  Clinton Foundation, Bill & Melinda Gates Foundation, Economist Intelligence Unit, and WORLD Policy Analysis Center. 2015. *The Full Participation Report: No Ceilings*. Full Participation Project. New York: Clinton Foundation.

Global Definitions of Education Levels

Education systems around the world can be quite different in structure and content. To help develop a global picture of education, in the 1970s the United Nations Educational, Scientific, and Cultural Organization (UNESCO) developed a system to classify various kinds of education. This classification system, which was last updated in 2011, outlines four main levels of children's education around the world:

- Early childhood education: defined as at least 2 hours per day for 100 days a year

- Primary education: typically 6 years, but varies between 4 and 7 years

- Lower secondary education: typically 3 years, but varies between 2 and 5 years

- Upper secondary education: typically 3 years, but varies between 2 and 5 years

Frequently, governments and other education actors refer to the first three levels—early childhood, primary, and lower secondary—as *basic education*. Basic education is most often understood to comprise the essential foundational levels of education, to which every child around the world has a right.

UIS. (2012). *International Standard Classification of Education: ISCED 2011.* UNESCO: Montreal.

A school-age girl can be counted as not enrolled in school in three main ways:

- She never had any opportunity to attend school, and hence has never made it to the school door.

- She entered school but dropped out early, unable to build on her initial education.

- She started school much later than the required age, and thus missed important learning in her early years.

Girls who make it into school, but at later than the required age, are described as overage students. Frequently, their learning is truncated by late entry and early leaving during adolescence. There are global measures capturing the overage student population in school in the developing world.

Depending on where a girl is born, she has a very different likelihood of being able to enroll in primary or lower secondary school. **The majority of girls who are not enrolled in school live in Africa and Asia:**

- In Sub-Saharan Africa, 16.6 million school-age girls are not enrolled in primary school and 11.3 school-age girls are not enrolled in secondary school.

- In Asia, 8.1 million school-age girls are not enrolled in primary school and 16.3 million school-age girls are not enrolled in secondary school.

Calculating Who Is In and Out of School—Net-Enrollment Ratios (NER) versus Gross-Enrollment Ratios (GER)

Calculating how many children and youth are in and out of school can be tricky business. In many countries, children enter school at a late age, leave early, and sometimes reenter after much time has passed. There are two main methods for calculating how many children are in and out of school. The first method gives a good sense of the numbers of school-age children who are in and out of school, and the second one gives a sense of the total numbers of children in school, including overage children:

- The net enrollment ratio (NER) is the share of children of school age who are enrolled in school. This can be calculated for different education levels, such as for primary school or lower secondary school. By definition, the NER cannot exceed 100 percent. For example, if all children in a country who are of primary school age are in school, then the primary school NER is 100; but if only half the children who are of primary school age are in school, then the primary school NER is 50.

$$\text{Primary NER} = \frac{\text{Number of children of primary school age enrolled in primary school}}{\text{Number of children of primary school age}}$$

- The gross enrollment ratio (GER) is an indicator related to the NER. It shows how many children, no matter what their age, are enrolled at a particular level of school, relative to the population of school-age children for that level. For example, if many adolescents are enrolled in primary school because their schooling was interrupted for several years and they have recently returned to school—something that frequently happens in the context of war—the primary GER will be more than 100 percent, indicating that many children who are not of primary school age are in school.

$$\text{Primary GER} = \frac{\text{Number of children of primary school age enrolled in primary school}}{\text{Number of children of primary school age}}$$

- In Arab states, 2.6 million school-age girls are not enrolled in primary school and 1.7 million school-age girls are not enrolled in secondary school.

UNESCO. 2015a. *Education for All 2000–2015: Achievements and Challenges—Education for All Global Monitoring Report 2015*. Paris: UNESCO.

2 Completing Their Education: How Many Girls Make It Through Secondary School?

- **In most parts of the world, school-age girls and boys are enrolled in primary school at higher rates than in secondary school**. The deficits at secondary education levels can be extreme, ranging from almost two-thirds of school-age girls out of school in Sub-Saharan Africa to more than half in South Asia and almost a full 40 percent in the Arab world (see figure 3.1).

King, Elizabeth, and Rebecca Winthrop. 2015. *Today's Challenges for Girls' Education*. Washington: Brookings Institution.

- Using UNESCO data from the World Bank's EdStats database, figure 3.1 shows the authors' calculations of regional net enrollment rates using averages over four years, so all developing countries have data included. However, these regional averages mask very deep disparities between girls and boys in some countries:

  - **Chad: 46 girls for every 100 boys are enrolled in secondary school.**

  - **Democratic Republic of Congo: 59 girls for every 100 boys are enrolled in secondary school.**

  - **Pakistan: 74 girls for every 100 boys are enrolled in secondary school.**

  - **Iraq: 75 girls for every 100 boys are enrolled in secondary school.**

Winthrop, Rebecca, and Eileen McGivney. 2014b. "Top 10 List You Don't Want to Be One: Dangerous Places for Girls' Education," blog post, Center for Universal Education, Brookings Institution. http://www.brookings.edu/blogs/education-plus-development/posts/2014/09/23-dangerous-places-girls-education-winthrop-mcgivney.

Enrolling girls in school is only the first step. And ensuring that girls stay in school can often be equally difficult. **Millions of girls who have enrolled in school drop out before they finish, from either primary or lower secondary school.** After enrolling girls, ensuring that they complete school is the second major challenge for girls' education today (see figure 3.2):

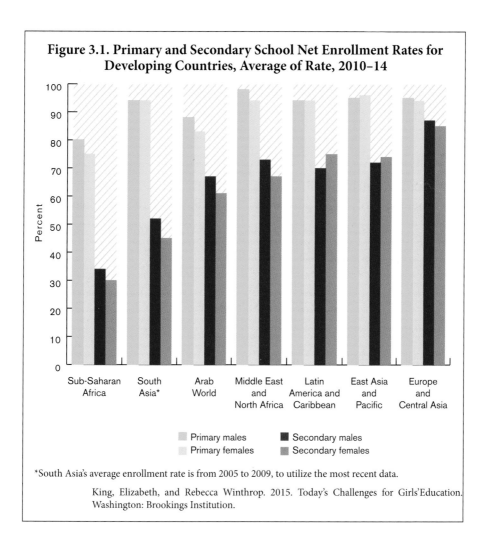

Figure 3.1. Primary and Secondary School Net Enrollment Rates for Developing Countries, Average of Rate, 2010–14

Primary males Secondary males
Primary females Secondary females

*South Asia's average enrollment rate is from 2005 to 2009, to utilize the most recent data.

King, Elizabeth, and Rebecca Winthrop. 2015. Today's Challenges for Girls' Education. Washington: Brookings Institution.

- **"In Sub-Saharan Africa, the drop-off is even starker, with 75 percent of girls starting school but only 8 percent finishing secondary."**

  Winthrop, Rebecca, and Eileen McGivney. 2014b. "Top 10 List You Don't Want to Be One: Dangerous Places for Girls' Education," blog post, Center for Universal Education, Brookings Institution. http://www.brookings.edu/blogs/education-plus-development/posts/2014/09/23-dangerous-places-girls-education-winthrop-mcgivney.

In many places, both boys and girls are dropping out of school before they finish. The equally small numbers of boys and girls completing their education in the developing world shows that there is a serious problem for both genders.

- **Even once they are enrolled, girls often are less likely to complete school than boys.** In Sub-Saharan Africa, from 1990 to 2008 the ratio of girls to boys who complete school increased from 0.78 to 0.91, but remained especially low in Central and West Africa, where only eight girls complete primary school for every ten boys.

  World Bank. 2012. *World Development Report 2012: Gender Equality and Development.* Washington: World Bank.

- **In Chad, girls' enrollment in primary school increased by 50 percent, but they are still 30 percent less likely than boys to remain enrolled.**

  GCE (Global Campaign for Education) and RESULTS Educational Fund. 2010. *Make it Right: Ending the crisis in girls' education.* Johannesburg and Washington D.C.: GCE and Results Education Fund.

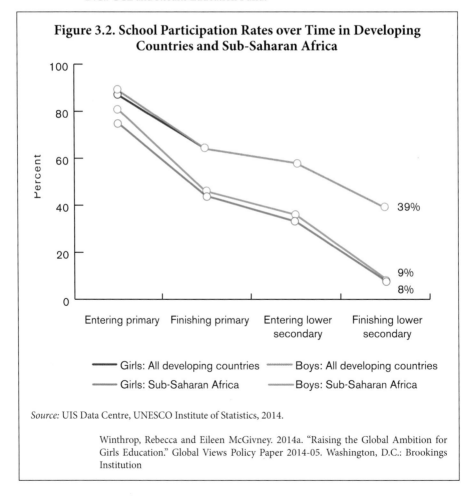

Figure 3.2. School Participation Rates over Time in Developing Countries and Sub-Saharan Africa

Source: UIS Data Centre, UNESCO Institute of Statistics, 2014.

Winthrop, Rebecca and Eileen McGivney. 2014a. "Raising the Global Ambition for Girls Education." Global Views Policy Paper 2014-05. Washington, D.C.: Brookings Institution

What is Gender Parity?

The important goal of ensuring that girls and boys are in school in equal numbers is tracked with a measure called gender parity, which is defined as the ratio of girls to boys at any given level of education, such as primary or lower secondary school. When an education system has between 97 and 103 girls enrolled for every 100 boys, it is considered to have an equal number of girls and boys—or, in the words of educationalists, the system is said to have reached gender parity. This is because at any given time, there may be slightly more girls or boys in the school-age population. When there are between 85 and 97 girls for every 100 boys, girls are considered to be disadvantaged vis-à-vis gender parity; and if there are fewer than 85 girls for every 100 boys, girls are considered to be severely disadvantaged vis-à-vis gender parity.

3 Are Girls Learning and Receiving a High-Quality Education?

Once girls enroll and stay in school, the third major hurdle they face is to ensure that they are learning well while there. Indeed, the quality of schooling and girls' ability to complete school are closely related. If girls are struggling to master their lessons, they are more likely to fall behind in school and ultimately drop out. We know from global student assessment data on reading and mathematics that it is the very same regions where girls struggle to enter and stay in school that have the poorest quality of schooling (see figure 3.3):

- In South and West Asia, only 48 percent of girls and boys in school meet basic proficiency standards for reading, and 28 percent for mathematics.

- In the Arab states, only 59 percent of girls and boys in school meet basic proficiency standards for reading, and 40 percent for mathematics.

- In Sub-Saharan Africa, only 67 percent of school girls and boys in school meet basic proficiency standards for reading , and only 62 percent for mathematics.

UNESCO. 2015b. "World Inequality Database on Education." http://www. education-inequalities.org/.

Winthrop, Rebecca, and Eileen McGivney. 2015. *Why Wait 100 Years? Bridging the Gap in Global Education*. Washington: Brookings Institution.

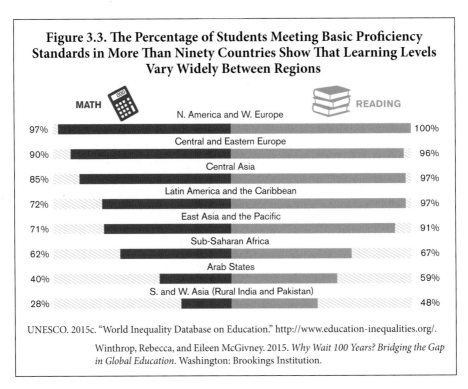

Figure 3.3. The Percentage of Students Meeting Basic Proficiency Standards in More Than Ninety Countries Show That Learning Levels Vary Widely Between Regions

MATH   **READING**

N. America and W. Europe
97%   100%

Central and Eastern Europe
90%   96%

Central Asia
85%   97%

Latin America and the Caribbean
72%   97%

East Asia and the Pacific
71%   91%

Sub-Saharan Africa
62%   67%

Arab States
40%   59%

S. and W. Asia (Rural India and Pakistan)
28%   48%

UNESCO. 2015c. "World Inequality Database on Education." http://www.education-inequalities.org/.

Winthrop, Rebecca, and Eileen McGivney. 2015. *Why Wait 100 Years? Bridging the Gap in Global Education.* Washington: Brookings Institution.

The quality of education affects both girls and boys who are in school, and ultimately with such poor learning results, educational quality is an urgent issue for both genders.

- **One global study estimates that 250 million children in the world do not meet basic proficiency standards for mathematics and reading—and this includes 130 million who are in school and 120 million who have never been to school.** Although many more children are enrolling in school, millions—boys and girls—are not learning even the most basic skills.

  UNESCO. 2015a. *Education for All 2000–2015: Achievements and Challenges—Education for All Global Monitoring Report 2015.* Paris: UNESCO.

- **A 2014 household assessment of all children living in rural areas of India finds that less than half of all fifth-grade students can read at a second-grade level.** Learning levels are also low in mathematics, with just over a quarter of fifth-grade students able to do division. In many states, these figures have actually been declining in recent years.

ASER (Annual Status of Education Report) Centre. 2015. *Annual Status of Education Report (Rural) 2014.* Provisional, January 13. http://img.asercentre.org.

- **Findings from a survey of 27,000 marginalized girls across twelve countries show that literacy levels for fourteen- and fifteen-year-olds were equivalent to the expected reading proficiency levels for seven-year-olds.** Additionally, nine- to eleven-year-old girls' average reading proficiency levels are below the expected levels for seven-year-olds, and they are about three years of schooling behind international norms.

  Additionally, "the average difference in literacy scores between 14–15- and 9–11-year olds was only 27 [words per minute], which roughly corresponds to an increase in reading fluency to the equivalent of less than 1.5 years of schooling, even though 14–15-year-old girls have spent between four and five additional years in school. This suggests that the literacy gap is increasing as girls get older. . . . Once there is a significant gap in literacy levels then these differences tend to maintain over the schooling years."

  Coffey International Development. 2015. *Baseline Report: Innovation Window— Evaluation Manager Girls' Education Challenge Fund.* London: UK Department for International Development.

4 How Are Girls Doing in the Hot Spots, the Countries Still Lagging Behind?

Despite the progress on girls' education to date, the job is far from done. The girls' education crisis has moved from touching most countries, as it did twenty-five years ago, to being a significant problem in approximately eighty countries around the world. These eighty countries are *girls' education hotspots*, many of which are the poorest in the world; a number of them struggle with armed conflict and political violence. Not surprisingly, most of them are located across Sub-Saharan Africa, in the Middle East, and in South and West Asia (see figure 3.4):

- **A recent study using World Bank data to compare multiple education indicators across all countries finds that there are eighty countries in the world where progress on girls' education is severely lagging behind.** "These countries are not meeting the education MDGs. They are stuck in an education bog—still struggling to enroll all girls and boys in primary school and close the gender gaps between boys and girls at both the primary and secondary levels…. The eighty countries where girls' education is stalled, today's *girls' education hotspots,* are primarily located across Sub-Saharan Africa, the Middle East and South West Asia."

- Today's girls' education hot spots are made up of the eighty countries listed below. All these countries have fewer school-aged girls and boys enrolled in primary and/or secondary school than the global average, and many of them have many more girls out of school than boys:

  ○ **Some of these countries are enrolling girls at low rates relative to global average, and also relative to boys:** Albania, Antigua and Barbuda, Azerbaijan, Cameroon, Comoros, Dominican Republic, Ghana, Guatemala, India, Kenya, Malaysia, Morocco, Mozambique, Papua New Guinea, Palau, Timor-Leste, and Zambia.

    ▪ **Some of these countries are significantly below global enrollment rates (1 standard deviation):** Afghanistan, Angola, Benin, Burkina Faso, Burundi, Cambodia, Central African Republic, Chad, Côte

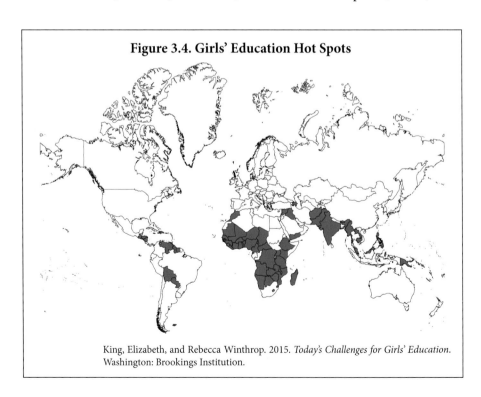

Figure 3.4. Girls' Education Hot Spots

King, Elizabeth, and Rebecca Winthrop. 2015. *Today's Challenges for Girls' Education.* Washington: Brookings Institution.

d'Ivoire, Democratic Republic of Congo (some data missing), Djibouti, Ethiopia, Guinea, Guinea-Bissau, Haiti (some data missing), Iraq, Laos, Jamaica, Liberia, Malawi, Mali, Niger, Nigeria, Pakistan, Sierra Leone, Solomon Islands, South Sudan, Syria, Togo, Uganda, and Yemen.

- ○ **Some of these countries are enrolling all children below the global average, girls and boys:** Bermuda, Bhutan, Bolivia, Botswana, El Salvador, Honduras, Maldives, Marshall Islands, Myanmar, Namibia, Nicaragua, Philippines, Paraguay, São Tomé and Príncipe, Senegal, Suriname, Tanzania, Turks and Caicos, Tuvalu, Vanuatu, Venezuela (some data missing), and Zimbabwe.

  - ▪ **Some of these countries are significantly below global enrollment rates:** Equatorial Guinea, the Gambia, Guyana, Lesotho, Madagascar, Mauritania, Puerto Rico, and Swaziland.

    King, Elizabeth, and Rebecca Winthrop. 2015. *Today's Challenges for Girls' Education*. Washington: Brookings Institution.

5 How Do Violence and Humanitarian Crises Affect Girls' and Boys' Education?

Violence and humanitarian crises affect girls and boys in terrible ways: families are displaced, communities are destroyed, and whole countries are affected as people desperately flee. Globally, one-third of all the girls and boys who are out of school live in countries that are afflicted with crises—from war to disasters to epidemics. These crises can shatter lives and communities, and many are long-lasting. Today, 60 million people around the world have been forced to flee their homes, more than the world has ever seen before. Sometimes it can take decades before children and their families can return home. An increasing phenomenon of attacking education—especially girls, female teachers, and girls' schools—only adds to the list of fear and disruption that violence and crisis brings to education. In these contexts, education becomes a right unfulfilled for most girls and boys (Sperling 2006a).

Crises: War, Disaster, and Epidemics

- • **Currently thirty-five countries are affected by an emergency or ongoing crisis—from war to natural disaster to health epidemics.** Although estimating populations affected by crises can be tricky, given the dynamic nature of the problem, researchers at the Overseas Development Institute have recently done a careful study of education in crisis contexts. Half the countries are plagued by war, and the rest are suffering from a mixture of natural disasters, health epidemics, and contexts where all three are present.

• **Within the countries that are affected by crises, approximately 37 million primary and lower secondary school-age girls and boys are out of school.** These children make up approximately one-third of all the school-aged children out of primary and lower secondary schools in the world.

• **"There are at least 14 million refugee and internally displaced children aged 3–15 in affected countries; very few go to preprimary, 1 in 2 to primary, and 1 in 4 to lower secondary school."**

• **"Girls are disproportionately affected, especially by conflict, with 4 of the 5 countries with the largest gender gaps in education experiencing war or insurgency."**

Nicolai, Susan, S. Hine, and J Wales. 2015. *Education in Emergencies and Protracted Crises: Towards a Strengthened Response.* Background paper for the Oslo Summit on Education for Development. London: Overseas Development Institute.

- **At the end of 2014, 60 million people were forced to flee their homes.** This is more than the world has ever seen before, with most of the situations lasting for more than twenty years.

- **The conflict in Syria, now on its fourth year, is today's single biggest driver of forced displacement.** There are 2.6 million children out of school in Syria, and in the neighboring countries of Turkey, Lebanon, Jordan, Iraq, and Egypt.

  UNHCR. 2014. *World at War: Global Trends in Forced Displacement in 2014.* Geneva: UNHCR.

  Jalbout, Maysa. 2015. *Reaching All Children with Education in Lebanon: Opportunities for Action.* London: Their World.

- **The recent earthquake in Nepal in April 2015 destroyed more than 36,000 classrooms, and an additional 17,000 classrooms were damaged, disrupting the education of more than 1 million children.**

  UNICEF. 2015. "Nepal Earthquake: New Appeal for Children Amid Growing Need." United Nations Children's Fund. http://www.unicef.org/infobycountry/media_81729.html.

- **The Ebola epidemic that started in 2014 in Liberia and spread across Sierra Leone and Guinea shut down education systems for more than 7 months in those countries, not to mention destroying girls' lives, families, and communities.**

  INEE. 2015. *EiE Crisis Spotlight: Ebola—West Africa.* http://www.ineesite.org/en/crisisspotlights/ebola-west-africa.

- **Adolescents and young adults living in war-torn North Kivu Province of the Democratic Republic of Congo are twice as likely to have less than two years in school—three times as likely for poor females—compared to the national average.** Conflict-affected areas are often sites of extreme disadvantage in education. Within these areas, the poor typically fare far worse than others, and poor girls worst of all.

- **In Northern Uganda, armed conflict nearly doubles the risk that girls from the poorest households have less than two years of school,**

though it appears to have had little impact on the educational opportunities of boys from the wealthiest households.

UNESCO. 2011. *The Hidden Crisis: Armed Conflict and Education: EFA Global Monitoring Report 2011*. Paris: UNESCO.

Political Violence and Attacks on Education

A more recent growing phenomenon has been the explicit and growing attacks on education, particularly on girls' education (Sperling 2001a). There are several high profile examples, including the near fatal shooting of education activist Malala Yousafzai by members of the Taliban on a school bus in Swat Valley, Pakistan, in October 2012, and the night kidnapping of nearly 300 Nigerian Chibok schoolgirls from their boarding school by the jihadist terrorist organization Boko Haram in April 2014. Although these have garnered much international attention to the horrible nature of attacking girls as a strategy of political violence, most attacks against girls' education do not make the headlines. Indeed, girls and boys in 70 countries around the world have their education disrupted by political violence targeted on schools.

What is the Malala Fund?

Malala Yousafzai was born in 1997 in Pakistan, a girl with a father dedicated to education. Growing up in the Swat Valley, she became an advocate for girls' education, speaking out against those that would wish to ban it for girls. In 2012, she was shot in the head by the Taliban on her way home from school. Her survival catapulted her to global fame, becoming a worldwide symbol of all girls braving school amid political violence and armed conflict. She continues to speak out for girls' education and before the age of 18 she has had a UN Day named after her and she has been awarded the Nobel Peace Prize. The Malala Fund is her foundation and the platform from which she conducts her advocacy and seeks to support efforts for secondary education for girls around the world.

- **Between 2009 and 2012, there were attacks on education in over 70 countries.**

  Global Coalition to Protect Education from Attack. 2014b. *Education under Attack: 2014*. New York: Global Coalition to Protect Education from Attack.

- **In Pakistan, a violent campaign by the Taliban outlawed girls schooling in the Swat district, forcing 120,000 girls to drop out of school.**

Nobel Peace Prize-winner Malala Yousafzai was shot in the head for speaking up for girls' right to an education. Even after the region restored government control, many girls were too scared to return to school. In Pakistan there are only 74 girls for every 100 boys enrolled in primary school.

- **In Northern Nigeria in 2014, the militant group Boko Haram, which translates literally to "Western education forbidden," kidnapped nearly 300 girls from a secondary school, many of whom are still missing at the writing of this report.** More than a third of girls in Nigeria are married before they are 18, and there are fewer than 9 girls in secondary school for every 10 boys.

- **In Afghanistan, girls' education has been attacked violently by gassing schools, bombing busses of schoolgirls, and threatening teachers and parents who educate girls.** In one instance, a teacher was fatally shot for continuing to teach girls after threats.

- **In the Democratic Republic of Congo, girls have been raped by military personnel on their way to school.**

- **In Colombia, girls were sexually harassed in their schools by police, and forced to be spies for armed groups.**

- **In India, girls have been raped in schools due to sectarian violence.**

  Global Coalition to Protect Education from Attack. 2014b. *Education Under Attack 2014.* New York, New York: Global Coalition to Protect Education from Attack.

  Winthrop, Rebecca, and Eileen McGivney. 2014b. "Top 10 List You Don't Want to Be One: Dangerous Places for Girls' Education," blog post, Center for Universal Education, Brookings Institution.http://www.brookings.edu/blogs/education-plus-development/posts/2014/09/23-dangerous-places-girls-education-winthrop-mcgivney.

6 How Are the Most Disadvantaged and Most Marginalized Girls Progressing?

In recent years, a number of studies have demonstrated with increasing clarity which girls exactly are still struggling to get an education. We know that globally the girls who need our attention primarily live in the poorest countries in the world, many of which are in countries struggling with war and humanitarian crisis as discussed above. We also know that within these countries, it is the girls from the poorest families who live in rural areas that are the farthest behind in terms of getting into school, completing school, and in learning well while there. Indeed, within the girls' education hotspots, the level of inequality can be significant. Many girls and boys from wealthy families and who live in urban centers are able to successfully progress through a full course of schooling. We also know that if girls are from an ethnic or linguistic minority, and speak a different mother-tongue from what is taught in school, they are very likely to be left behind.

The Poorest Countries Is Where the Girls Farthest Behind Live

- **"The largest gender gaps in enrollment are in the poorest countries.** In highly indebted poor countries, the average net enrollment rate at the primary level is 75.6 percent for girls compared with 80.9 percent for boys. The average girls' net enrollment rate in these countries is more than 5 percentage points lower than the average for low-income countries, more than 16 percentage points lower than for middle-income countries, and more than 20 percentage points lower than for in high-income countries. **At the secondary level, the deficits for girls in the heavily indebted countries are much larger. . . . To illustrate, the average girls' net enrollment rate is 25.9 percent, as compared with 63.6 percent in middle-income countries and 90.0 percent in high-income countries."**

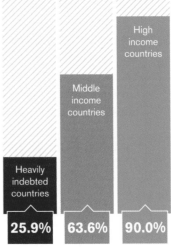

King, Elizabeth, and Rebecca Winthrop. 2015. *Today's Challenges for Girls' Education*. Washington: Brookings Institution.

Within Poor Countries: The Poorest Girls Living in Rural Areas are the Farthest Behind

- **Within poor countries, it is poor and rural girls that are most behind. At current rates, in Sub-Saharan Africa it will take poor girls seventy years longer to reach universal lower-secondary school completion than rich boys** (see figure 3.5).

- **Data from demographic and health surveys for twenty-four low-income countries shows that being a poor, rural girl is a triple disadvantage.** Living in a rural area and belonging to a family in the lowest income group is a disadvantage for any child. But additionally being a girl in these circumstances decreases the likelihood she will complete primary school even further (see figure 3.6).

    King, Elizabeth, and Rebecca Winthrop. 2015. *Today's Challenges for Girls' Education*. Washington: Brookings Institution.

- **A sixty-one-country study finds that the poorest children are more than three times as likely to be out of school as the richest children.** "Poverty, gender and location are the most pervasive factors linked to disparities in school attendance in children of primary-school and lower-secondary school age. An analysis of sixty-one household surveys from developing countries between 2006 and 2012 shows that children of primary-school age from the poorest 20 percent of households are over three times more likely to be out of school than children from the richest 20 percent of households. Among the poorest households, girls are more likely to be excluded from education than boys. Disparities in school participation linked to place of residence also persist. Rural

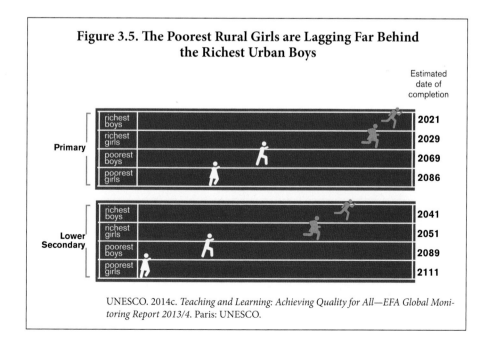

Figure 3.5. The Poorest Rural Girls are Lagging Far Behind the Richest Urban Boys

Estimated date of completion

Primary
- richest boys — 2021
- richest girls — 2029
- poorest boys — 2069
- poorest girls — 2086

Lower Secondary
- richest boys — 2041
- richest girls — 2051
- poorest boys — 2089
- poorest girls — 2111

UNESCO. 2014c. *Teaching and Learning: Achieving Quality for All—EFA Global Monitoring Report 2013/4*. Paris: UNESCO.

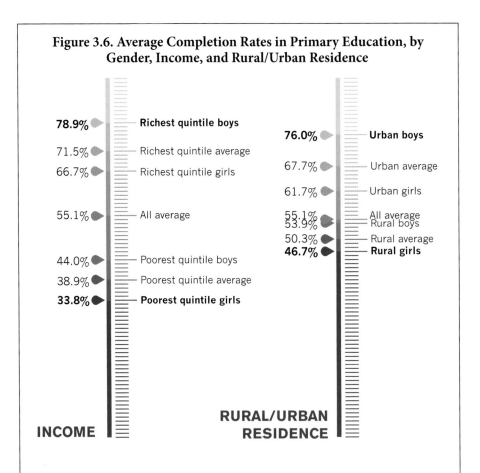

Figure 3.6. Average Completion Rates in Primary Education, by Gender, Income, and Rural/Urban Residence

INCOME

78.9% — Richest quintile boys
71.5% — Richest quintile average
66.7% — Richest quintile girls
55.1% — All average
44.0% — Poorest quintile boys
38.9% — Poorest quintile average
33.8% — Poorest quintile girls

RURAL/URBAN RESIDENCE

76.0% — Urban boys
67.7% — Urban average
61.7% — Urban girls
55.1% — All average
53.9% — Rural boys
50.3% — Rural average
46.7% — Rural girls

Note: Aggregates for low-income countries are averages for twenty-four low-income countries for wealth disaggregates and for urban/rural disaggregates weighted by primary school-age population.

Source: Authors' calculations using latest available data from Demographic and Health Surveys, 2000–2011.

King, Elizabeth, and Rebecca Winthrop. 2015. *Today's Challenges for Girls' Education.* Washington: Brookings Institution.

primary school-aged children are twice as likely to be out of school compared with their urban counterparts. In Sub-Saharan Africa, only 23 percent of poor, rural girls complete their primary education."

United Nations. 2014. *Millennium Development Goals Report 2014.* New York: United Nations.

- "The combination of sex and location of residence reveals that girls from rural areas are more likely to be out of school than boys from rural areas and children of either sex from urban areas. The biggest disparity exists between rural girls and urban boys." According to household survey data from thirty countries, 2003–10, the average out-of-school rate for rural females was 33 percent, compared with 29 percent for rural boys.* Similarly, urban girls and boys in these thirty countries had out-of-school rates of 16 and 14 percent, respectively.

UNESCO. 2012. 2012a. *Reaching Out-of-School Children Is Crucial for Development: UIS Fact Sheet No. 18.* Paris: UNESCO.

*The data are from international household surveys conducted between 2003 and 2010: (1) Demographic and Health Surveys: Philippines, 2003; Chad, Morocco, and Turkey, 2004; Ethiopia, Guinea, and Senegal, 2005; Burkina Faso, India, Mali, Nepal, Niger, and Uganda, 2006; Indonesia, Pakistan, Ukraine, and Zambia, 2007; Egypt, Ghana, and Nigeria, 2008; Kenya and Madagascar, 2009; Colombia and United Republic of Tanzania, 2010. (2) Multiple Indicator Cluster Surveys: Cameroon, Central African Republic, and Côte d'Ivoire, 2006; Mauritania, 2007; Mozambique, 2008. (3) Pesquisa Nacional por Amostra de Domicílios: Brazil, 2006.

- **Household survey data from forty-two countries for 2000 to 2008 show that rural girls are more likely to be out of school (31 percent) than rural boys (27 percent), and they are twice as likely to be out of school as urban girls (15 percent).**

  UNDP. 2010. *Millennium Development Goals Report.* New York: UNDP.

- **"In 2010, the poorest women in rural areas in both low- and lower-middle-income countries had spent less than three years in school, compared with the richest urban young men, who spent 9.5 and 12 years, respectively."**

  Clinton Foundation, Bill & Melinda Gates Foundation, Economist Intelligence Unit, and WORLD Policy Analysis Center. 2015. *The Full Participation Report: No Ceilings.* Full Participation Project. New York: Clinton Foundation.

A number of country case studies illustrate just how far behind the most disadvantaged and marginalized girls are:

- **Among rural communities in Peru, only 43 percent of young rural women between the ages of twenty and twenty-four had finished secondary school, compared with 58 percent of young men of that age.** Additionally, findings from the study show that 83.7 percent of twelve- to sixteen-year-olds in urban areas attended secondary school, compared with 66.4 percent of that age group in rural areas.

Ames, Patricia. 2012. "Constructing New Identities? The Role of Gender and Education in Rural Girls' Life Aspirations in Peru." *Gender and Educations* 25, no. 3.

- **In Niger, 61 percent of rural girls are out of school, compared with 51 percent of rural boys and only 18 percent of urban girls.**

- **In Afghanistan, 59 percent of rural girls are out of school, compared with only 39 percent of rural boys. In urban areas, 27 percent of girls are out of school, compared with only 17 percent of urban boys.**

- **In Burkina Faso, only 15 percent of urban boys are out of school, compared with 57 percent of rural girls.**

UNESCO. 2015b. "World Inequality Database on Education." http://www.education-inequalities.org/.

- **"In Niger and Guinea, approximately 70 percent of the poorest girls had never attended school—notably higher than the share of the poorest boys—compared with less than 20 percent of the richest boys."**

UNESCO. 2015b. *Education for All 2000–2015: Achievements and Challenges—Education for All Global Monitoring Report 2015*. Paris: UNESCO.

- **"Household surveys in the thirty countries accounting for 34 million of the 61 million children worldwide who are out of school found that among primary-school age children, 43 percent of those out of school are girls from the poorest household quintile, and only 9 percent are boys from the richest household quintile."**

Clinton Foundation, Bill & Melinda Gates Foundation, Economist Intelligence Unit, and WORLD Policy Analysis Center. 2015. *The Full Participation Report: No Ceilings*. Full Participation Project. New York: Clinton Foundation.

- **"Among those aged 5 to 15 in developing-country partners with recent MICS survey data, the likelihood of never having attended school was 1.2 times higher for girls than for boys, 2.1 times higher for rural children than for urban children, and 3.4 times higher for poor children than for children of wealthy families."**

- **In Afghanistan, Burkina Faso, and Mozambique, poor female rural children had less than one chance in ten of completing primary education.**

GPE (Global Partnership for Education). 2015. *Results for Learning Report 2014/2015: Basic Education at Risk.* Washington: GPE.

- **In Ethiopia, only 11 percent of poor rural girls complete primary school, while 85 percent of rich urban boys finish primary school. Each characteristic contributes starkly to the disparity.**

  UNESCO. 2015c. "World Inequality Database on Education." http://www.education-inequalities.org/.

- **In Afghanistan, location of residence and income level exacerbate the existing gender disparity in primary completion. Although 47 percent of boys complete primary school, only 19 percent of girls do so; and only 4 percent of poor rural females complete primary school, compared with 74 percent of rich urban boys.**

  UNESCO. 2015c. "World Inequality Database on Education." http://www.education-inequalities.org/.

- **In Rwanda, household surveys find that fewer than 5 percent of rural girls complete secondary school.** These data stand in contrast to the secondary education statistics produced by the Rwandan government.

- **In Iraq, poor rural girls are also far behind. For rich urban boys, the lower secondary completion rate was 58 percent, whereas it was only 3 percent for poor rural girls, according to Iraq Multiple Indicator Cluster Surveys in 2000 and 2011.**

  Gross enrollment ratio: UIS database; completion rate: *EFA Global Monitoring Report* team calculations, 2013, based on Demographic and Health Survey data.

  UNESCO. 2014c. *Teaching and Learning: Achieving Quality for All—EFA Global Monitoring Report 2013/4.* Paris: UNESCO.

Rural Girls from Ethnic or Linguistic Minorities Are Being Especially Left Back

- **"Speaking a minority language compounds even further the marginalization of being a woman."**

- **"In Nigeria, 97 percent of poor Hausa-speaking girls and over 90 percent of rural Hausa women between the ages of seventeen to twenty-two have fewer than two years of education."**

- "In Turkey 43 percent of Kurdish-speaking girls from the poorest households have fewer than two years of education, while the national average is 6 percent."

- "In Guatemala 62 percent of Spanish-speaking girls complete primary school compared with only 26 percent of girls who speak indigenous languages."

  Romaine, Suzanne. 2013. "Keeping the Promise of the Millennium Development Goals: Why Language Matters." *Applied Linguistics Review* 4, no. 1: 1–21.

- Bolivia and Mozambique are two examples that show that girls living in rural areas who do not speak the national language are the farthest behind in terms of average years of schooling, even farther behind than their male peers (see figure 3.7).

Learning Levels Low for Marginalized Girls

- "In Benin, around 60 percent of rich boys stay in school and attain basic numeracy skills, compared with only 6 percent of poor girls."

- "In the Democratic Republic of Congo, only 23 percent of poor young women age fifteen to twenty-four are able to read in everyday situations, compared with 64 percent of poor young men."

- "In Burkina Faso, 72 percent of rich young men have basic literacy skills, compared with 54 percent of rich young women, but only 13 percent of poor men and 6 percent of poor women."

- "In Ethiopia, only 30 percent of young women in rural areas were literate in 2011, compared with 90 percent of urban young men."

- "In Senegal, the percentage of rural young women able to read in everyday situations was only 20 percent in 2010, compared with 65 percent of urban young men."

- "In northwest Nigeria, only 2 percent of young women can read."

  UNESCO. 2014c. *Teaching and Learning: Achieving Quality for All—EFA Global Monitoring Report 2013/4*. Paris: UNESCO.

Figure 3.7. Gender Gaps in Mozambique and Bolivia, by Urban/Rural Residence and Language Group

Bolivia (DHS data 2008)

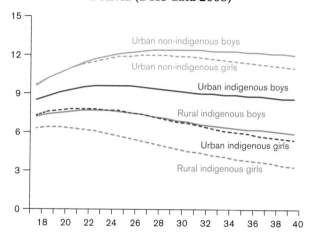

Note: Nonindigenous population is defined as those people whose native language is Spanish; the indigenous population is defined those whose native language is Quechua, Aymara, Guarani, or other native languages. By this definition, the non-indigenous population in rural areas is small and we have omitted them here. A STATA smoothing function has been applied to extract the age pattern in the data.

Mozambique (DHS data 2003-04)

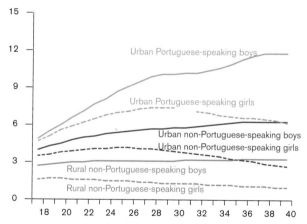

Note: The curves for the lusophone (or Portuguese-speaking) groups fluctuate more than the other curves, even after applying a STATA smoothing function to extract the age pattern, so we have omitted them; they represent a small population compared to the other groups.

King, Elizabeth M. and Rebecca Winthrop. 2015. *Today's Challenge in Girl's Education.* Washington DC: Brookings Press.

- **The evidence suggests that "the development of social and emotional skills and other noncognitive skills may be just as important as the development of cognitive skills."** Evidence from longitudinal studies of nine OECD countries found that the development of competencies and character skills such as perseverance, self-esteem, and sociability may have a bigger influence on addressing social challenges such as crime, health decisions, and ensuring success in the labor market. In turn, developing soft skills also improves academic achievement. Additionally, differences in soft skills can explain many of the differences between genders in their higher education enrollment and completion rates.

King, Elizabeth, and Rebecca Winthrop. 2015. *Today's Challenges for Girls' Education*. Washington: Brookings Institution.

Kautz, Tim, et al. 2014. *Fostering and Measuring Skills: Improving Cognitive and Non-cognitive Skills to Promote Lifetime Success*. NBER Working Paper 20749. Cambridge, Mass.: National Bureau of Economic Research.

OECD. 2015b. *Skills for Social Progress: The Power of Social and Emotional Skills*. Paris: OECD Publishing. http://dx.doi.org/10.1787/9789264226159-en.

Progress in Girls' Education to Date

There is still a long way to go before all girls will be able to go to school, stay in school, and learn well while there. However, during the past twenty-five years, there has been significant forward momentum upon which today's girls' education advocates can build. In 1990 and then again in 2000, two major sets of global education goals were agreed to by governments around the world, and girls' education has been a priority in both. For the Education for All goals, and then, later, the MDGs, enrolling girls and boys in primary school in equal numbers was a central focus, and both sets of goals sunset in 2015.

The progress made over the last twenty-five years is in many ways a testament to the effectiveness of having many actors work collaboratively to solve global problems. Indeed, the global girls' education community has a strong forward momentum, with a number of important actors taking up the issue and working jointly with parents, communities, and governments on the ground. This momentum and collaboration must continue in order to finish the job of ensuring that all girls around the world get an education.

The Education for All Initiative and the Millennium Development Goals

Education for All Goals	Millennium Development Goals
Goal 1 Expanding and improving comprehensive early childhood care and education, especially for the most vulnerable and disadvantaged children.	**Goal 1** Eradicate extreme poverty and hunger.
Goal 2 Ensuring that by 2015 all children—particularly girls, children in difficult circumstances, and those belonging to ethnic minorities—have access to, and complete, free and compulsory primary education of good quality.	**Goal 2** Achieve universal primary education. **Goal 3** Promote gender equality and empower women.
Goal 3 Ensuring that the learning needs of all young people and adults are met through equitable access to appropriate learning and life-skills programs.	**Goal 4** Reduce child mortality. **Goal 5** Improve maternal health.
Goal 4 Achieving a 50 percent improvement in levels of adult literacy by 2015, especially for women, and equitable access to basic and continuing education for all adults.	**Goal 6** Combat HIV/AIDS, malaria, and other diseases. **Goal 7** Ensure environmental sustainability.
Goal 5 Eliminating gender disparities in primary and secondary education by 2005, and achieving gender equality in education by 2015, with a focus on ensuring girls' full and equal access to and achievement in basic education of good qualtiy.	**Goal 8** Develop a global partnership for development.
Goal 6 Improving all aspects of the quality of education and ensurng the excellence of all, so that recognized and measurable learning outcomes are achieved by all, especially in literacy, numeracy, and essential life skills.	

Increasing Numbers Are Enrolling in School

- **Between 1999 and 2009, an extra 52 million children enrolled in primary school."**

  Krishnaratne, Shari, Howard White, and Ella Carpenter. 2013. *Quality Education for All Children? What Works in Education in Developing Countries.* 3ie Working Paper 20. New Delhi: International Initiative for Impact Evaluation (3ie).

- **In 2000, 109.9 million girls of primary and lower-secondary school age were not in school. This means that since 2000, the number of out-of-school girls has nearly halved, and enrollment has increased by 8 percent.**

  UNESCO Institute for Statistics. "UIS StatCentre: Education Statistics." Retrieved July 21, 2015.

- **From 1990 to 2012, the number of countries closing the gender gap in enrollment in primary school rose from 86 to 124, and in secondary school it rose from 40 to 69** (see figure 3.8).

  Winthrop, Rebecca. December 12, 2014. "Mobilizing Children's Rights, Supporting Local Leaders and Improving Girls' Education." PowerPoint presentation. Center for Universal Education, The Brookings Institution.

- **Today, 89 percent of low-income countries, 97 percent of middle-income countries, and all high-income countries have made primary education tuition-free.** Girls are more likely than boys to be kept out of school because of financial hardship, so free schooling has helped propel more girls into primary school.

  WORLD Policy Analysis Center. 2015. "Facilitating Girls' Access to Quality Education: Global Findings on Tuition-Free and Compulsory Education." WORLD Education Database. http://www.worldpolicyforum.org.

- **This recent progress in girls' education has followed several decades of education expansion around the world.** Especially after 1948, when education was declared a universal human right, developing countries in particular began to develop mass schooling systems for their populations. We can see this progress over time by looking at the average number of years of schooling women in a particular country have.

  Winthrop, Rebecca, and Eileen McGivney. 2015. *Why Wait 100 Years? Bridging the Gap in Global Education.* Washington: Brookings Institution.

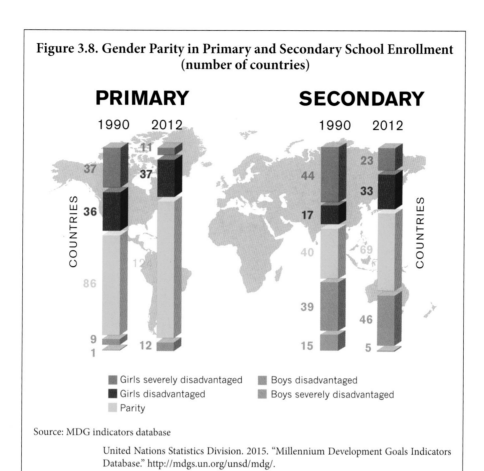

Figure 3.8. Gender Parity in Primary and Secondary School Enrollment (number of countries)

PRIMARY

SECONDARY

Girls severely disadvantaged
Girls disadvantaged
Parity

Boys disadvantaged
Boys severely disadvantaged

Source: MDG indicators database

United Nations Statistics Division. 2015. "Millennium Development Goals Indicators Database." http://mdgs.un.org/unsd/mdg/.

- The average number of years of school women complete is also on the rise, and "today, women and girls age fifteen and over spend an average of 7.3 years in school, compared to 5.6 years in 1990."

  Clinton Foundation, Bill & Melinda Gates Foundation, Economist Intelligence Unit, and WORLD Policy Analysis Center. 2015. *The Full Participation Report: No Ceilings*. Full Participation Project. New York: Clinton Foundation.

- In the Middle East and North Africa, average years of school completed for women rose from less than one in 1950 to more than seven in 2010 (see figure 3.9).

  King, Elizabeth, and Rebecca Winthrop. 2015. *Today's Challenges for Girls' Education*. Washington: Brookings Institution.

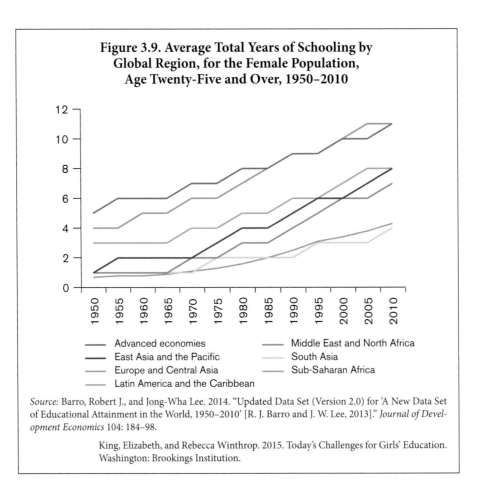

Figure 3.9. Average Total Years of Schooling by Global Region, for the Female Population, Age Twenty-Five and Over, 1950–2010

Advanced economies
East Asia and the Pacific
Europe and Central Asia
Latin America and the Caribbean
Middle East and North Africa
South Asia
Sub-Saharan Africa

Source: Barro, Robert J., and Jong-Wha Lee. 2014. "Updated Data Set (Version 2.0) for 'A New Data Set of Educational Attainment in the World, 1950–2010' [R. J. Barro and J. W. Lee, 2013]." *Journal of Development Economics* 104: 184–98.

King, Elizabeth, and Rebecca Winthrop. 2015. Today's Challenges for Girls' Education. Washington: Brookings Institution.

Building Momentum in the Global Girls' Education Community

The political momentum around girls' education has been building over time and at multiple levels. From village leaders in rural Africa whose opinions on girls' education are highly influential in their community to civil society campaigns to philanthropists and business leaders, girls' education has been an issue that has needed multiple players to work together to catalyze action.

At the global level, attention to the issue has increased rapidly in recent years—a positive signal that there are ready actors who can work together to address the very deep and urgent crisis of girls' education. This girls' education movement builds on global advocacy energy in both the education and women's empowerment sectors.

"The rights of girls is becoming the hot topic of 2013, as a new movement of empowered young women discovers that it has the momentum to force big issues—girls' health, girls' education and the protection of girls against violence—to the centre of the global agenda."

Gordon Brown, Former Prime Minister of the UK and the UN Special Envoy for Global Education

Civil society mobilization around the education MDGs has been led by a range of organizations, including the Global Campaign for Education, which led some of the initial global advocacy efforts around ensuring a free primary education for all. Recently new actors have joined the effort, particularly since the appointment in 2012 by the UN Secretary General of former UK Prime Minister Gordon Brown to be the first UN Special Envoy for Global Education. A long-time advocate of girls' education, Brown together with his wife, Sarah Brown, have catalyzed A World At School, an international campaign for global education leveraging the business community, the youth movement, the faith community, and a range of civil society organizations. Education International, the global network representing teacher organizations around the world, has also increasing engaged in global education advocacy and policy debates.

The women's movement has also played a role in advocating for girls' education globally, including organizations like Vital Voices that seeks to support and empower women leaders around the world, including those working on education issues. The Half the Sky Movement, which evolved out of Nicholas Kristof and Sheryl WuDunn's book (2009a) and documentary series (Bennett et al. 2012), *Half the Sky: Turning Oppression into Opportunity for Women Worldwide,* has done much to garner public attention to human rights violations like sex trafficking and gender-based violence against girls and women globally. The movement aims to mobilize global political will through various modes of engagement—including mobile games in India and East Africa—to overcome widespread cultural barriers in the way of achieving gender equality, ultimately working to transform the way society views girls and women from the problem to the solution to fighting global poverty and extremism (Kristof and Wu-Dunn 2009b). Education is an important piece of the Half the Sky Movement; indeed, Kristof and WuDunn argue it is "the single most important way to encourage women and girls to stand up for their rights," and that we as society "can do far more to promote universal education in poor countries" (Kristof and WuDunn 2009a).

Two recent reports have discussed this increasing momentum at the global level, and they give good insights particularly about the girls' education players and momentum needed to help finish the job of ensuring that all girls get a high-quality education. Xanthe Ackerman's 2015 survey of global girls' education actors and funders provides a useful timeline, and Elizabeth King and Rebecca Winthrop's 2015 review of recent girls' education data helps describe the key actors and their role in the global girls' education community.

- **The global advocacy and momentum for girls' education been building slowly over the past decade, but in the last three years it has accelerated rapidly** (see figure 3.10).

"Commentators and scholars on girls' education have noted the emergence of girls' education from a technical field within international development to a global movement" (Ackerman 2015). Noted examples include the establishment in 1992 by five female African ministers of

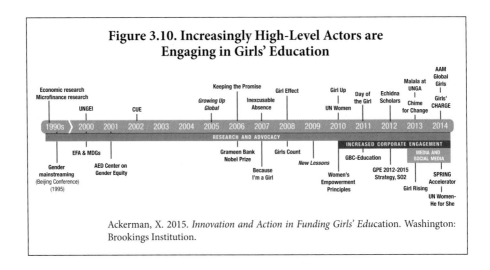

Figure 3.10. Increasingly High-Level Actors are Engaging in Girls' Education

Ackerman, X. 2015. *Innovation and Action in Funding Girls' Edu*cation. Washington: Brookings Institution.

education of the Forum of African Women Educationalists (FAWE). Today, FAWE is a pan-African organization working closely with the association of African ministers of education to advance policy and practice on girls' education issues in Africa. In 2000, the United Nations increased its focus on girls' education by establishing the UN Girls' Education Initiative (UNGEI), a network of organizations focused on actions to close the gender gap in primary and secondary schools. Today, UNGEI deploys diverse strategies for advancing girls' education, including providing technical tools and advocacy for national education plans to be developed using a gender lens.

What is the United Nations Girls' Education Initiative?

Founded in 2000, the United Nations Girls' Education Initiative (UNGEI) is a network of organizations focused on actions to close the gender gap in primary and secondary schools. Today, UNGEI deploys diverse strategies for advancing girls' education, including providing technical tools and advocacy for national education plans to be developed using a gender lens.

In the last ten years, the girls' education movement has taken on new momentum with growing global advocacy efforts. These include Plan International's Because I Am a Girl campaign (2007), the Nike Foundation's Girl Effect (2008), and the Documentary Group's Girl Rising (2013), to name a few. The United Kingdom's David Cameron has identified girls' education as a top priority for his country's overseas development assistance, and in 2012 he launched a significant program of investment named the Girls' Education Challenge, with the aim of investing £300 million and reaching 1 million girls. Globally prominent advocates are also increasingly speaking out, including Graça Machel, Archbishop Desmond Tutu, and other members of the Elders, an independent group of global leaders who work together for peace and human rights, who have taken up the issue of child marriage, in partnership with the civil society movement Girls Not Brides. In 2014, former US secretary of state Hillary Clinton and former Australian prime minister Julia Gillard jointly launched Collaborative for Harnessing Ambition and Resources for Girls' Education (CHARGE), a girls' education collaborative of more than forty organizations focused on "second-generation" issues with a shared commitment to reach 15 million girls. In 2015, US first lady Michelle Obama launched Let Girls Learn, an initiative focused on supporting developing-country grassroots leadership in girls' education. Finally, the joint Nobel Peace Prize award to Kailash Satyarthi and Malala Yousafzai for their work on children's rights, in particular girls' right to get an education, has put the global spotlight on the issue in a way never yet seen" (King and Winthrop 2015).

What is the Global Partnership for Education?

The Global Partnership for Education (GPE), which was founded in 2000, is a multilateral partnership focused on supporting the poorest countries in the world as they seek to improve their education systems. Membership in GPE is diverse and represents the main actors working on education globally, including the governments of both donor countries and developing countries, United Nations organizations, civil society networks, teacher organizations, and corporate and philanthropic organizations. GPE manages a pooled fund valued at approximately $2 billion for supporting developing countries' plans to reach children with education.

CHAPTER 4

What Works: A Catalogue of Evidence on Addressing Girls' Education Needs

I t is now well established that girls' education is a great investment and that girls want to go to school. Yet, by virtue of their gender, girls still face serious and unique barriers—economic (e.g., direct, indirect, and opportunity costs), cultural, and safety barriers. Many carefully monitored and evaluated interventions have shown, however, that smart policy and thoughtful program design can overcome these barriers.

To date, a wide range of policies, approaches, and interventions have been tried, tested, and evaluated to help girls attend and stay in school. The main focus of many of these efforts has been at the primary level, with governments and other girls' education actors emphasizing "basic" education (see Global Definitions of Education Levels in chapter 3). Although the authors of this book believe that experts and policymakers should strongly focus on primary school, important studies have also already been done on the high returns from secondary education and on those interventions that help promote secondary school access and completion for girls. This book thus deliberately emphasized studies and evidence focused on secondary education in order to roughly balance the number of studies reviewed at the primary and secondary education levels.

This chapter provides a catalogue of the latest information about what works in girls' education, as well as lessons learned from practice, to help guide policymaking and program design. It builds on the 2004 publication, as well as on six major recent reviews of hundreds of impact evaluations of education interventions for both boys and girls and two major reviews of education interventions specifically targeting girls (see Previous Studies of What Works in Education).

This book clusters the evidence on what works in girls' education into seven groups of interventions:

Previous Studies of What Works in Education

Six recent and important studies reviewing what works in education are listed below. These studies provide an important evidence base for improving education for children, even though they did not look specifically at the differences between girls and boys:

1. Conn, K. 2014. "Identifying Effective Education Interventions in Sub-Saharan Africa: A Meta-Analysis of Rigorous Impact Evaluations." Unpublished manuscript, Columbia University, New York.

2. Glewwe, Paul, Eric Hanushek, Sarah Humpage, and Renato Ravina. 2011. *School Resources and Educational Outcomes in Developing Countries: A Review of the Literature from 1990 to 2010.* NBER Working Paper 17554. Cambridge, Mass.: National Bureau of Economic Research.

3. Kremer, Michael, Conner Brannen, and Rachel Glennerster. 2013. "The Challenge of Education and Learning in the Developing World." *Science* 340: 297–300.

4. Krishnaratne, Shari, Howard White, and Ella Carpenter. 2013. *Quality Education for All Children? What Works in Education in Developing Countries.* 3ie Working Paper 20. New Delhi: International Initiative for Impact Evaluation (3ie).

5. McEwan, P. J. 2014. "Improving Learning in Primary Schools of Developing Countries: A Meta-Analysis of Randomized Experiments." *Review of Education Research* 20, no. 10: 1–42.

6. Murnane, R. J., and A. J. Ganimian. 2014. *Improving Educational Outcomes in Developing Countries: Lessons from Rigorous Evaluations.* NBER Working Paper 20284. Cambridge, Mass.: National Bureau of Economic Research.

Two recent and important studies have been done on interventions that specifically support the education of girls:

1. Lloyd, C. B., and J. Young. 2009. *New Lessons: The Power of Educating Adolescent Girls—A Girls Count Report on Adolescent Girls.* New York: Population Council.

2. Unterhalter, Elaine, Amy North, Madeleine Arnot, Cynthia Lloyd, Lebo Moletsane, Erin Murphy-Graham, Jenny Parkes, and Mioko Saito. 2014. "Interventions to Enhance Girls' Education and Gender Equality." Education rigorous literature review, UK Department for International Development, London. http://r4d. dfid.gov.uk/pdf/outputs/HumanDev_evidence/Girls_Education_Literature_ Review_2014_Unterhalter.pdf.

1. **Interventions that help make schools affordable**: Reduce direct costs to families by eliminating school fees. Reduce indirect and opportunity costs through scholarships, stipends, cash, and in-kind transfers.

2. **Interventions that help girls overcome health barriers**: Provide school meals and take-home rations. Provide deworming treatments. Improve water, sanitation, and hygiene infrastructure.

3. **Interventions that reduce the time and distance to get to school**: Build schools closer to girls' homes. Establish community schools to reduce the cultural distance between home and school. Employ flexible school schedules to accommodate girls' work.

4. **Interventions that make schools more girl-friendly**: Provide preschool and child care programs. Eliminate school-related gender-based violence.

5. **Interventions that improve school quality**: Hire more qualified teachers who attend school regularly. Improve how teachers teach.

6. **Interventions that increase community engagement**: Mobilize the community to sustain gains made in girls' education.

7. **Interventions that sustain girls' education during emergencies**: Ensure that girls' education continues during emergencies caused by wars, natural disasters, and epidemics—albeit usually taking a different form.

On the basis of the evidence, it is now commonly known that having affordable, nearby, and girl-friendly schools is an important first step to get girls to school. When this evidence is paired with interventions that improve the quality of schooling, mobilize communities to sustain the progress they make, and increase the supply of and demand for high-quality secondary girls' education, policymakers and practitioners now have a powerful recipe for realizing the education dream for all girls.

1 Making Schools Affordable

For many years, school was not free in developing countries. Governments charged students and their families fees to attend school—in part to help offset the high costs of schooling, given limited government budgets. In many countries, students were also expected to buy school uniforms and textbooks, and if they did not have these they were not allowed to enroll. Although the costs were

Overview of This Book's Methodology

The literature reviewed for this book was identified through a comprehensive and systematic search of academic databases, online resource depositories (e.g., the World Bank's Open Knowledge Repository), and nongovernmental organizations' (NGOs') websites and publication holdings, as well as through personal communications with subject experts and researchers in the field. This process gathered information from nearly 1,000 academic studies, published and unpublished reports, program evaluations, and documents using a wide variety of quantitative, qualitative, and mixed research designs and methodologies that investigate various dimensions of girls' education in developing countries. Nearly 500 of these studies informed the main themes and central findings of this book. However, to understand specifically the most effective interventions for girls' education, 138 studies that investigate the effects of an intervention were chosen for in-depth review, on the basis of subject relevancy and the rigor and validity of the research conducted. The breakdown of these 138 studies by type of education is as follows:

Type of education	Number of studies
Primary	59
Secondary	58
Tertiary	3
Vocational/technical	6
Nonformal	8
No level specified	27

These 138 studies constitute a very robust set of evidence of what works in girls' education. Evidence was categorized as strong if the research was peer reviewed and/or met at least one of the following criteria: included a control group, measured outcomes before and after an intervention, isolated and controlled for variables, or was conducted over a sustained period of time to adequately investigate the impact of interventions. Evidence from empirical research not meeting these criteria was categorized as promising. Findings derived from anecdotes or from nonrigorous investigation were flagged as needing more research.

not large individually, if added together across multiple children, the costs would immediately become an insurmountable barrier for poor families. With parents unable to afford to pay fees for all their children, many poor, disadvantaged, and marginalized families were forced to choose which of their children to enroll. More often than not, a preference for boys meant that millions of girls were kept out of school. Indeed, it would be hard to devise a policy more likely to deny

The Cost of Schooling

When understanding how to make schools more affordable for girls, the global education community commonly breaks down the costs of schooling into three main categories:

- **Direct costs**: Tuition or school fees paid annually or at each term.

- **Indirect costs**: The price of uniforms, school supplies, transportation, parent–teacher association fees, and the like.

- **Opportunity costs**: The "services" lost by a family when their daughter or son attends school—for example, water collection, child care of younger siblings, lower bride price, or the time that an adult must spend accompanying a girl to school.

Aikman, Sheila, and Elaine Unterhalter. 2007. *Practising Gender Equality in Education*. Oxford: Oxfam Great Britain.

Herz, Barbara, K. Subbarao, Masooma Habib, and Laura Raney. 1991. *Letting Girls Learn: Promising Approaches in Primary and Secondary Education*. World Bank Discussion Paper 133. Washington: World Bank.

girls an education than charging poor families an individual fee for each child they send to school. Though eliminating fees and direct and indirect costs for children going to school is important for achieving universal education for all children, it is crucial for girls.

In developing nations, parents in poor families may perceive that schooling is more costly for girls, both in terms of real financial cost and opportunity costs. To illustrate, for such parents, sending a girl to school means forgoing her labor in the household or the wages she may earn; in some societies, it also means spending more human and financial resources supervising her, concealing her, and keeping her safe on the way to, from, and in school. Thus, even though school may be allegedly free, parents often find that they cannot afford to send their daughters to school.

A range of approaches has been tested to reduce and offset these costs for girls and boys. Abolishing school fees is important, especially eliminating or at least reducing the direct costs of educating girls. Research has shown that the most direct and fastest way for governments to boost girls' enrollment is to ban schools from collecting fees. However, experience suggests that governments must also prepare extensively for the increases in enrollment that are likely to follow by building schools and training additional teachers. Policies to both make school truly free and compulsory, together with careful planning to handle increased enrollment, are critical for achieving universal girls' education, especially because fees per student will be a greater barrier to girls' than to boys' education. In addition to eliminating school fees, cash transfers (conditional and unconditional), scholarships, and stipends have been among the most prominent and most researched interventions targeting the cost of schooling. In a review of 146 social protection interventions aimed at improving education outcomes, UNESCO documents nearly two-thirds have had some element of cash transfers (UNESCO 2015a). These programs are premised on the notion that cash assistance to families helps to underwrite real or opportunity costs that influence whether families send their girls to school and keep them in school (Arnold, Conway, and Greenslade 2011; GPE 2014).

This section provides evidence on both these approaches, as well as summarizes the lessons learned on how to effectively design and implement interventions that make schools affordable for girls.

Reduce the Direct Costs of Schooling

In the early 2000s, many countries around the world moved to legislate universal basic education, abolishing government fees for attending school and making basic education free and compulsory. The school fee abolition initiative, led by a range of global education organizations, including the Global Campaign for Education, which mobilized considerable pressure from civil society, was spurred by the global Education for All (EFA) goals and by the Millennium Development Goals. Ultimately, the elimination of school fees and related free primary education policies have greatly contributed to reducing the direct costs of schooling and have led to dramatic progress in increasing girls' enrollment.

Recent studies, however, have begun to show that though crucial, gains from eliminating fees are not enough for girls from especially poor households (Chepleting et al. 2013; Lincove 2009). Even if the direct cost of schooling has been removed, indirect and opportunity costs, like having an adult take time out of his or her day to accompany a girl on her walk to and from school, mixed with cultural barriers, like limited mobility for adolescent girls, may still be factors in parents' decisions to keep daughters at home. This indicates that additional policies or interventions, like cash transfers, are required that especially target the additional barriers experienced by girls (Lincove 2009; Lucas and Mbiti 2012).

Additionally, researchers have learned that reducing costs is not enough to ensure high-quality learning. Interventions targeting access must be paired together with interventions targeting quality:

- **Attendance doubled in Tanzania after the elimination of fees.** Tanzania eliminated fees for primary school in January 2002, and estimated that 1.5 million additional students, primarily girls, began attending primary school almost immediately. This success has also raised critical issues related to crowding and education quality, as Tanzania's new challenge became the building and staffing of 46,000 new classrooms to cope with the expected 3 million children who were to enter the system.

  Bruns, Barbara, Alain Mingar, and Ramahatra Rakotomalala. 2003. *Achieving Universal Primary Education by 2015: A Chance for Every Child.* Washington: World Bank.

  Coalition for Health and Education Rights. 2002. *User Fees: The Right to Education and Health Denied.* Policy Brief. New York: Coalition for Health and Education Rights.

- **Enrollment jumped 70 percent after fees were cut and major reforms undertaken in schooling in Uganda.** In Uganda, when free schooling was introduced in 1997, primary school enrollment immediately doubled, from 3.4 million to 5.7 million children, and rose to 6.5 million by 1999. Total girls' enrollment went from 63 percent to 83 percent, while enrollment among the poorest fifth of girls went from 46 percent to 82 percent. By 2000, there was virtually no gap between male and female net enrollment ratios (89.3 percent vs. 88.8 percent), though the gender gap worsened in some areas. By 2003, enrollment climbed again, to 7.5 million. (The elimination of fees was part of broader education reforms, so it may not have been responsible for the entire enrollment increase.)

Enrollment increases, however, led to serious problems with crowding and education quality. In response, as part of a broader set of reforms, a teacher recruitment initiative was initiated. More than 10,000 teachers upgraded their qualifications, and the share of untrained teachers in classrooms declined by 10 percent.

Deininger, Klaus. 2003. "Does the Cost of Schooling Affect Enrollment by the Poor? Universal Primary Education in Uganda." *Economics of Education Review* 22, no. 3: 291–305.

Tomasevski, Katarina. 2003. *Education Denied: Costs and Remedies.* New York: Zed Books.

- **Malawi's efforts to reduce fees and costs helped boost enrollment 63 percent.** When Malawi abolished fees for primary school and made uniforms optional in 1994, enrollment of both boys and girls shot up, from 1.9 million to 3.1 million students. By 1996, more than 91 percent of both boys and girls age six to eleven were enrolled in school, compared with just over 50 percent in 1992 (the gender gap then was minimal and actually favored girls).

  Although the increase in enrollment was a success, the Malawi case also illustrates the importance of advance planning and mustering resources to support fee reductions. The increase in enrollment nearly overwhelmed Malawi's education system, significantly increasing class size and increasing concerns about education quality. Moreover, "free school" was seen as part of a new move toward democratization, and some scholars found that in some cases parents began to regard education as a government responsibility, weakening traditional parental participation.

  Rugh, Andrea. 2000. *Starting Now: Strategies for Helping Girls Complete Primary*. SAGE Project. Washington: Academy for Educational Development.

  Filmer, Deon. 2000. *The Structure of Social Disparities in Education: Gender and Wealth*. Policy Research Working Paper 2268. Washington: World Bank.

- **Kenya eliminated fees in January 2003 and saw primary enrollment soar. Shortly thereafter, 1.3 million students entered the school system, for a total of 7.2 million.** As in other countries, the influx of students created formidable challenges. Classrooms became so overcrowded that administrators had to defer students' admission. Trained teachers were scarce, and another 1.5 million children were still out of school. Studies examining test scores by subject found that free primary education actually led to a relative deterioration of girls' scores in English and mathematics. However, in science, the subject with the highest gender gap in scores before free primary school, girls' scores improved. Again, lessons from Kenya reinforce the importance of combining school fee abolition with other reforms to ensure and sustain school quality, such as hiring and training more teachers.

  Lacey, Mark. 2003. "Primary Schools in Kenya, Fees Abolished, Are Filled to Overflowing." *New York Times*. January 7.

  Lucas, Adrienne M., and Isaac M. Mbiti. 2012. "Does Free Primary Education Narrow Gender Differences in Schooling? Evidence from Kenya." *Journal of African Economies* 21, no. 5: 1–32.

  UNICEF. 2003. *State of the World's Children 2004*. New York: UNICEF.

- **Asian countries saw enrollment rise after fees were reduced.** A number of Asian countries—including China, South Korea, and Sri Lanka—reduced school fees. The fee reductions were in conjunction with strong government advocacy of education for girls as well as for boys, awareness campaigns, and other efforts to promote girls' education. Sometimes these governments have exempted girls but not boys from the fees, and sometimes just poor girls. Rigorous evaluations of these measures are not available, but enrollment rates for both girls and boys have risen in these countries and compare well with those of countries with similar income levels.

  Herz, Barbara, K. Subbarao, Masooma Habib, and Laura Raney. 1991. *Letting Girls Learn: Promising Approaches in Primary and Secondary Education*. World Bank Discussion Paper 133. Washington: World Bank.

Reduce the Indirect and Opportunity Costs of Schooling

Eliminating school fees is an essential first step to making school more affordable. But as discussed above, this step needs to be followed by efforts to offset the indirect and opportunity costs that keep children out of school as well as efforts to sustain and improve school quality. Over the years, specific sets of interventions have been tried and tested under the names of scholarships, stipends, education subsidies, bursaries, and cash transfers. Despite this variety, their central principle is the same: to provide families with resources that help underwrite the costs influencing parents' decisions about sending their daughters to school (Arnold, Conway, and Greenslade 2011).

Cash and in-kind transfers make up a set of interventions that is perhaps the most popular (and most researched) strategy for getting girls into primary and secondary school, due largely to the success and the successful scaling up of a few flagship programs in countries across South America, South Asia, and Southeast Asia. This book highlights a number of both small- and large-scale programs that have been rigorously evaluated, many with randomized control trials that demonstrate the effectiveness of this strategy (see Eleven Effective Programs). *The evidence linking cash transfers with increased school enrollment for girls is strong—sometimes with enrollment increases as large as 20 to 30 percentage points* (Filmer and Shady 2008, 2011).

Eleven Effective Programs That Have Made Schools Affordable for Girls

The following programs have been rigorously evaluated and shown to be effective in making schools affordable for girls. Their impact and how they work are reviewed in detail in this section.

- Female Stipend Program, Bangladesh

- Progresa (now Oportunidades), Mexico

- Punjab Female School Stipend Program, Pakistan

- Japan Fund for Poverty Reduction Scholarship Program, Cambodia

- Child Sponsorship Program, Kenya

- Chief Minister's Bicycle Program, India

- Zomba Cash Transfer experiment, Malawi

- Cambodia Education Sector Support Project Scholarship Program, Cambodia

- Subsidios Condicionados a la Asistencia Escolar, Colombia

- Apni Beti Apna Dhan, India

- Girls' Scholarship Program, Kenya

From this extensive evidence, researchers have also learned that the effectiveness of cash and in-kind transfer programs relies heavily on well-designed and implemented programs. The evidence shows overwhelmingly that resource transfers linked to behavior (e.g., enrollment, attendance, and graduation)—something educationalists call conditions or conditional cash transfers—are the most effective way of getting girls to go to and stay in school.

Yet, though the idea is straightforward, the details in the design can be tricky. If not done well, resource transfers can have some negative unintended consequences. Conditional criteria should thus be thoughtfully designed to mitigate all risks to girls. For example, if the criteria for selecting recipients of scholarships are not transparent, tension can erupt between recipients and nonrecipients. Care must be taken to ensure that the mechanism for receiving a transfer are explicit and transparent and that it never places girls at risk of engaging in forced transactional sex to receive their payment. They should also avoid discriminating against girls from low education households where a girl may not have the resources at home to help her study and to make the grades necessary to receive a transfer conditioned on minimum test scores, turning a stipend into a merit-based scholarship that is out of reach (Raynore and Wesson 2006). Eligibility rules should also be carefully considered, as they may inadvertently lead families with two or more children to reallocate child work to ineligible siblings, to direct educational investments away from a sibling who did not receive a scholarship, or to enroll a son in a higher-quality private school using the resources that have been freed up by a cash transfer. In this case, a cash transfer program can create inequalities and gender disparities in educational attainment within the household (Alam, Baez, and Del Carpio 2011; Barrera-Osorio et al. 2011). These examples drive home the importance of program design when trying to reach those girls who are most in need.

Also, to truly ensure girls' success in school, well-designed cash transfer programs must be paired with interventions focused on improving girls' learning outcomes and school quality (Kim 2014; 3ie 2010; Akresh, de Walque, and Kazianga 2013; Baird et al. 2013, 2015; Filmer and Shady 2009; Muralidharan and Prakash 2013; Schurmann 2009, Slavin 2010).

Ultimately, well-designed programs offsetting the indirect and opportunity costs for girls' education—by providing either cash or other resources, such as uniforms or bicycles—have been shown across many countries to be an effective intervention for getting girls into both primary and secondary schools.

- **Secondary school stipends offered through Bangladesh's Female Stipend Program lifted girls' enrollment to almost double the national average.** The program began in 1982 in conjunction with the Bangladesh Rural Action Committee (BRAC) and was first scaled up by the national government to cover one-fourth of all administrative districts. During its first five years, when the program ran in pilot areas, girls' enrollment rose from 27 percent to 44 percent, almost double the national average. Under popular pressure, in 1992 the Bangladesh government eliminated girls' tuition and extended the stipend program to all rural areas nationwide. Girls' and boys' enrollment climbed to 55–60 percent, but girls' enrollment climbed faster than boys'.

  How it works: The stipends cover full tuition, paid directly to the school, and as much as 50 percent of costs of exams, textbooks, school supplies, uniforms, transportation, and kerosene for lamps paid directly to a bank account in her name. Any girl in grades 6–10 is eligible for the stipends in all 460 rural counties (*thanas*) across Bangladesh, as long as she meets three basic criteria: (1) She attends school regularly (75 percent of the time), (2) she achieves certain minimum grades (45 percent), and (3) she does not marry while she is in school.

Khandker, Shahidur R., Mark M. Pitt, and Nobuhiko Fuwa. 2003. *Subsidy to Promote Girls' Secondary Education: The Female Stipend Program in Bangladesh.* MPRA Paper 23688. Munich: Munich Personal RePEc Archive. http://mpra. ub.uni-muenchen.de/23688/.

Schurmann, Anna T. 2009. "Review of the Bangladesh Female Secondary School Stipend Project Using a Social Exclusion Framework." *Journal of Health, Population and Nutrition* 27, no. 4: 505–17.

World Bank. 2001. *Engendering Development through Gender Equality in Rights, Resources, and Voice.* World Bank Policy Research Report. New York: Oxford University Press.

• **The Mexican Progresa scholarship program (now renamed Oportunidades) has increased across-the-board enrollment in primary and secondary school and has been successfully scaled up and replicated.** A rigorous randomized evaluation found that nearly all eligible families took advantage of the program, increasing average enrollment by 3.4 percent for all students in grades 1–8. Girls' enrollment improved, especially for children finishing primary school and entering secondary school. The most significant increase (15 percent) was for girls completing grade 6. In addition, in 1998, the program increased girls' transition rates from elementary to junior secondary school by 14.8 percentage points and boys' by 6.5 percentage points. In part because randomized evaluation of the Progresa program allowed for such clear documentation of the program's positive effects, the program was expanded within Mexico, and by 2000 it had reached 2.6 million families, or 10 percent of the families in Mexico. (The program's budget was also substantial, at $800 million, or 0.2 percent of gross domestic product.)

How it works: Families receive monthly payments for each child in school, which increase with the age of the child, from about $7 through the third year of primary school to about $25 through the third year of secondary school—contingent on children maintaining 85 percent attendance. Transfers were about 13 percent higher in the case of a daughter's attendance relative to a son's. Participants also received free health care services, contingent on regular attendance at clinics and educational sessions.

Behrman, Jere R., Piyali Sengupta, and Petra Todd. 2005. "Progressing through Progresa: An Impact Assessment of a School Subsidy Experiment in Rural Mexico." *Economic Development and Cultural Change* 54, no. 1: 237–75.

Creighton, Mathew, and Park, Hyunjoon. 2010. "Closing the Gender Gap: Six Decades of Reform in Mexican Education." *Comparative Education Review* 54, no. 4: 513–37.

Kremer, Michael, Conner Brannen, and Rachel Glennerster. 2013. "The Challenge of Education and Learning in the Developing World." *Science* 340: 297–300.

Morley, Steven, and David Coady. 2003. *From Social Assistance to Social Development: Targeted Education Subsidies in Developing Countries.* Washington: Center for Global Development and International Food Policy Research Institute.

Schultz, T. Paul. 2004. "School Subsidies for the Poor: Evaluating the Mexican Progresa Poverty Program." *Journal of Development Economics* 74: 199–250.

- **In Pakistan, the Punjab Female School Stipend Program increased middle school enrollment for girls by 10 percentage points in just two years, increased completion rates by 4.5 percent, and saw transition rates to high school improve as well.** Girls in the program were 3 to 6 percentage points more likely to complete middle school, 4 to 6 percentage points more likely to transition to high school, and 6 percentage points more likely to complete at least grade 9 of high school, compared with girls in the control group. Also, their labor force participation decreased by 4 to 5 percentage points, translating into at least two to three fewer hours worked per day compared with girls not in the program. Girls in the poorest households experienced nearly double the amount of reduced labor force participation as the rest of the program beneficiaries.

How it works: Female students received a quarterly stipend of approximately PKR 600 (roughly $10). Beneficiaries were targeted based on residency in a district with literacy rates below 40 percent in the province, and enrollment in grades 6–8 in public schools. Eligibility was conditional on a minimum school attendance rate of 80 percent, reported regularly by the school. Eventually, the program was extended to grades 9 and 10.

Alam, Andaleeb, Javier E. Baez, and Ximena V. Del Carpio. 2011. *Does Cash for School Influence Young Women's Behavior in the Longer Term? Evidence from Pakistan.* Policy Research Working Paper 5669. Washington: World Bank.

Chaudhury, N., and D. Parajuli. 2008. "Conditional Cash Transfers and Female Schooling: The Impact of the Female School Stipend Program on Public School Enrollments in Punjab, Pakistan." *Journal of Applied Economics.*

- **The Japan Fund for Poverty Reduction Scholarship Program in Cambodia encouraged girls to transition to secondary school, increasing girls' secondary school enrollment and attendance by about 30 percent.** The effects were largest for the most disadvantaged girls: girls from the poorest households, girls from households with lower parental education levels, and girls who lived far away from a secondary school.

How it works: Cash transfers of $45 in the form of a scholarship were awarded to poor girls completing the sixth grade (the last grade of primary school) and beginning the seventh grade (lower secondary). Families received the transfer, provided that their daughter was enrolled in school, maintained a passing grade, and was absent fewer than ten days a year.

Filmer, Deon, and Norbert Schady. 2008. "Getting Girls into School: Evidence from a Scholarship Program in Cambodia." *Economic Development and Cultural Change* 56, no. 3: 581–617.

- **Colombia improved enrollment in secondary education through vouchers with a randomized evaluation finding that students were 10 percent more likely to complete eighth grade and score a full grade level higher on texts.** Colombia launched a national education voucher program in 1992 to promote continuation from primary to secondary school. Because government schools were overcrowded but there was excess capacity in private schools, the government ran a lottery to award and fund vouchers for parents to send their children to private schools. A randomized evaluation found that voucher lottery winners were 15 to 20 percent more likely to attend private school, 10 percent more likely to complete eighth grade, and scored the equivalent of a full grade level higher (0.2 standard deviation) on standardized tests compared with students in the control group. The costs of the program were similar to the costs of providing places in public schools.

King, Elizabeth M., Peter Orazem, and Darin Wohlgemuth. 1999. "Central Mandates and Local Incentives: The Colombia Education Voucher Program." *World Bank Economic Review* 13, no. 3: 467–91.

Angrist, Joshua, Eric Bettinger, Erik Bloom, Elizabeth King, and Michael Kremer. 2002. "Vouchers for Private Schooling in Colombia: Evidence from a Randomized Natural Experiment." *American Economic Review* 92, no. 5: 1535–58.

- **In Kenya, providing free uniforms to children in primary school significantly reduced girls' school dropout rate, from 19 to 16 percent, and reduced the teen pregnancy rate, from 16 to 13 percent.** In some areas of Kenya, parents are normally required to purchase school uniforms, at a cost of $6 (a significant expense in a country with an average annual per capita income of $340). In one program, grade 6 students were provided with two free school uniforms during the last three years of primary school to help subsidize the cost of education. An innovative study tracked students in the program for seven years, from age 13.5 to 20.5 years. They found that after three years of the education subsidy (the uniforms), the primary school dropout rate fell significantly, from 19 percent to 16 percent for girls and from 13 percent to 10 percent for boys. In addition, girls' teen pregnancy rates fell from 16 percent to 13 percent in that same period; four years later, there was still a 7 percent gap in the childbearing rate between girls who received uniforms (46 percent) and girls who did not (49 percent).

- **Another Kenya program that provided free uniforms to orphans reduced absenteeism by 7 percentage points, especially for girls.** The Child Sponsorship Program distributed school uniforms by lottery to primary school children who had experienced one or two parent deaths (i.e., were orphans). A randomized evaluation found that receiving a uniform reduced absenteeism by 7 percentage points (39 percent), from a base of 18 percent school absenteeism. The program's impact was larger on girls than boys, and even larger on children who had not owned a uniform before.

- **A rigorous evaluation of a school supplies program in Kenya found that after five years, students participating in the program had completed 15 percent more schooling as compared with students in control schools.** This program provided free uniforms, textbooks, and classroom construction to seven of fourteen poorly performing schools.

Duflo, Esther, Pascaline Dupas, and Michael Kremer2014. *Education, HIV, and Early Fertility: Experimental Evidence from Kenya*. NBER Working Paper 20784. Cambridge, Mass.: National Bureau of Economic Research. http://www.nber.org/papers/w20784.pdf.

Evans, David, Michael Kremer, and Muthoni Ngatia. 2008. "The Impact of Distributing School Uniforms on Children's Education in Kenya." Poverty Action Lab. http://www.povertyactionlab.org/publication/impact-distributing-school-uniforms-childrens-education-kenya.

Kremer, Michael, Sylvie Moulin, and Robert Namunyu. 2002. *Unbalanced Decentralization: Results of a Randomized School Supplies Provision Program in Kenya*. Cambridge, Mass.: Harvard University.

- **Providing girls in India with bicycles increased girls' age-appropriate enrollment in secondary school by 30 percent and reduced the gender gap in age-appropriate enrollment by 40 percent.** Increases in enrollment took place primarily in those villages that were furthest away from secondary schools, suggesting that bicycles helped to reduce the time and safety costs of school attendance. In addition, the number of girls who stayed in school long enough to take the high-stakes Secondary School Certificate examination increased by 9.5 percent, although there was no impact on the number of girls who passed the examination, which vividly shows that increases in enrollment do not necessarily translate into increases in learning.

  How it works: The Chief Minister's Bicycle Program provided all girls who enrolled in grade 9 (secondary school) with funds (approximately $40) to buy a bicycle to make it easier to go to school. Girls received funds through their schools in public ceremonies attended by local officials and elected representatives. School principals were required to collect the receipts and provide a utilization certificate to show that the funds had been used to purchase a bicycle.

  Muralidharan, Karthik, and Nishith Prakash. 2013. *Cycling to School: Increasing Secondary School Enrollment for Girls in India.* IZA Discussion Paper 7585. Bonn: Institute for the Study of Labour.

- **A Gambian girls' scholarship program increased secondary enrollment by nearly 10 percent.** A nationwide scholarship program for secondary school girls in the Gambia saw girls' enrollment increase by 8 to 9 percentage points. This positive effect was even experienced by girls in primary school, whose enrollment also increased significantly, by about 9 percentage points. These findings suggest that the removal of school fees caused parents to further invest in the schooling of their younger daughters, in anticipation of lower costs for future levels of schooling.

  Gajigo, Ousman. 2012. *Closing the Education Gender Gap: Estimating the Impact of Girls' Scholarship Program in the Gambia.* Working Paper 164. Abidjan: African Development Bank Group.

Designing Effective Cash and In-Kind Transfer Programs for Girls: Issues to Consider

On the basis of the evidence, policymakers and practitioners also now have a better idea of what components of scholarship and cash transfer packages matter the most for girls' educational outcomes. For example, cash transfers with

What We Know About Providing Cash to Offset Indirect and Opportunity Costs

- Conditional cash transfers (CCTs) have the edge in improving girls' educational outcomes, whereas unconditional cash transfers (UCTs) may be more effective in improving girls' health outcomes.

- The type of condition matters (e.g., if targeting participation, transfers should be conditioned upon monthly attendance; if targeting learning, scholarships should be awarded based on merit).

- Transfers to mothers may be more effective than transfers to fathers; we do not yet know whether transfers directly to girls are more effective than transfers to their mothers.

- Incentives need to be appropriately timed with the behavior targeted for change (e.g., if targeting transitions, transfers should be distributed at the time of reenrollment; if targeting completion, transfers should be distributed at the time of graduation; if targeting seasonal fluctuations in attendance, transfers should be distributed at the time of harvest), with consideration given to the timing of payment and the timing of school costs.

- Cash transfers can be as small as 2 percent of median household consumption to be effective—although the context matters.

- Monitoring of recipients' satisfaction of eligibility and conditionality requirements is recommended.

- Selection criteria for targeting beneficiaries should focus on those most in need; determining the right target group depends on the context.

- Eligibility rules should be made public and transparent; unintended within-family and within-classroom consequences should be considered.

- Logistical measures for transferring funds efficiently and systematically to recipients must be in place, especially in rural areas, where transactional costs to individual accounts can be quite high. In this case, transfers made directly to schools to administer to recipients may be more cost-effective, not to mention add an additional accountability measure to reinforce girls' attendance and retention.

conditionalities attached are critical for improving girls' enrollment (both primary and secondary), attendance, retention, transition, and completion, as well as reducing dropout rates. This is especially true for girls from resource-poor settings and poor households, where parents are forced to make a choice between sending their daughters to school or not (Akresh, de Walque, and Kazianga 2013; Unterhalter et al. 2014).

Research from behavioral economics also has helped to explain the importance of matching the timing of scholarships, stipends, and cash transfers to the timing of school fees in order to increase the cost-effectiveness of programs (FHI360 2013; Kremer, Brannen, and Glennerster 2013). Also, other research has illustrated how interventions like merit-based scholarships can have positive spillover effects to nonrecipients, particularly by motivating students to attend school more often, work harder, and study harder (Kremer, Brannen, and Glennerster 2013; Kremer, Miguel, and Thornton 2009).

Policymakers and practitioners also have a better idea of the kinds of questions they need to be asking when designing programs, such as, *Who will benefit the most?* A series of studies of the Zomba Cash Transfer experiment, for example, illustrate the need to carefully target cash transfers to the right group. Researchers found that the girls who benefited the most from cash transfers and who were able to hold onto these gains across more time were girls who were out of school at the baseline and who, upon receiving the cash transfers, were able to return to school and accumulate the knowledge and skills that they otherwise would not have made out of school. Girls who were already enrolled in school at the baseline did not sustain their gains beyond the program's conclusion because these girls were likely to continue schooling without the extra cash incentive (Baird et al. 2015). Similarly, Khandker and colleagues (2003) found that those from the poorest households (the land poor) benefited more than those with larger land wealth from the Female School Stipend Program in Bangladesh.

- **CCTs distributed in the Zomba Cash Transfer experiment in Malawi more than doubled the reenrollment of girls between thirteen and twenty-two years old who were out of school at the baseline.** Although girls who received UCTs were also significantly more likely to be enrolled in school compared with the control group, their gains in enrollment were less than half of that achieved by girls who received CCTs. Of particular importance, a program's impact was even more pronounced if recipient girls were monitored for compliance and penalized for noncompliance, with a 60 percent improvement in the odds of enrollment compared with an 18–25 percent improvement in the odds of enrollment for recipients who either received UCTs or whose satisfaction of condition requirements were not monitored.

- **By the end of the two-year experiment, girls in the UCT treatment group were 44 percent less likely to ever be married and were 27**

percent less likely to be ever pregnant than girls in the control group. Similar effects were not observed for girls in the CCT treatment group. Girls who dropped out of school after the start of the program experienced the most substantial delays in fertility and marriage.

How it works: In order to determine whether the amount of cash transferred to households influenced educational outcomes, researchers randomly assigned parents to receive a monthly transfer of $4, $6, $8, or $10, and girls received $1, $2, $3, $4, or $5 per month depending on a lottery. These transfers were conditional upon girls' attending school at least 80 percent of the month. In addition, girls' tuition was paid directly to the school. Households could potentially have more than one daughter participate in the program at once.

Researchers found that the smallest transfer amounts ($4 per month to the parents and $1 per month to the schoolgirl) were sufficient to attain the average schooling gains observed by the girls who received CCTs. They found no evidence that increasing the amount of transfers made directly to the girls themselves was effective in improving any of the educational outcomes observed.

Baird, Sarah, Craig McIntosh, and Berk Ozler. 2011. "Cash or Condition? Evidence from a Cash Transfer Experiment." *Quarterly Journal of Economics* 126, no. 4: 1709–53.

Baird, Sarah, Francisco H. G. Ferreira, Berk Ozler, and Michael Woolcock. 2013. "Relative Effectiveness of Conditional and Unconditional Cash Transfers for Schooling Outcomes in Developing Countries: A Systematic Review." *Campbell Systematic Reviews* 8.

- **Girls who were out of school before the Zomba Cash Transfer program began sustained the education gains after the program ended, and over the long run they were 10 percentage points less likely to have been married and 4 percentage points less likely to have been pregnant.** However, for other girls, the gains from the experiment appear to have been short-lived. Two years after the program ended, the educational gains (especially school completion rates) made by girls in the CCT treatment group were sustained only for those girls who had been out of school at the baseline.

Meanwhile, girls who were in the UCT treatment group suffered from "bounce back," whereby their marriage and fertility outcomes eventually

"I performed really well in school. My father traveled a lot and my uncle was responsible for us. When my husband came to marry me, my uncle—who married his daughters early—asked me for my opinion. I was too embarrassed to say I didn't want to marry, so I left school although I was a very good student. My husband is really nice, but every night I dream that I am back at school. And when my children have exams, I dream that I go with them and sit for the exams. I swear, I was really good [at school]."

A Palestinian woman who married early

caught up to the same level that they would have reached if they had never participated in the program. In other words, "the cash transfer program was akin to pushing a pause button for these school-aged girls for two years, but once that button was released they engaged in these behaviors at rates *higher* than the counterfactual."

- **Researchers suggest that the durable gains made by some of the girls—those who were out of school at the baseline and in the CCT treatment group—can be explained by the positive effects of schooling.** That is, the CCT provided out-of-school girls, who were unlikely to return to school on their own, with the opportunity to reenroll in school and to accumulate a meaningful combination of skills, knowledge, information, and networks. Thus, the transitory impact of the UCT treatment can be attributed to the absence of any significant accumulation of capital (human, social, or physical) that the girls could have used to set a different trajectory in life.

Baird, Sarah, Ephraim Chirwa, Craig McIntosh, and Berk Ozler. 2015. *What Happens Once the Intervention Ends? The Medium-Term Impacts of a Cash Transfer Program in Malawi*. 3ie Grantee Final Report. New Delhi: International Initiative for Impact Evaluation.

- **In Burkina Faso, a randomized experiment found that CCTs are more effective than UCTs in improving school enrollment, increasing the enrollment of marginalized girls by 20.3 percent.** The intervention focused on enrolling "marginal" children—those children who are initially not enrolled in school or are less likely to go to school, including girls, younger children, and children with lower abilities. Researchers randomly assigned 540 households in 75 villages in Nahouri province into four treatment groups (with CCTs paid to the father, CCTs paid to the mother, UCTs paid to the father, and UCTs paid to the mother) and a control group. CCT households experienced statistically significant increases in enrollment of 20.3 percent for girls, 37.3 percent for younger children, and 36.2 percent for lower-ability children relative to the mean enrollment of those subgroups. UCT transfers had no significant impact. An ongoing analysis is determining whether program effects differed between households where transfers were given to the mother and where transfers were given to the father.

How it works: For each child under the age of seven, the mother or the father would receive quarterly payments of $8.80 (or about 4 percent of household per capita expenditures), conditional upon the child meeting quarterly visits to the local health clinic for growth monitoring. For each child between seven and ten years (or in grades 1 to 4), the mother or father would receive quarterly payments of $17.60 (or roughly 8 percent of household per capita expenditures) conditional upon meeting school enrollment and attendance target rates above 90 percent each quarter. For each child between eleven and fifteen years (or in grades 5 or higher, but younger than the age of fifteen), the mother or father would receive quarterly payments of $35.20 (or approximately 16 percent of household per capita expenditures), also conditional upon enrollment and 90 percent attendance. Each child in CCT households was given a booklet in which school attendance or health clinic visits were recorded by schoolteachers or clinic staff members. Record books of 20 percent of CCT students were randomly cross-checked by village committee members against school and health clinic administrative records to confirm whether a child was satisfying the conditionality requirements needed to receive their transfer.

Akresh, Richard, Damien de Walque, and Harounan Kazianga. 2013. *Cash Transfers and Child Schooling: Evidence from a Randomized Evaluation of the Role of Conditionality*. Policy Research Working Paper 6340. Washington: World Bank.

- **The Cambodia Education Sector Support Project Scholarship Program demonstrates that a $45 scholarship was more effective in improving transitions to lower secondary school and increasing attendance (by 25 percentage points) compared with a $60 scholarship.** The $45 scholarship is equivalent to about 2 percent of median household consumption in Cambodia, which is small compared to the value offered by programs in other countries. For example, 22 percent of household income for recipients of Oportunidades in Mexico, 29 percent for recipients of Red de Protección Social in Nicaragua, 17 percent for recipients of Familias en Acción in Colombia, and 6 percent for recipients of Bolsa Familia in Brazil and Bono de Desarrollo Humano in Ecuador.

  How it works: Scholarships were awarded to sixth-grade students in "feeder" schools, conditional on enrolling in the seventh grade (the first year of lower secondary school). The selection of students was based on an application that was used to predict the likelihood of dropping out of school. In each recipient school, the twenty-five students with the lowest score on the application were offered a $60 scholarship and the next twenty-five students with the lowest scores were offered a $45 scholarship. (Researchers studied the effect of the two different scholarship amounts on students at the $45/$60 cutoff, making the two groups similar to each other in terms of academic performance.) Lists of scholarship recipients were posted in schools. Scholarships were renewable for three years on three conditions: (1) enrollment, (2) regular attendance, and (3) on-time promotion to the next grade. Scholarships were transferred to parents, and program officials did not monitor how the money was spent.

  Filmer, Deon, and Norbert Schady. 2011. "Does More Cash in Conditional Cash Transfer Programs Always Lead to Larger Impacts on School Attendance?" *Journal of Development Economics* 96: 150–57.

- **In Colombia, the impact of the Subsidios Condicionados a la Asistencia Escolar ("Conditional Subsidies for School Attendance") program showed the effectiveness of paying part of the cash transfer at reenrollment time; enrollment increased by 4 percentage points for secondary school.** The program also increased enrollment in tertiary institutions by 9.4 percentage points, without reducing daily attendance. Even more significantly, incentivizing graduation rather than just attendance led to an increase in matriculation rates at tertiary institutions by 48.9 percentage points. These effects of the program were even larger for

unquestionably leads to the increased participation of children in terms of enrollment, attendance, and completion." Indeed, today BRAC community schools account for 50 percent of total enrollment in rural areas in Bangladesh.

DeStefano, Joseph, Audrey-marie Schuh Moore, David Balwanz, and Ash Hartwell. 2007. *Reaching the Underserved: Complementary Models of Effective Schooling*. USAID and Equip2.

Rugh, Andrea, and Heather Bossert. 1998. *Involving Communities: Participation in the Delivery of Education Programs*. Washington: USAID.

- **Colombia's Escuela Nueva "New School" program of multigrade community schools contributed to a 30 percent increase in rural enrollment.** Escuela Nueva was implemented in 1975 by Colombia's Education Ministry as a way to target rural areas, which, as in many countries, lagged far behind urban areas in educational attainment. The program established Escuela Nueva schools in poor rural communities, where students of different ages, grades, and abilities were taught in the same classroom and were provided with more flexible schedules. Because of the challenge of teaching such a variety of students, teachers were trained in active learning techniques and were encouraged to break from the rote methods taught in conventional schools. In contrast to BRAC, Escuela Nueva provided an alternative within (rather than outside) the formal education system.

Escuela Nueva's piloting process was slow and difficult, and the program faced strong initial resistance. But the program was eventually brought to scale in the late 1980s, in 18,000 classrooms. A study in 1992 found that rural enrollment increased from about 50 percent to 80 percent, with girls attending Escuela Nueva schools more frequently than boys. In 1994, the Escuela Nueva approach was implemented in poor areas of Cali and Bogotá and has been replicated in a number of other Latin American countries. A later study found that teacher innovation is a strong component of the success of the community-based, multigrade school approach, and that Escuela Nueva in Colombia is an example of "one of the most successful multigrade schooling programs."

Benveniste, L., and P. J. McEwan. 2000. "Constraints to Implementing Educational Innovations: The Case of Multi-Grade Schools." *International Review of Education* 46, nos. 1–2: 31–48.

Rugh, Andrea, and Heather Bossert. 1998. *Involving Communities: Participation in the Delivery of Education Programs*. Washington: USAID.

- **A sixteen-country review in Africa shows that community schools generally increase enrollment, retention, and quality and, on average have lower dropout rates.** Despite differences in approach (new construction vs. support of existing schools; varying levels of government vs. NGO involvement), the study found broadly consistent trends. For example, World Learning in Ethiopia has seen girls' enrollment increase by 13.8 percent; the Community School Alliances project in Ghana reported that nearly every child in participating communities was enrolled by the end of the project; girls' enrollment in southern Sudan increased 96 percent as a result of the work of community education committees sensitizing parents and the community on the need to educate girls; and in Malawi, children in community-based schools scored 30 percent higher than children in government schools on national tests.

Miller-Grandvaux, Yolande, and Karla Yoder. 2002. *A Literature Review of Community Schools in Africa*. Washington: USAID.

- **Community schools in Mali have raised girls' enrollment by 67 percent.** Mali's efforts to promote community participation to encourage girls' education are historically well-known in Africa. Between 1989 and 1993, a program to encourage and support local community schools increased girls' overall enrollment by 67 percent and increased by 83 percent the number of seven-year-old girls entering primary school. In 2000, 1,500 community schools were operating, serving about 8 percent of Mali's schoolchildren. Communities are now building more locally accessible schools and are involving communities in the design and operation of the schools so that they meet cultural norms. The program is also setting quotas for both boys and girls, developing more relevant "life skills" in the curriculum, and using local languages in instruction. Rigorous research is not available on the impact of more recent programs, but early indications are that girls' enrollment and test scores are increasing. A number of studies and field practitioners have found that community schools are less expensive to set up and run than more traditional, centralized schools. One study in Mali found that it cost $36 per year to educate a student at a community school compared with $42 per year at the regular district school. Practitioners have found similar results in comparable countries.

DeStefano, Joseph, Audrey-marie Schuh Moore, David Balwanz, and Ash Hartwell. 2007. *Reaching the Underserved: Complementary Models of Effective Schooling.* USAID and Equip2.

Rugh, Andrea. 2000. *Starting Now: Strategies for Helping Girls Complete Primary.* SAGE Project. Washington: Academy for Educational Development.

Tietjen, Karen. 1999. *Community Schools in Mali: A Comparative Cost Study.* SD Publication Series Technical Paper 97. Washington: USAID.

- **In Upper Egypt, community schools not only increased access to primary education for girls in rural hamlets, they also improved academic performance with 97 percent of fifth graders passing national examinations, compared to 73 percent of students in public schools in the districts.** As part of a UNICEF and Egyptian Ministry of Education joint initiative, these schools were implemented through local NGOs and managed by community education committees who provided a school site, determined the hours and days school is in session, and participated in teacher selection. The Ministry of Education paid teacher salaries, UNICEF supplied school materials, and the community education committees ensured that schooling was truly free. The community schools use a modified curriculum that accommodates a local view of the learning relationship between teachers and students and that enables multiage teaching. The schools also offered courses outside of regular school hours, including parenting classes, preschool and daycare, nonformal adolescent education, and hygiene, health, and nutrition classes. Schools were visited at least once per month by teacher support staff who observe instruction and provide immediate, on-the-spot feedback and professional development. And, new community school teachers were provided with mentoring opportunities and networks with experienced community school teachers. The government has since worked to apply lessons learned from the community schools program to its public schools.

DeStefano, Joseph, Audrey-marie Schuh Moore, David Balwanz, and Ash Hartwell. 2007. *Reaching the Underserved: Complementary Models of Effective Schooling.* USAID and Equip2.

Flexible School Schedules

In general, offering flexible schedules in both regular and informal schools helps boost enrollment by accommodating children's work, making it easier for children to care for younger siblings, do chores, or even work for wages while enrolled in school. These options have been most effectively implemented in community school settings, where it is easier for the community to support and sustain flexible approaches. For example, in India, efforts to provide flexible hours through nonformal education helped draw working children, especially girls, into primary school. Colombia's Escuela Nueva program includes flexible schedules for different grades. Also, part-time and flexible scheduling helped raise girls' enrollment in China (Herz et al. 1991).

Such efforts do pose a dilemma: They make it easier for children to attend but may make it harder for them to spend time studying. Yet for many poor children, offering flexible school schedules may be the most realistic option for receiving an education. Ultimately, it is important to help children gain time to go to school and to study, and, where children are in informal schools, to enable them to make the transition to regular schools.

- **A study of Bangladesh's BRAC program finds that flexible "satellite" schools raise girls' primary enrollment.** Satellite schools, including two or three small schools serving at least the first three primary grades, were established closer to the community and supervised by a more distant main primary school. Satellite schools operated only 2.5 hours daily, mainly with women teachers, and school schedules were set to suit rural children's work. Participation rates were greater than what was expected, girls constituted 63 percent of students enrolled, and fewer than 1 percent dropped out.

  Herz, Barbara, K. Subbarao, Masooma Habib, and Laura Raney. 1991. *Letting Girls Learn: Promising Approaches in Primary and Secondary Education.* World Bank Discussion Paper 133. Washington: World Bank.

- **Double sessions in Pakistan's Northern Areas enrolled girls for the first time.** Parents asked government schools to have double sessions, with boys attending until 2 pm, and girls attending afterward. Such schedules and the hiring of female teachers helped boost girls' enrollment.

  World Bank. 1996. *Improving Basic Education in Pakistan.* Report 14960-PAK. Washington: World Bank.

Herz, Barbara. 2002. *Universal Basic Education: What Works.* Paper prepared for Coalition for Basic Education. Washington: Academy for Educational Development.

 4 Making Schools Girls-Friendly

Although having a basic school nearby is an important first step to getting girls into school, it may not suffice to bring all girls into school or to keep them there. Moreover, practitioners' experience suggests that girls' enrollment rates and test scores may respond even more when those schools are equipped with girl-friendly amenities and features. Building on UNICEF's child-friendly schools framework, researchers and practitioners advocating for girl-friendly schools are calling for transforming the school climate and school culture into one that is not only gender-sensitive but also promotes parity in the enrollment and achievement of girls and boys; reduces constraints on gender equity and eliminates gender stereotypes; and provides facilities, curricula, and learning processes that are welcoming to girls.

In creating girl-friendly schools, cultural requirements for privacy must be understood. Depending on the context, these may entail separate schools for girls, separate hours for girls in schools shared with boys, boundary walls for girls' schools, female teachers, and the like. Such efforts are critical not only for increasing enrollment and achieving gender parity but also for creating high-quality learning environments and community cultures for girls. Involving communities has emerged as the best way to find out what matters most to parents and how to proceed (Herz 2002; World Bank 2001).

Interventions that have attempted to make schools more girl-friendly have typically implemented a package of interventions targeted at improving school quality and gender equality simultaneously. Research is needed to determine which components girls are responding to and which are most effective. Here are two examples of girl-friendly schools that employ a package of some of the best practices in girls' education:

- **Case Study: BRIGHT Program in Burkina Faso. As a model for girl-friendly schools offering a diverse package of services, the Burkinabe Response to Improve Girls' Chances to Succeed (BRIGHT) schools in**

Burkina Faso raised girls' enrollment, attendance, and participation by 5 percentage points more than boys within 2.5 years of the program. The BRIGHT program is a government effort designed to increase the supply of primary schools in 132 rural villages in Burkina Faso via infrastructure development. School construction under this program specifically equipped schools with girl-friendly amenities. Funded by the Millennium Challenge Corporation and implemented by NGOs under the supervision of the US Agency for International Development (US-AID), BRIGHT schools included three classrooms, a multipurpose hall, one office, one storage room, housing for three teachers, separate toilets for girls and boys, and a water pump. Each BRIGHT school also included student and teacher desks, chairs, metal bookshelves, and a playground. Incentives were also provided to encourage children to attend school, and programs were initiated to mobilize the community in support of education, especially girls' education. Students received school uniforms and textbooks, as well as school meals each day they attended school. Girls were eligible for take-home rations, conditional on 90 percent attendance each month. Parents were also targeted by information campaigns that highlighted the benefits of education, especially for girls, and mothers were encouraged to attend an adult literacy program. Finally, the program also sought to place more female teachers in BRIGHT schools, and teachers and ministry officials received gender sensitivity training.

In addition to increasing enrollment and attendance for girls, test scores for both girls and boys improved by an average of 0.41 percentage point—no gender differences were found—and for those students who were out of school before a BRIGHT school was constructed, test scores increased by 2.2 standard deviations. Estimating the specific effects of BRIGHT schools' girl-friendly amenities—improvements targeting the quality of the school environment in reference to its female students—researchers found that BRIGHT schools' girl-friendly features improved enrollment by 13 percentage points more than the effect on enrollment of providing a regular (non-BRIGHT) school (27 percentage points). Compared with boys, girls responded even more favorably to BRIGHT schools' girl-friendly amenities; the amenities account for the difference of 6.6 percentage points in enrollment above boys' enrollment. BRIGHT school girl-friendly features improved the academic performance of girls *and* boys, accounting for an increase in test scores for all children in the village by 0.35 standard deviation above the 0.32 standard deviation effect on test scores of providing a regular school.

Kazianga, Harounan, Dan Levy, Leigh L. Linden, and Matt Sloan. 2013. "The Effects of 'Girl-Friendly' Schools: Evidence from the BRIGHT School Construction Program in Burkina Faso." *American Economic Journal: Applied Economics* 5, no. 3: 41–62.

- **Case Study: Forum for African Women Educationalists (FAWE) in Africa.** Starting in 1999, FAWE began to transform ordinary (girls only and co-ed) schools across African countries into gender-responsive schools that attend to the physical, academic, and social dimensions of both girls' and boys' education. These Centers of Excellence provide girls (and boys) with teachers who are trained in gender-responsive pedagogy, school directors who are trained in gender-responsive school management, learning materials that portray girls and women in positive and equitable ways, a school environment that is welcoming and conducive to learning, and a community of adults who support them and are engaged in school management. Additional features include stipends for underprivileged girls; puberty and menstrual hygiene management education; a science, mathematics, and technology program for girls; and empowerment training for both girls and boys. Although no formal external evaluations have been conducted, FAWE's own program evaluations have demonstrated improved academic performance and achievement for girls, greater participation by girls in classroom processes, higher retention rates, more girls in school committees and leadership roles, a reduction in teenage pregnancies, and higher gender awareness among boys. Centers of Excellence have now been introduced in Burkina Faso, Chad, Comoros, the Gambia, Guinea, Kenya, Madagascar, Namibia, Rwanda, Tanzania, Togo, Uganda, Zambia, and Zanzibar.

FAWE. (2009). "Centres of Excellence." http://fawe.org/activities/interventions/COEs/index.php.

Lloyd, Cynthia B. 2013. "Education for Girls: Alternative Pathways to Girls' Empowerment." Integrated Approaches to Improving the Lives of Adolescent Girls Issue Paper Series. GirlEffect.org.

Preschool and Child Care Programs

Although rigorous evidence is scarce, some studies suggest that providing affordable child care or lowering the cost of community-based child care can help girls who care for their siblings to attend school (Miske Witt and Associates 2007).

- **A village preschool program in India helped to boost enrollment rates.** One study discusses India's effort to set up centers offering early education classes near or in village primary schools. These were intended to promote early childhood development and to help substitute for the child care that may keep girls from attending primary school. The centers do not accept children younger than two years of age, however, so toddlers often roam fairly freely in villages. The study indicates that the centers help introduce poor children from illiterate families to the school environment, and these children tend to continue into the formal primary school program.

  Rugh, Andrea. 2000. *Starting Now: Strategies for Helping Girls Complete Primary.* SAGE Project. Washington: Academy for Educational Development.

- **A Nepali program in early childhood development and parental training particularly boosts girls' attendance.** Roughly 13,000 children participated in this program. They tend to enroll at higher rates in primary school, have low repetition and high promotion rates, and are less likely to

What is Early Childhood Development?

In addition to helping out an older sister, who is usually tasked with taking care of younger siblings, to continue with her schooling, preschool and child care programs provide an additional benefit to the child being cared for. Early childhood development (ECD) programs, which includes preschool, kindergarden, or early childhood care and education, have been shown to have some of the largest effects on how children perform in school, with many of these effects persisting into adulthood. As they stimulate brain development early, ECD interventions can take place in formal school settings or during day care, or can even target improving parents' practices at home. The first 1,000 days, or three years, of a child's life represent a crucial time for brain development and nutrition that can set children on a path toward success. Considering that estimates from the World Bank find that there are 200 million children under five in the world who are not fulfilling their developmental potential due to poverty and poor nutrition, expanding access to ECD programs could have a huge impact.

Studies have shown that high-quality early childhood interventions can have a large impact on the future of children—not to mention allowing older siblings to continue with their schooling:

- A preschool program in Mozambique had beneficial impacts on further schooling, with participating children more likely to enroll in primary school and more likely to start school at the right age. Participants showed an 87 percent increase over the control group on overall school readiness, especially in cognitive development. Once in school, they also spent more time on homework and school related activities.

Martinez, Sebastian, Sophie Naudeau, and Victor Pereira. 2012. "The Promise of Preschool in Africa: A Randomized Impact Evaluation of Early Childhood Development in Rural Mozambique." Washington: The World Bank Group and Save the Children.

- In Vietnam, an early childhood education intervention had lasting effects on the cognitive development of school-aged children in rural areas. Children in grades 1 and 2 with the most nutritional deficits benefited the most from the program in terms of improvements in cognitive test scores.

Watanabe, Koichiro, Rafael Flores, Junko Fujiwara, and Lien Thi Huong Tran. 2005. "Early Childhood Development Interventions and Cognitive Development of Young Children in Rural Vietnam." *Journal of Nutrition* 135, no. 8: 1918-25.

- The Turkish Early Enrichment Project had positive impacts on children's schooling performance and developmental trajectories into young adulthood. The program offered both early childhood enrichment (center-based) and training of mothers (home-based) in low-income areas of Istanbul. A ten-year follow-up study showed that 86 percent of the children in the program were still in school, compared to 67 percent of the children in the control group. Twenty-two years later, positive results for participants endured in terms of educational attainment, occupational status, age of beginning gainful employment, and some indicators of integration into modern urban life, such as owning a computer.

Kagitcibasi, Cigdem. 1992. "A Model of Multipurpose Nonformal Education: The Case of the Turkish Early Enrichment Project." Proceedings from the First International Council on Education for Women.

Kagitcibasi, Cigdem, Diane Sunar, Sevda Bekman, Nazli Baydar, and Zeynep Cemalcilar. 2009. "Continuing Effects of Early Enrichment in Adult Life: The Turkish Early Enrichment Project 22 Years Later." *Journal of Applied Development Psychology* 30, no. 6: 764-79.

- An early childhood home-visiting program in Jamaica also had a large impact. Severely disadvantaged and growth-stunted children whose mothers received help stimulating their children's cognitive and psychosocial skills for two years earned 25 percent higher wages twenty years following the program, catching up to the earnings of a nonstunted comparison group. These effects were higher than those of providing nutritional supplements to stunted children alone.

Gertler, Paul, et al. 2014. "Labor Market Returns to an Early childhood Stimulation Intervention in Jamaica." *Science* 344, no. 6187: 998–1001.

drop out. Enrollment rates for girls and for very poor and low-caste children who participated in the program are similar to those for high-caste boys, and they are succeeding as well. The parents of participating children are also more likely to engage with the children's teachers and schools.

> Save the Children. 2000. *What's the Difference? The Impact of Early Childhood Development Programs*. Kathmandu: Save the Children.

Eliminate School-Related Gender-Based Violence

Making schools girl-friendly also means eliminating a range of explicit and implicit acts or threats of sexual, physical, or psychological violence against girls in and around schools. Around the world, girls are subjected to school-related gender-based violence (SRGBV), with documented cases in numerous countries. For example, one study found that 30 percent of girls in South Africa are raped in and around school (UNGEI, UNESCO, and EFA 2015; King and Winthrop 2015). Examples of this type of school violence range widely, as seen in figure 4.1, and can include when a teacher asks a student for sex in exchange for better grades or punishes a student with poor grades if she or he rejects the teacher's sexual advances (Irish Consortium 2013). Girls are especially vulnerable to these types of violence, and it is reinforced by gender inequality in the society writ large, but boys can also be subjected to this type of abuse.

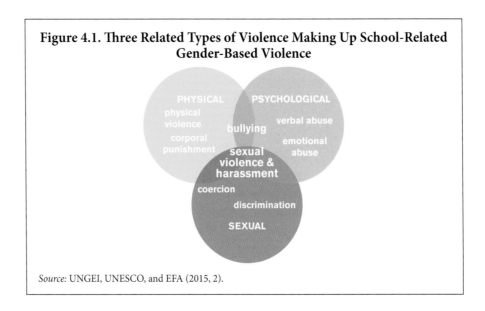

Figure 4.1. Three Related Types of Violence Making Up School-Related Gender-Based Violence

Source: UNGEI, UNESCO, and EFA (2015, 2).

Effective SRGBV interventions address both prevention and response, which means efforts take on coordinated, multilevel, and multifaceted "whole-school" approaches. Tackling SRGBV requires cultural change, involving teachers, students, parents, community members, and local organizations (Camfed 2010; Michau et al. 2015; USAID 2008a, 2008b). Such an integrated approach also means recognizing that GBV within schools is related to GVB outside schools, making it essential to change attitudes and improve awareness toward violence beyond school walls (UNGEI, UNESCO, and EFA 2015). This section presents evidence for several promising interventions that help make schools more girl-friendly.

School Safety Policies and Codes of Conduct for Teachers

Reforming teachers' codes of conduct and other safety policies can help quickly raise awareness of SRGBV, protect children from GBV, and enhance teacher–student interaction, especially when teachers, students, and whole schools are involved in creating these codes and policies. Not to mention, codes of conduct can help change the institutional climate concerning violence by strengthening mechanisms for reporting code violations and holding perpetrators of violence accountable (ICRW 2015). In addition, strengthening the legislative and policy frameworks dealing with violence against girls can help enhance linkages to services for victims:

- **USAID's safe schools program increased the amount of teachers who knew how to report an incident of GBV.** Following the USAID Safe Schools Program, which included the revision of teachers' code of conduct, 97 percent of teachers in Ghana and Malawi reported having seen the code, compared with about 75 percent of teachers in the baseline survey. A total of 94 percent of teachers in Ghana believed that the revised code adequately protected children, and about 75 percent of teachers thought it was fair to teachers. The proportion of teachers trained in the code also increased significantly following reform: 71 percent of teachers in Ghana and 67 percent of teachers in Malawi reported having received training, up by 34 percentage points among teachers in Ghana and 15 points among teachers in Malawi from baseline. The program increased the amount of teachers who said they knew how to report a violation by more than one-third, of whom nearly all said they had a responsibility to report violations.

  USAID 2008b. *Safe Schools Program: Final Report.* Washington: USAID.

- **Learning from Nigeria and Tanzania shows that girls are more likely to report SRGBV if schools have established mechanisms for doing so.** Cross-country analyses in Nigeria and Tanzania demonstrate that teachers and members of school management committees who reported incidences of SRGV did so through formal structures rather than informal structures. Moreover, findings from Tanzania show that girls' confidence in reporting incidences of violence correlated positively with their schools' capacity to respond, reinforcing the importance of establishing policies and official mechanisms for reporting incidences of violence, along with increasing schools' and communities' capacities to respond to and support victims.

    Unterhalter, Elaine, and Jo Heslop. 2012. *Transforming Education for Girls in Nigeria and Tanzania: A Cross-Country Analysis of Endline Research Studies.* Washington: ActionAid.

- **In Mozambique, a community outreach program showed improved outcomes for girls, including greater confidence to speak out against acts of violence perpetrated against them.** The community outreach and advocacy performed by youth participating in ActionAid's Stop Violence Against Girls in School project helped improve knowledge about child protection processes and strengthened community-based structures that link informal and formal judicial systems.

    Parkes, Jenny, and Jo Heslop. 2013. *Stop Violence Against Girls in School: A Cross-Country Analysis of Change in Ghana, Kenya and Mozambique.* Johannesburg: ActionAid International.

In terms of eliminating corporal punishment in schools, however, studies point to the challenge of changing teacher-student power dynamics, especially given the poor conditions in which many teachers are expected to teach, along with changing parents' beliefs about the value of corporal punishment in building character and maintaining classroom discipline (Parkes and Heslop 2013; Reilly 2014; USAID 2008a). In some cases where corporal punishment was prohibited from the top-down and without training in other disciplinary techniques, teachers were left without knowledge of and the capacity to use alternative forms of positive discipline (Parkes and Heslop 2013; Reilly 2014).

- **In Sierra Leone, activities implemented under Plan International's Building Skills for Life project helped raise teacher and community awareness of the Teachers' Code of Conduct and equipped teachers with knowledge of alternative classroom discipline.** For example, instead of receiving floggings, students reported that teachers disciplined students by having them sweep or clean the classroom. Perhaps such a change in teacher behavior can be attributed to one particularly popular activity undertaken in this project that involved the school community in painting murals related to the code on school walls and helping to reinforce messages delivered during training, as well as creating a stronger school culture of accountability to the code.

Reilly, A. 2014. "Adolescent Girls' Experiences of Violence in School in Sierra Leone and the Challenges to Sustainable Change." *Gender and Development* 22, no. 1: 13–29.

More research is needed to determine the effectiveness of policy-level interventions like teachers' codes of conduct in actually reducing incidences of GBV in schools or increasing feelings of safety. In the example given above for Sierra Leone, even after measures were taken to train teachers in alternative disciplines and to raise awareness about issues of SRGBV, only 65 percent of girls reported feeling safe in school (Reilly 2014). This reminds us that we need to think holistically about school safety. Enforcing legislation is not enough; policies and codes of conduct need to be accompanied by curricular change, institutional-level change, and individual-level change.

Gender Sensitivity Training for Teachers and Students

Practitioners and researchers alike suggest that the prevention of SRGBV is key. Promising programs take measures to prevent violence at school, including initiatives like gender sensitivity training, especially training that seeks to transform gender norms (Barker, Ricardo, and Nascimento 2007). Programs' intensity and duration are also connected to their effectiveness, with training for children suggested at 20 hours or more for 270 days or more and training for teachers suggested for at least 10 hours for four days or longer (CARE 2014).

Research suggests that gender sensitivity training programs should focus on transforming the unequal relations of power that perpetuate and tolerate both physical and psychological violence against girls and women. These power dynamics manifest interpersonally as well as systemically within the community and in broader society (Michau et al. 2015). However, it should also be kept in mind that communication about the issues of SRGBV needs to be both strategic and inclusive and not demonize or alienate innocent male teachers and boys. Instead, communication about SRGBV needs to balance negative images with positive and constructive ones (Fleming et al. 2013; USAID 2008a).

- **In a rigorous study of USAID's Safe Schools Program in Ghana and Malawi, an impact evaluation revealed that training for students, teachers, and community counselors led to positive changes in knowledge, attitudes, and practice regarding GBV and sexual harassment.** For example, before the Doorways training program, 45 percent of teachers knew how to report a violation related to SRGBV; after the program, 75 percent knew how. In Malawi, 75 percent of teachers thought whipping boys was unacceptable before the program, whereas 96 percent of teachers thought it was unacceptable after the program. In addition, teachers' awareness of sexual harassment of girls and boys at school increased from 30 percent to 80 percent and from 26 percent to 64 percent, respectively. Positive changes in attitudes by students were similarly observed. In Ghana, the proportion of students who believed they have the right not to be hurt increased from 57 percent to 70 percent. In Malawi, 90 percent of girls believed that it was wrong for a teacher to get a girl pregnant as long as he married her, compared with 70 percent of girls before the program. The Doorways program has had similar positive impact on teachers' and students' attitudes toward SRGBV in other countries, including Burkina Faso.

The Doorways program for students was designed to help them improve their ability to prevent and respond to SRGBV by learning about GBV, health issues, and gender stereotypes. They learned communication and negotiation skills, along with how to report SRGBV incidences. The curriculum for teachers focused on changing knowledge, attitudes, and practices by teaching them about children's rights and responsibilities, alternative teaching practices that promote safe learning environments, and how to respond to SRGBV. They also learned basic counseling and listening skills, and received training in the Teachers' Code of Conduct. The program for community counselors similarly focused on counseling and listening skills, children's rights, GBV, and developing a response network for SRGBV. Counselors were to act as contact persons and support personnel for students who had experienced SRGBV.

Queen, Emily Forsyth, Lorena Gonzalez, and Shannon Meehan. 2015. "Doorways: Preventing and Responding to School-Related, Gender-Based Violence in West Africa." In *Educating Adolescent Girls Around the Globe: Challenges and Opportunities*, edited by Sandra L. Stacki and Supriya Baily, 96-117. New York: Routledge.

USAID 2008b. *Safe Schools Program: Final Report*. Washington: USAID.

- **An evaluation of ActionAid's Stop Violence Against Girls in School program found similar effects for its in-service teacher training program on teachers' awareness about children's welfare and about reporting mechanisms.** Such training programs were viewed positively by the school community; however findings revealed weak school policy frameworks. This suggests that even though individual teachers were reporting improved attitudes toward SRGBV, the effects of training were not feeding into school-level practice.

  Parkes, Jenny, and Jo Heslop. 2011. *Stop Violence Against Girls in School: A Cross-Country Analysis of Baseline Research from Ghana, Kenya, and Mozambique.* Developed for ActionAid International. London: Institute of Education of the University of London.

As is the case for many of the strategies covered in this section, it is important to recognize that changing teachers' attitudes to physical and psychological punishment requires on-going training, and that teachers need continuous support not only to make their teaching practices and pedagogies more gender-sensitive but also to manage their classrooms more effectively (Reilly 2014). This means also addressing the awareness and skills of personnel at all levels of the school, including district-level and ministry-level education officials, as well as those of judicial officials, community leaders, and the media through broader public advocacy (UNESCO 2014a; USAID 2008a).

In terms of shifting the attitudes and knowledge of students:

- **Results from a randomized experiment with 123 sixth- and seventh-grade classrooms in the United States illustrate that gender sensitivity training aimed at reducing GBV in schools is more effective if students learn about the legal penalties and consequences for perpetrators of violence than if students learn only about setting and communicating boundaries in relationships.** Students assigned to a five-session course focused on laws, definitions, information, and data about penalties for sexual assault demonstrated more consistent and significant changes in knowledge and attitudes related to gender violence than students assigned to a five-session course that made students struggle with subjectivity and ambiguity about friendships and intimacy.

  Taylor, Bruce., Stein, Nan., and Burden, Frances. (2010). The effects of gender violence/harassment prevention programming in middle schools: a randomized experimental evaluation. Violence and victims, 25(2), 202-223.

Girls' Clubs and Safe Spaces

Safe spaces and girls' clubs are popular features of girl-friendly schools as well as popular strategies for increasing girls' confidence and capacity to stand up against GBV and other issues of gender inequality. In a review of forty-nine studies of interventions in low- and middle-income countries that made reference to girls' health as an outcome, more than half included provisions for safe spaces (Hallman et al. 20130).

Safe spaces, generally meaning girls-only spaces, are important components to interventions seeking to improve social and psychological outcomes for girls, especially because public spaces are often reserved for men and shared spaces like the school lobby, the canteen, and the classroom can become sites of violence or harassment (Bhatla et al. 2015). Finding safe spaces may involve helping girls map locations where they feel safe, like community halls, youth centers, or even empty shipping containers in some cases (Baldwin 2011). Although widely supported among practitioners, their impact on girls' educational outcomes is inconclusive. However, an ongoing randomized impact evaluation of a large-scale safe spaces project in Zambia—the Adolescent Girls Empowerment Program, led by the Population Council and funded by the UK Department for International Development (DFID)—will provide much needed empirical data on this intervention (Lloyd 2013).

Similarly, girls' clubs can play an important role both in girls' empowerment and in improving GBV outcomes.

- **In Ghana, researchers evaluating the program found that girls' clubs that engaged in critical self-reflection and questioning led by trained female mentors can provide important spaces for combating discriminatory and oppressive gender norms.** Coordinated by ActionAid in forty-five primary schools and their communities in Ghana, Mozambique, and Kenya, the Stop Violence Against Girls project used girls' clubs led by trained female mentors—in addition to gender policy advocacy in schools, community outreach and sensitization, and in-service teacher training—to increase the capacity of girls to challenge violence and gender inequality. Overall, researchers observed positive changes in girls' attitudes toward gender and violence, as well as increased knowledge about how and where to report incidences of violence, compared with girls who did not participate. However, there was great variation in whether girls actually reported violence. Researchers found that managing critical dialogue about sensitive, taboo topics, including sex and relationships, requires a skilled leader who needs ongoing training and support. In addition, better integration of these clubs within the larger school culture and community is needed to prevent the appearance of being an elite, NGO-run intervention.

Parkes, Jenny, and Jo Heslop. 2013. *Stop Violence Against Girls in School: A Cross-Country Analysis of Change in Ghana, Kenya and Mozambique.* Johannesburg: ActionAid International.

Parkes, Jenny, Jo Heslop, Samwel Oando, Susan Sbaa, Francisco Januario, and Asmara Figue. 2013. "Conceptualising Gender and Violence in Research: Insights from Studies in Schools and Communities in Kenya, Ghana and Mozambique." *International Journal of Educational Development* 33, no. 6: 546–56.

- **In three coeducational secondary schools in Swaziland, girls' clubs helped increase girls' social assets (e.g., friendship or participation in extracurricular activities) and their awareness of and attitudes against SRGBV.** But, like the Stop Violence Against Girls project implemented in Ghana, Mozambique, and Kenya mentioned above, girls' clubs had mixed effects on changing girls' behaviors—in this case, their odds of declining sexual advances from fellow students or teachers. In this intervention, coordinated by the Swaziland Action Group Against Abuse (SWAGAA) for a 12-month period, girls age sixteen years and older were invited to participate in weekly girls' clubs. Each girls' club was structured with groups of approximately twenty girls and was led by a trained female mentor, between the age of eighteen and twenty-five years, who was recruited from the community surrounding the school and trained by SWAGAA. Club sessions took place in preidentified safe spaces, and included interactive discussions on issues related to sexual violence and GBV.

Manzini-Henwood, Cebile, Nokwanda Dlamini, and Francis Obare. 2015. "School-Based Girls' Clubs as a Means of Addressing Sexual And Gender-Based Violence in Swaziland." *BMC Proceedings* 9 (supplement 4): A5–A7.

The evidence suggests that there are limits to empowering girls with knowledge about GBV without actually transforming gender relations and power dynamics that would allow girls to stand up against acts of violence. Emerging insights from communities of practice also agree that interventions that build girls' economic assets should be pursued more systematically, pointing to economic insecurity as being a factor that is little understood but often talked about that makes girls vulnerable to SRGBV (Caton et al. 2014). Girls' clubs—although effective in increasing awareness, attitudes, and self-confidence, as well as providing important psychosocial support networks for girls—should thus be accompanied by specific strategies that enhance a girl's livelihood capabilities and economic empowerment and work to transform the social attitudes of members in the communities where she lives.

5 Improving Quality Education

A major lesson learned during the last decade is that improving access is not enough to achieve sustainable gains in girls' education; assuring that a girl has a high-quality learning experience and a high-quality education while in school may be equally if not more important. Studies find that a first and critical step is to have enough qualified teachers who attend school regularly and are able to engage students in their lessons. Beyond teachers, the quality of a girl's physical learning environments and the culture of her surrounding environment also play critical roles. This section discusses these two primary areas for which research has generated some evidence. In chapter 5, we propose other components of and discuss promising approaches to improving educational quality, including strategies for cultivating both "hard" and "soft" skills.

Hire Good Teachers Who Attend School and Engage Students

Teachers are a key component to improving the quality of education. Extensive evidence exists linking good teachers to the schooling success of both girls and boys. For example, in the United States, researchers have found that having a good teacher is equivalent to an average gain in learning of one school year; and having a great teacher is equivalent to 1.5 years of learning; but having a weak teacher means mastering less than half of the expected subject content (Hanushek and Rivkin 2010, in King and Winthrop 2015). The same policies and interventions that focus on hiring good teachers are best for both girls *and* boys. In other words, recruiting well-trained teachers and providing them with support inside and outside the classroom help provide a high-quality education to all children. Indeed, evidence suggests that good teachers matter even more for girls' learning success, whose average years of schooling is fewer than boys'. Good teachers help to ensure that girls acquire basic competencies and foundational skills during their limited number of years in school.

But how does one hire more qualified teachers? A special issue of the *EFA Global Monitoring Report* on teaching and learning points to the first hurdle: entry requirements to the profession (UNESCO 2014c). These must be carefully designed to encourage the best and most talented candidates, while balancing the need to recruit candidates from a wide range of backgrounds, including rural and ethnic-linguistic minority communities, and in equal numbers of women and men. In some cases, especially in remote areas experiencing teacher shortages, hiring parateachers (teachers who are hired on short, flexible contracts, often in primary schools or nonformal education centers) is a promising solution (Education for Change 2013; Kim, Alderman, and Orazem 1998). Indeed, teacher shortages are severe; UNESCO (2014c) estimates that 5.1 million more teachers are needed to achieve universal lower secondary education by 2030. Half of these teachers are needed in Sub-Saharan Africa, and an additional 1 million lower secondary school teachers are required in South and West Asia.

One persistent challenge in developing countries is not only hiring more teachers, many of whom are not well educated themselves, but also getting teachers to attend school regularly. In some countries, teachers have been recorded to miss nearly a quarter of the school year (Glewwe, Ilia, and Kremer 2003; Kremer et al. 2005). In many places, teachers have multiple roles in the community or have multiple jobs, all taking them away from classtime. However, randomized experiments on teacher incentives have identified a few promising strategies, not only for recruiting teachers but also for encouraging them to do their job well; here are some of them:

- **Indonesia's experience shows that more teachers, not just more schools, are key to improving girls' and boys' educational access.** When Indonesia built thousands of new schools in a drive to increase enrollment, it also provided additional qualified and trained teachers to maintain class-size norms. As a result, despite rapid expansion in the school system, student academic performance held up.

  Duflo, Esther. 2001. "Schooling and Labor Market Consequences of School Construction in Indonesia: Evidence from an Unusual Policy Experiment." *American Economic Review* 92, no. 4: 795–813.

- **In South Korea, an incentive program offering better pay and better working conditions attracts a larger proportion (77 percent) of qualified teachers to disadvantaged schools in villages and small towns**

than in large cities (32 percent). Specifically, teachers serving in a difficult area are given salary incentives, smaller class sizes, reduced teaching time, the chance to choose their next school (teachers rotate every five years), and links to promotion to administrative positions.

Kang, N. H., and M. Hong. 2008. "Achieving Excellence in Teacher Workforce and Equity in Learning Opportunities in South Korea. *Educational Researcher* 37, no. 4: 200–207.

Luschei, Thomas F., Amita Chudgar, and W. Joshua Rew. 2013. "Exploring Differences in the Distribution of Teacher Qualifications across Mexico and South Korea: Evidence from the Teaching and Learning International Survey." *Teachers College Record* 115, no. 5: 1–38.

- **In India, offering teachers incentives helped reduce teacher absenteeism and improved student achievement.** In a randomized experiment in fifty-seven single-teacher, nonformal education centers in rural India, parateachers whose attendance was monitored daily, and whose salaries were made a function of the number of days they were present, significantly reduced teacher absenteeism by 21 percentage points relative to the control group, and improved students' test scores by 0.17 standard deviation. Specifically, the NGO named Seva Mandir gave teachers cameras with tamper-proof date and time functions and instructed teachers to have students take a picture of them (with students) in the class at the start and close of each school day. The intervention impact was larger for low-quality teachers; for them, there was an increase of 24 percentage points in attendance, compared with an increase of 15 points for high-quality teachers.

Duflo, Esther, Rema Hanna, and Stephen P. Ryan. 2012. "Incentives Work: Getting Teachers to Come to School." *American Economic Review* 102, no. 4: 1241–78.

- **Research from Africa and Asia shows the importance of hiring teachers who have sufficient education in the fields they teach.** Teachers' own educations consistently affect children's learning. Teacher training does not always compensate; it often focuses on teaching methods. Making sure that teachers meet minimum education qualifications may be particularly important in low-income countries, where teachers may not even have a complete secondary education and thus may have subject knowledge that does not far exceed their students'. A study in Pakistan found that only three out of five teachers could pass primary school mathematics examination, compared with two out of five of their students.

Ridker, Ronald G., ed. 1997. *Determinants of Educational Achievement and Attainment in Africa: Findings from Nine Case Studies.* SD Publication Series, Technical Paper 62. Washington: USAID.

Warwick, Donald, and Fernando Reimers. 1995. *Hope or Despair? Learning in Pakistan's Primary Schools.* Westport, Conn.: Praeger.

- **In rural India, local teachers improve students' test scores.** In some cases, like rural India, recruiting more teachers from within the community being served may be a better approach, as it reduces the social and demographic distance between students and teachers. Modeling the fixed effects of student and teacher characteristics, researchers found that when students are taught by a teacher whose demographic characteristics (religion, caste, and gender) match those of the students, the students score about 0.25 standard deviation higher than if they are taught by a teacher whose demographic characteristics do not match. Specifically, students taught by teachers of the same gender performed 0.04 standard deviation better than students taught by a teacher of a different gender. Having a teacher of the same religion improves performance by 0.17 standard deviation, and having a teacher of the same caste improves performance by 0.04 standard deviation. Learning effects were not gender disaggregated. Researchers suggest that two things may be going on. First, teachers who share the same gender, religion, and caste may be providing students with a role model, improving their attitudes toward education and their effort in school. And second, teachers of the same gender, religion, and caste are less likely to treat students differently because of their demographic characteristics or because they belong to a particular social group.

Rawal, Shenila, and Geeta Kingdon. 2010. *Akin to My Teacher: Does Caste, Religious, or Gender Distance Between Student and Teacher Matter? Some Evidence from India.* Department of Quantitative Social Science Working Paper 10-18. London: Institute of Education of University of London.

- **Many countries have tried to recruit women teachers with reduced experience or qualifications to work in rural areas to encourage girls' enrollment.** In Mozambique and Botswana, voluntary or interim teachers were hired, with plans to improve recruiting and in-service training for those areas. While community or interim teachers lack sufficient educational qualifications and resources to ensure quality, they are often well situated and eager to teach in their rural areas, especially where teaching is one of the first jobs open to women. (see The Gender of Teachers).

Nilsson, Paula. 2003. "Education for All: Teacher Demand and Supply in Africa." Education International Working Paper 12. Brussels: Education International.

- **In Nigeria and Tanzania, improvements in teacher qualifications, when matched with increased teacher engagement, helped improve girls' empowerment.** An initiative to offer primary and junior secondary teachers in the TEGINT (Transforming Education for Girls in Nigeria and Tanzania) project schools training in gender, HIV, and participatory methods showed that even though higher percentages of teachers were meeting minimum qualifications, this did not necessarily correlate with improvements in girls' empowerment. However, where teachers met qualifications *and* scored high on the Teacher Engagement Index, girls were more likely to have higher scores on the Girls' Empowerment Index (a measure of their change in confidence in dealing with GBV and their knowledge of and attitudes toward HIV/AIDS and gender equality). This shows that teacher qualifications alone are not enough, but that high-quality, engaged teachers who are able to put their training into practice are critical to girls' performance in school.

  Unterhalter, Elaine, and Jo Heslop. 2012. *Transforming Education for Girls in Nigeria and Tanzania: A Cross-Country Analysis of Endline Research Studies.* Washington: ActionAid.

Improve How Teachers Teach

If the quality of education is only as good as teachers, how do we ensure that teachers are great? Researchers like Robin Alexander (2015) and pan-institutional research initiatives like the Multi-Site Teacher Education Research Project (MUSTER), have been trying to answer this exact question, by systematically exploring teacher education, teacher training, and teacher pedagogy around the world. Some of the major challenges the MUSTER studies have identified in teacher education in Africa, for example, include:

- patchy and incomplete teacher education curricula that do not match the levels of achievement of preservice teachers (teachers who are being trained before they enter a classroom), many of whom have only achieved minimum entry-level qualifications;

- teacher training practices that are dominated by instructors and treat preservice teachers as passive learners—which many of the teachers go on to replicate in their own classrooms; and

The Gender of Teachers: A Note on the Evidence

Much attention has been given to the link between female teachers and improved educational outcomes for girls, especially as they approach adolescence. Practitioners' wisdom points to the positive effects that female teachers have on girls as role models and how their presence may even make girls safer in school by decreasing their vulnerability to sexual harassment and abuse from male students and teachers.

However, the evidence behind the link between female teachers and girls' educational outcomes is really context specific. In some cases, the gender of teachers does not matter, but rather hiring more qualified, gender sensitive, and engaged teachers is more important (Chudgar and Sankar 2008; Lloyd et al. 2003; Seged et al. 1991; Unterhalter and Heslop 2012). For example, in the case of mathematics achievement in Pakistan, where students of female teachers performed worse, the gender gap in learning could actually be attributed to the urban or rural location of the school, the formal education level of the teacher, and the coverage of the mathematics curriculum by the teacher (Warwick and Jatoi 1994). The gender of the teachers was not as important as the teachers' knowledge of mathematics and their teaching strategies. In this case, interventions targeted at improving teacher qualifications or providing them with training in teaching mathematics are needed.

In other contexts, the gender of teachers does matter for girls' educational outcomes, especially in socially conservative cultures, where girls and women are isolated or segregated into sex-specific spaces and have less mobility, or where concerns are strong about physical or sexual violence or abuse against girls by teachers or students (Chin 2004; Kim, Alderman, and Orazem 1998; Makwati, Audinos, and Lairez 2003; Muralidharan and Sheth 2014; Rawal and Kingdon 2010). Research also suggests that hiring more female teachers is necessary in contexts where there is a great disparity in the ratio between male and female teachers and where social norms prevent girls from attending school with male teachers (Kirk 2004).

A study in Yemen, for example, where only 27 percent of teachers are female, found that school committees in rural schools that used school grants—issued through technical cooperation with Japan—to increase their share of female teachers sustained their gains in gender parity in enrollment after the cooperation ended (Yuki et al. 2013). In India, distributing female teachers to one-teacher schools through Operation Blackboard raised primary school completion rates for girls from poor households by up to 4 percentage points, compared with 2 points for boys (Chin 2004). But beyond affecting girls' school enrollment and retention in contexts like Yemen and India, it is not yet known *whether* and *how* female teachers improve girls' learning outcomes.

In cases where a girl's enrollment, attendance, and participation in school depend on the gender of her teachers, the following recommendations have been put forward to help recruit, hire, and retain female teachers, especially in cases where it is difficult to find enough qualified women (e.g., rural areas) or when urban women with more education will not move to rural areas to work (Kirk 2004, 2006):

- Encourage more gender-balanced recruitment and hiring targets.

- Relax age restrictions for entry into teaching.

- Develop more flexible and creative teacher training programs that accommodate the needs of women who have caregiving responsibilities, either by allowing teachers to bring children and babysitters with them or by incorporating distance learning components.

- Ensure that teacher training content addresses the priorities and concerns of female (and male) teachers and that gender equality is a specific topic of study.

- Provide incentives to attend preservice teacher training.

- Use creative deployment strategies that will help attract well-qualified women teachers to rural schools.

- Hire committed local women who may not have the necessary formal qualifications.

- Work with community organizations to encourage community-wide support for female teachers.

- Create local networks of women teachers who can support each other and share experiences, concerns, and ideas.

- Ensure that professional development opportunities are accessible.

- Ensure that female teachers are fully involved in decisionmaking processes at school.

It is important to remember, however, that hiring female teachers is not enough to create supportive environments for girls' education, and that one cannot assume that just because a teacher is a woman that she will always be supportive of girls' education needs (Camfed 2012; Kirk 2006). The gender of teachers is only one dimension that influences the teaching and learning process; a focus on the gender of teachers should not detract from also attending to other dimensions of teaching and learning, like teacher pedagogy—that is, how teachers teach (Chudgar and Sankar 2008).

- economic and logistical obstacles to providing appropriate practical experience to preservice teachers in countries with a poor educational infrastructure (Lewin and Stuart 2003).

In the most comprehensive review to date of 489 studies of pedagogy, curricula, teaching practices, and teacher education in developing countries, researchers who had been commissioned by DFID identified three interactive strategies and six engaging teaching practices that effective teachers use in the classroom:

Three interactive teaching strategies:

1. Provide feedback, sustained attention, and inclusion.

2. Create a safe environment in which students are supported in their learning.

3. Draw on students' backgrounds and experiences.

Six engaging teaching practices:

1. Flexible use of whole-class, group, and pair work where students discuss a shared task.

2. Frequent and relevant use of learning materials beyond the textbook.

3. Open and close questioning, expanding on student responses, encouraging student questioning.

4. Demonstrating and explaining, drawing on sound pedagogical content knowledge.

5. Using local languages and code-switching.

6. Planning and varying lesson sequences.

Researchers also found that effective teachers had positive attitudes toward their training and their students. This helped to position them in the best frame of mind to shape the teaching and learning process in ways that are interactive, engaging, and participatory, provoking visible responses from students and providing indication that learning is taking place (Westbrook et al. 2013).

But can policymakers and practitioners improve teacher pedagogy—that is, how teachers teach, engage, and interact with their students? There is an increasing international consensus that teachers should move away from teacher-centered pedagogies (e.g., teacher-dominated, lecture-driven, rote-learning methods, and passive learning) and toward student- or learner-centered pedagogies (e.g., where teachers actively co-construct knowledge with students through activities, group work, reflection, and promote critical thinking). But few studies have identified what it takes to successfully make this shift in classroom instruction in developing country contexts.

Training teachers and providing them with continued support for improving how they teach can be effective in improving quality learning opportunities for girls and boys. Multiple studies show that it is important to complement teacher training with initiatives that remove possible barriers that prevent teachers from implementing what they have learned. For example, ensuring teachers have sufficient materials to use in the classroom, adjusting exam systems to support interactive pedagogy, and ensuring that parents understand and support learner-centered teaching methods can all help teachers put into practice what they have learned (Chapman et al. 2005; Nguyen, Terlouw, and Pilot 2006; O'Sullivan 2004; Serbessa 2006; Schweisfurth 2011; Vavrus 2009). Whether the right focus of teacher training should be on teaching teachers to use student-centered pedagogies, or teaching teachers to be better at teacher-centered pedagogies, or teaching teachers how to combine a bit of both is something that needs more research and experimentation (Barrett 2007; Vavrus, Thomas, and Bartlett 2011). The lesson learned from existing studies is that teacher training must be simultaneously accompanied by a focus on improving the conditions in which teachers teach and on providing them with continuous professional support and opportunities for training and gaining further qualifications (Unterhalter 2012):

- **Studies find good training enables young, undereducated women to teach primary school effectively**. In countries such as Bangladesh, Pakistan, and India, girls often need to be taught by women, and with relatively few women being literate, some provinces have relaxed age and education requirements so they can hire enough teachers. This happens particularly in remote rural areas, where many women are reluctant to be posted, and thus young women from local communities are needed. Yet these young women have proved that they can teach effectively at the primary level if they have enough training and community support. It helps to provide programmed curricula and lesson plans, and coming from the communities they serve helps these teachers reach the children.

Kim, Jooseop, Harold Alderman, and Peter Orazem. 1998. *Can Cultural Barriers Be Overcome in Girls' Schooling? The Community Support Program in Rural Balochistan*. Working Paper on Impact Evaluation of Education Reforms 10. Washington: World Bank.

Khandkher, Shahidur. 1996. *Education Achievements and School Efficiency in Rural Bangladesh*. World Bank Discussion Paper 319. Washington: World Bank.

Rugh, Andrea. 2000. *Starting Now: Strategies for Helping Girls Complete Primary*. SAGE Project. Washington: Academy for Educational Development.

World Bank. 1997. *Pakistan: New Approaches to Education—The Northern Areas Community School Program*. Washington: World Bank.

- **In Liberia, the EGRA Plus program that trained teachers in how to teach reading improved reading performance, especially of girls, by 1.43 standard deviations.** In Liberia, teachers in the full treatment group of an early grade reading teacher training program (EGRA Plus) received training on reading instruction and methods of continuously assessing student performance. They were also provided with frequent school-based teaching support, resource materials, and books. An external program evaluation found that female students of teachers in the full treatment group had the greatest absolute gains in reading performance, with an average effect size of 1.43 standard deviations, compared with boys, at 1.21 standard deviations. This illustrates that if teachers are well-trained, can implement their training in the classroom, and receive teaching support, girls can narrow or even close the gender gap in learning.

  Piper, Benjamin, and Medina Korda. 2010. *EGRA Plus: Liberia*. Program Evaluation Report. Research Triangle Park, NC: RTI International.

- **A Swaziland study found that teacher training helped raise girls' enrollment and helped girls and boys move on to secondary school.** The government hired more teachers and trained the teacher corps in curriculum content as well as participatory learning, giving them objectives for each lesson. The government set up regional resource centers, trained professors for its three teachers' colleges, and improved feedback systems for teachers. By 1990, most teachers were qualified. Enrollment climbed, with girls participating as much as boys. By 1997, three-fourths of Swazi children had completed grade 4, and almost half went on to secondary school.

  Gilmore, Julianne. 1997. *Phoenix Rising*. USAID Technical Paper 76. Washington: USAID.

- **A flexible, school-based teacher training program for 47,000 primary school teachers in Kenya helped to close the gap between teacher training and teacher practice, raising the quality of teacher pedagogy in English, mathematics, and science across the country.** The program combined six months of distance-learning and school-based professional development, including follow-up in the classroom, and was led by key resource teachers in each school and supported by head teachers. Compared with a national baseline study, systematic analysis of 144 video-recorded classroom lessons illustrated that teachers engaged in more interactive whole-class teaching, made greater use of group work, and used lesson plans, teaching resources, and flexible classroom layouts—all elements of effective teaching.

  Hardman, Frank, Jan Abd-Kadir, Catherine Agg, James Migwi, Jacinta Ndambuku, and Fay Smith. 2009. "Changing Pedagogical Practices in Kenyan Primary Schools: The Impact of School-Based Training." *Comparative Education* 45, no. 1: 65–86.

  UNESCO. 2015a. *Education for All 2000–2015: Achievements and Challenges—Education for All Global Monitoring Report 2015*. Paris: UNESCO.

- **A recent study of the Nali Kali program in Karnataka State in India further demonstrates the impact of combining teacher training and continuous teaching support on student performance outcomes.** Spearheaded by the teachers themselves, the Nali Kali program includes innovative hands-on experimentation with teaching and learning materials as well as teaching practices that incorporate art, craft, song, dance, and other activity-oriented methods. In 1995, its first year of implementation, 13,691 lower primary school standard 1 and 2 teachers were trained. Now the program is being implemented in standards 1 through 3 in all public schools across the state. Because of its learner-centered approach and active learning strategies, the program demands more participation and work by teachers than conventional teaching practices, making it a challenge to scale. Researchers have found that the program's success is largely due to the support that the teachers provide each other, including sharing problems with Nali Kali methods and finding common solutions, especially for teachers in single-teacher schools or in classes with more than thirty students. Cluster Resource Centers, which are centers of teacher empowerment and where teachers share their experiences and practices, provide an important mechanism for this peer support.

Raj, S. N. Rajesh; Kunal Sen, Vinod B. Annigeri, Arun K. Kulkarni, and D. R. Revankar. 2015. "Joyful Learning? The Effects of a School Intervention on Learning Outcomes in Karnataka." *International Journal of Educational Development* 40: 183–95.

Practitioners' wisdom and academic research also verify that an important element in enhancing how teachers teach is to improve teachers' attitudes toward girls and how teachers interact with female students. Teaching is a gendered and relational act, and teachers—who are subject to the social norms and gender identities of the larger society—can potentially reinforce harmful gender stereotypes (Education for Change 2013; Plan International 2013).

Research has shown that teachers' attitudes and expectations vis-à-vis girls can influence girls' educational outcomes; thus, whether teachers think that mathematics is important for girls and whether boys and girls receive and feel they receive equal treatment in the classroom substantially affects girls' probability of success in school. Moreover, if teachers think girls are less able, girls tend to underperform, whereas boys are less affected by teachers' views (Aikman, Unterhalter, and Challender 2005; Lloyd et al. 2000; Mlama et al. 2005; Plan International 2013a). In Nigeria, for example, boys are given more opportunities to ask and answer questions, to use learning materials, and to lead groups; girls are given less time on task than boys in science. Such findings would also be common for many countries in South Asia (Lloyd, Mensch, and Clark 2000; UNICEF 2001, 2002).

Training teachers to use gender-sensitive approaches can help combat gender stereotypes and improve the learning environment for girls. In Turkey, a study of a one-term preservice teacher education course on gender equity found that female teachers' gender attitudes and awareness were significantly improved after the course, illustrating that such short courses can be effective in raising teachers' awareness of how the selection of teaching materials, for example, can have a different impact on girls compared with boys (Erden 2009). In a study of thirty co-educational government secondary schools in Bihar, India, researchers found that gender-sensitive classroom dynamics—especially non-discriminatory treatment by teachers, positive feedback by teachers, and teachers' expression of gender egalitarian attitudes—were positively correlated with academic performance, especially among girls in mathematics (Santhya et al. 2015). In Africa, thirteen countries—including Ethiopia, Guinea, Rwanda, and Senegal—have adapted the model of teacher training followed by the Forum for African

Women Educationalists' Gender-Responsive Pedagogy, which trains teachers in the design and use of gender-responsive lesson plans, language in the classroom, classroom interaction, and setting up classrooms, among other things (Mlama et al. 2005). Effective approaches include encouraging respect for girls and boys equally; making sure that girls can participate in class equally with boys; encouraging girls to study subjects such as mathematics and science, where fewer girls than boys have done so; expressing similar expectations for boys and girls in learning performance; and suggesting nontraditional occupations for girls (Arnot 2006; King and Hill 1993; UNICEF 2001). Although research on the impact of specific programs is scarce, such efforts are under way in a number of countries and should be explored and analyzed more intensively.

6 Increasing Community Engagement

An important component that is often talked about among practitioners and academics as being key to sustaining the progress made in girls' education is engaging the community, parents, and especially mothers in the management of a school and its committees. However, because community engagement, outreach, and advocacy are usually part of a larger package of interventions, their effects are hard to disentangle. Moreover, unless community engagement is specifically targeted at improving girls' education outcomes, studies tend not to discuss its impact on girls specifically.

Nevertheless, insights into successful community engagement are emerging and help point the direction to how community participation might be harnessed for girls' education. Successful approaches include explicit agreements within the community to educate girls as well as boys, community influence over teacher recruitment and selection, greater community involvement in and management of school operations, and genuine partnerships between communities and the federal government. Often, local NGOs play an important role in helping to organize such community participation and parent–teacher associations.

- **In Niger, a pilot program run by the Ministry of Education and the World Bank increased parental participation in and responsibility for school management by giving school committees full control over school grants**. Using an experimental design, all school committees in the experiment were trained in how to manage schools. Parents in those schools that were randomly assigned to receive grants were more engaged in school activities, like attending meetings; spending in these schools went primarily to infrastructure improvements, but also to festivals and playground equipment that improved the overall quality of the school environment. Unfortunately, a political coup interrupted the program and researchers were unable to continue with the evaluation to determine how parental involvement may have had an impact on the quality of students' learning experiences. Early evaluations do not appear promising, as findings point to little change in the parental supervision of teachers or teacher accountability, suggesting that even though parents were willing to increase quality through participation, they were unable to influence what goes on in the classroom.

Beasley, Elizabeth, and Elise Huillery. 2014. "Willing but Unable: Short-Term Experimental Evidence on Parent Empowerment and School Quality." Working paper. http://www.povertyactionlab.org/publication/willing-unable-short-term-experimental-evidence-parent-empowerment-and-school-quality-0.

- **In Indonesia, a randomized experiment found that community engagement with schools improved student learning, especially for girls.** To better explain the relationship between community engagement, educational quality, and student learning outcomes, researchers conducted a randomized field experiment on school committee structures in Indonesia. They found that grant and training interventions aimed at reinforcing and strengthening the internal operations and functioning of existing school committee structures had a limited impact on learning. However, interventions targeted at fostering ties between school committees and nonschool parties (e.g., the village council) had a demonstrably positive impact on student learning, especially by girls. Two years after the project started, schools whose school committees had collaborated with village councils and had been democratically elected (instead of being appointed by the principal) saw average test scores improve between 0.17 and 0.22 standard deviation. In mathematics, girls improved by 0.11 standard deviation.

Researchers suggest that improving relationships between school committees and their communities not only raise community awareness about school committee activities but also generate interest by elite members of the community who can promote concrete actions, like enforcing study hours in the village, that reinforce and sustain gains made in school. Community groups also take on greater responsibility in following up on and monitoring compliance with an elected school committee's action plans, along with monitoring teacher performance. In fact, the researchers found that teachers in schools that received "linkage and election" interventions spent an average of 1 hour more per day on lesson preparation, classroom teaching, and grading inside and outside the classroom. The increased effort and engagement even extended to households; parents of students attending these schools spend on average 80 minutes more per week helping their children with homework.

Because of the randomized nature of this study, the researchers can conclude that equipping school committees with resources and skills alone is insufficient, as is democratically electing school committees alone. Instead, a school that elects its committee *and* cooperates with influential leaders in the community is necessary for community engagement to advance learning.

> Pradhan, Menno, Daniel Suryadarma, Amanda Beatty, Maisy Wong, Armida Alishjabana, Arya Gaduh, and Rima Prama Artha. 2014. "Improving Educational Quality through Enhancing Community Participation: Results from a Randomized Field Experiment in Indonesia." *American Economic Journal: Applied Economics* 6, no. 2: 105–26.

- **In Mali, parents were willing to enroll their daughters in community schools as long as school management committees insisted on gender parity.** Activities initiated by school management committees to improve girls' educational outcomes do matter, especially in places where parents prefer to send their sons to school and to hold their daughters back to perform household labor. Community schools in Mali also sought to accommodate parents' concerns about competition between the school and the household over the child's time, offering flexible school schedules. Once school committees dropped their gender equity guidelines, however, gender bias in enrollment decisions reemerged.

> Laugharn, Peter. 2007. *Negotiating "Education for Many": Enrolment, Dropout and Persistence in the Community Schools of Kolondieba, Mali*. Create Pathways to Access Research Monograph 14. Brighton: Consortium for Research on Educational Access, Transitions, and Equity.

- **In Yemen, specifically engaging mothers' committees as part of larger participatory school committees not only increases women's**

participation in school planning but also means that the school environment and courses offered are more relevant to girls. In Yemen, where mothers' committees were activated as part of the BRIDGE community schools' initiatives, schools were more likely to use school grants in ways that attracted girls to school. For example, at the start of the BRIDGE project, 10 percent of project schools hired a sewing trainer for a sewing class that would give girls the skills to make handicrafts, a traditional activity for women; three years later, more than 50 percent of schools had done so at the request of mothers' committees. Schools that incorporated mother's priorities for their daughters were not only more likely to enroll girls but also more likely to maintain their positive gains in gender parity during the project period. Once the project ended, however, sustaining the effects of the school improvement projects initiated by the mothers' committees was dependent on whether postintervention budgets had allocated resources to continue training, guidance, and monitoring activities. This illustrates that even though mothers' committees may shape school management in ways that favor girls' educational outcomes, their decisions must be supported by wider systemic changes in school management processes.

Yuki, Takako, Keiko Mizuno, Keiichi Ogawa, and Sakai Mihoko. 2013. "Promoting Gender Parity in Basic Education: Lessons from a Technical Cooperation Project in Yemen." *International Review of Education* 59: 47–66.

- **A study of six communities in Ghana identified key elements, including leadership and social cohesion, in the sustainability of community participation in schools.** Communities that had been successful in sustaining an externally financed project's impact had dynamic leaders who invested their time and personal resources over and above expectations. Findings suggest that the varying style of leadership (collaborative, hierarchical, or traditional) did not matter, as long as the leader had the ability to unify the community—especially across traditional and nontraditional leadership—through a common agenda of school improvement, and the community had a clear understanding of how disputes and their resolutions had an impact on school objectives. Leaders were also influential in planning, mobilization, and the effective utilization of resources; they set the standards for transparency in decisionmaking and the use of school funds; and they delegated responsibility to and secured commitment from community members. Collective action, a common vision among the community's members, and clarity about roles and responsibilities further enhanced communities' ability to sustain activities. Moreover, women's participation and commitment were essential to the effectiveness of community participation strategies. Women were more likely than men to attend meetings, participate in communal labor activities, and pay their dues and their children's fees, even though they were less financially stable and had less disposable income. Men also were more likely to trust women as committee treasurers, although committees did not explicitly attempt to harness female leadership.

Nkansa, Grace Akukwe, and David W. Chapman. 2006. "Sustaining Community Participation: What Remains After the Money Ends?" *International Review of Education* 52, no. 6: 509–32.

 7 Sustaining Education during Emergencies

Believe it or not, it is possible to sustain education amid crises and emergencies. It may not look the same; in other words, it may not be a school with four walls and a certified teacher that young people attend every day. But with a little creativity, it is not only possible to sustain education amid crises but also highly recommended to do so. Numerous studies of children's physical and psychosocial well-being amid crises have showed that restoring education and other regular activities is crucial for helping children adjust and adapt to their difficult surroundings (Loughry and Eyber 2003). Girls and boys are, it turns out, surprisingly resilient if given the most basic support, such as games, activities, and classes with a caring adult. This type of intervention has increasingly been shown to be crucial for children's long-term health and development, not only physically but also psychologically and socially (Boyden 2003; Reyes 2013). Although sustaining education during emergencies helps both boys and girls, it also remains a crucial intervention for the millions of girls affected by war, disasters, and epidemics.

During the past two decades, the global education community has made a particular effort to understand how children are affected by violence and crises, and especially how to respond in a way that meets their needs. In 1996, Graça Machel, the wife of Nelson Mandela and global children's advocate, released a report titled *Impact of Armed Conflict on Children*. She researched and wrote the report at the request of the United Nations secretary-general, and her findings rocked the humanitarian community. According to her report, not only were millions of children deeply affected by conflict and crisis, but, perhaps worse, the interventions aimed at assisting people in these contexts were focused on assisting adults, with children's needs all but forgotten. A wide range of issues—from protecting children from abuse to sustaining their education—were at the top of her agenda.

Machel's report sparked attention and action among a number of actors, including those within the education community. During the last fifteen years, the topic of sustaining education amid crises has been a focus among humanitarians, who have been experimenting with how and in what form education can or should continue for children; among campaigners and advocates, who have been raising the issue of children's education in emergencies; and increasingly among researchers, who have been studying children's development in these most difficult contexts. A global body, the Inter-Agency Network for Education in Emergencies, today is the most effective mechanism for linking these different actors together, serving both as a clearinghouse for data and discussion on the topic and as a technical resource for developing good practices and practitioner guidance.

Sustaining Education in Emergencies Is Essential to Girls' and Boys' Mental Health

The Inter-Agency Standing Committee is the UN body that works across all UN agencies to review evidence and set standards in relation to humanitarian emergencies. Its *IASC Guidelines on Mental Health and Psychosocial Support in Emergencies*, on which numerous academics and experts worked, identifies education as one of the crucial interventions to support children's development and well-being. They state:

"In emergencies, education is a key psychosocial intervention: it provides a safe and stable environment for learners and restores a sense of normalcy, dignity and hope by offering structured, appropriate and supportive activities. Many children and parents regard participation in education as a foundation of a successful childhood. Well-designed education also helps the affected population to cope with their situation by disseminating key survival messages, enabling learning about self-protection and supporting local people's strategies to address emergency conditions. It is important to (re)start non-formal and formal educational activities immediately, prioritising the safety and well-being of all children and youth, including those who are at increased risk or who have special education needs.

Loss of education is often among the greatest stressors for learners and their families, who see education as a path toward a better future. Education can be an essential tool in helping communities to rebuild their lives. Access to formal and nonformal education in a supportive environment builds learners' intellectual and emotional competencies, provides social support through interaction with peers and educators and strengthens learners' sense of control and self-worth. It also builds life skills that strengthen coping strategies, facilitate future employment and reduce economic stress."

Inter-Agency Standing Committee. 2007. *IASC Guidelines on Mental Health and Psychosocial Support in Emergencies.* Geneva: Inter-Agency Standing Committee.

Because contexts of violence and emergency make research and the monitoring and evaluating of interventions extremely challenging, the evidence base for effective strategies is not nearly as extensive as in other areas of education. However, there is accumulated knowledge about the most promising strategies for addressing children's needs during emergencies, with much of it coming directly from practitioners in the thick of finding ways to deliver education to girls and boys in the direst circumstances.

What is the Inter-Agency Network for Education in Emergencies?

The Inter-Agency Network for Education in Emergencies (INEE) is an 8,000-member global network of practitioners, policymakers, researchers, educators, and young people. It has collected practitioner lessons and developed a set of standards and guidelines that articulate the minimal level of educational quality and access needed to support girls' and boys' right to education even in the most difficult contexts. The INEE Minimum Standards represent the experiences and best practices of an extensive network of more than 2,250 practitioners, academics, and policymakers from more than fifty countries, gathered through a year-long consultative process, and points ways forward to ensuring a high quality of educational preparedness, response, and recovery.

The INEE Minimum Standards include nineteen standards organized into five domains:

1. *Foundational standards* focus on coordination, community participation, and analysis, especially with regard to understanding the local context and contextualizing standards to that context;

2. *Access and learning environment* focus on access to safe and relevant learning opportunities, highlighting critical linkages to other sectors, such as water and sanitation;

3. *Teaching and learning* focus on promoting effective teaching and learning, including curricula, training, pedagogy, learning processes, and assessment;

4. *Teachers and other education personnel* focus on administration and management of human resources, including recruitment and selection, conditions of service, and supervision and support; and

5. *Education policy* focuses on policy formulation and implementation.

Since 2004, the INEE Minimum Standards have guided the promotion of high-quality education from the start of an emergency through recovery in eighty countries. These standards also serve as an accountability tool for education providers and donor agencies.

> INEE. 2010. *Minimum Standards for Education: Preparedness, Response, Recovery*. New York: INEE Coordinator for Minimum Standards and Network Tools.

"We had to leave behind all of our posessions. The only thing we could bring with us is what we had in our heads, what we had been taught—our education. Education is the only thing that cannot be taken from us."

A Woman who fled from Darfur to Chad, 2004

The accepted wisdom from practitioners and academics studying this area is that even amid conflict and crisis, one can find ways to help girls and boys continue their education. Going to school—even if it does not look like a school from the outside—not only assures them of their right to education; if done well and safely it can also offer children (1) physical protection, by providing a safe and structured place to learn and play, as well as a positive alternative to military recruitment; (2) psychosocial protection, by providing continuity and a daily routine, as well as offering a sense of the future beyond the immediacy of violence and crisis; and (3) cognitive protection, by strengthening children's analytical and evaluative skills in responding to propaganda or disparate sources of information (Nicolai and Triplehorn 2003). Continuing education during an emergency and through recovery also means that children can transition more quickly to formal learning after the crisis is over.

To sustain education during emergencies, practitioners deploy a wide range of strategies, which are often invented on the spot based on the circumstances. Three important strategies that have been shown to be effective in helping girls and boys continue their learning are highlighted here: harnessing community demand, child-friendly spaces, and back-to-school campaigns.

Harnessing Community Demand

A key feature of the different interventions that have been shown to help girls and boys during emergencies is both to ensure that humanitarian actors are prepared to sustain children's education—something that historically they have not been—and to ensure that community initiative is fully integrated into the intervention's design and implementation.

Indeed, repeatedly across crisis contexts, the communities affected by crises have been the first ones to restore education to their children. Multiple global reviews of education in contexts of crisis and conflict, as well as several in-depth country case studies, have shown that affected communities are on the front lines in sustaining children's education. Not only is education repeatedly a high priority for affected communities—along with things such as shelter, food, and water—but it is also the community's initiative and contributions that quickly restore education and keep it going—from using existing teachers, to finding safe spaces for classes, to organizing food and logistics. Community members and parents, even amid a crisis, want their children to have daily activities that provide enjoyment and lay the groundwork for their long-term success in life. For many, restoring schooling is the lifeline to do just that.

- **Crisis-affected communities consistently prioritize education as important, together with life-saving assistance such as shelter, food and water, and health.** Data from rapid surveys of the needs and prioritizes of crisis-affected populations in multiple emergency contexts show that affected communities consistently identify assistance with education as one of their top priorities for international support.

  Martone, G. 2007. *Educating Children in Emergency Settings: An Unexpected Lifeline.* New York: International Rescue Committee.

- **In East Timor, parents and community members played a crucial role in sustaining education during the war for independence.** This initiative from parents and community members to find ways to support the continued schooling of their children during the height of the emergency was also crucial in laying the foundations for rebuilding the education system after the conflict was over.

  Nicolai, Susan. 2004. *Learning Independence: Education in Emergency and Transition in Timor-Leste since 1999.* Paris: UNESCO International Institute for Educational Planning.

- **At least four global reviews of the evidence about education in crises and conflict have highlighted the crucial role that communities play in sustaining education during crises, citing a wide variety of examples ranging from Afghanistan to Pakistan to South Sudan.** In the words of one particular study, "One of the strongest assets in the field of education and fragility, the importance of which cannot be emphasized enough, is the prioritization of education by individuals and communities affected by crises. All around the world, people find ways to maintain schooling in some form when neither governments nor the international community are able or willing to assist them. . . . Sustaining education in these contexts frequently takes great ingenuity and personal courage, but always relies on parents' strong beliefs that educational continuity amid a crisis is of the utmost importance" (Winthrop and Matsui 2013).

Smith, A., and T. Vaux. 2003. *Education, Conflict and International Development.* London: UK Department for International Development.

Buckland, P. 2005. *Reshaping the Future: Education and Post-Conflict Reconstruction.* Washington: World Bank.

UNESCO. 2011. *The Hidden Crisis: Armed Conflict and Education: EFA Global Monitoring Report 2011.* Paris: UNESCO.

Winthrop, Rebecca, and Elena Matsui. 2013. *A New Agenda for Education in Fragile States.* Washington: Brookings Institution.

Child-Friendly Spaces

In emergency settings, *child-friendly spaces* are a more effective approach to sustain education than setting out to build schools, training or bringing in teachers, or awaiting government-approved textbooks. The premise is simple: To quickly find safe spaces where children can gather with caring adults and regularly engage in enriching activities, including games and expressive activities, in addition to traditional school subjects such as reading and mathematics. Using whatever materials are available in the context (from gathering under trees and drawing in the sand to reading books and hearing traditional stories from elders), this approach has been shown to effectively reach large numbers of children very rapidly. There is also increasing evidence to demonstrate that this approach helps support children's psychosocial well-being, boosting their ability to bounce back from their difficult experiences. This approach works across the different types of contexts where emergencies strike: refugee settings, natural disasters, and armed conflict. It also can lay the foundations for, over time, developing more formal learning environments, which are crucial to the full restoration of schooling.

What Are Child-Friendly Spaces?

Child-friendly spaces is a term that comes out of UNICEF and its extensive work on education in emergencies; other terms, such as *safe spaces* or *child-centered spaces,* are also used for this approach. An accepted definition of child-friendly spaces is programs that "support the resilience and well-being of children and young people through community organized, structured activities conducted in a safe, child friendly, and stimulating environment."

> CPWG (Child Protection Working Group). 2012. *Minimum Standards for Child Protection in Humanitarian Response.* Geneva: CPWG.
>
> UNICEF. 2011. *Guidelines for Child-Friendly Spaces in Emergencies.* New York: UNICEF.

- **Five thousand girls and boys affected by an earthquake and tsunami in the Solomon Islands rapidly benefited from a child-friendly spaces intervention over the course of four months.** Save the Children USA implemented eighty-nine Safe Spaces in the Solomon Islands after an earthquake and tsunami in April 2007, and as a result about five thousand children benefited from the program over the course of four months. The earthquake and tsunami had displaced into substandard tent cities more than ten thousand people, more than 60 percent of whom were children. Focus group sessions with both parents and children revealed that the children participating in Safe Spaces reportedly had increased their self-confidence, cooperation with others, concentration, and perceived safety.

How it works: Safe Spaces' facilitators are trained to design and implement gender- and age-appropriate activities such as local games, expressive activities, health promotion, arts and crafts, sports, and schoolwork for young children in the morning and adolescents in the afternoon. Notably, toward the end of 2007, Save the Children, UNICEF, and the Solomon Islands Ministry of Education made concerted efforts to transition from Safe Spaces to formal schooling through village committees, even converting several Safe Spaces to government preschools where they had not previously existed.

> Madfis, Josh, Daryl Martyris, and Carl Triplehorn. 2010. "Emergency Safe Spaces in Haiti and the Solomon Islands." *Overseas Development Institute: Disasters* 34, no. 3: 845–64.

- **One of the most extreme adaptations of the child-friendly spaces approach was successfully used by the International Rescue Committee (IRC) to sustain education for girls in Afghanistan under the Taliban.** In 1997 in Afghanistan, in response to the Taliban's violent repression of girls' education, the IRC began supporting safe spaces for girls to study. These safe spaces were inside the homes of brave men and women who were willing to secretly help continue education for girls. After the fall of the Taliban, these girls' schools were evolved into government community schools. Academic studies indicate that since that time, these schools have been successful in increasing girls' participation in school, improving enrollment by 52 percentage points, and are able to provide girls with a high-quality education, increasing girls' average test scores by 0.65 standard deviation.

  How it works: The locations of these alternative, community-based girls' schools were frequently moved, and the arrival and departure of students was staggered to avoid unwanted attention. These schools offer girls a safe, alternative form of education, maintaining low visibility, minimizing their commute, and being heavily integrated into their home communities.

  Burde, Dana, and Leigh L. Linden. 2013. "Bringing Education to Afghan Girls: A Randomized Controlled Trial of Village-Based Schools." *American Economic Journal: Applied Economics* 5, no. 3: 27–40.

  Groneman, Christine. 2011. *Study on Field-Based Programmatic Measures to Protect Education from Attack.* New York: Global Coalition to Protect Education from Attack.

- **For refugee girls and boys fleeing the Democratic Republic of Congo, child friendly spaces boosted their social and emotional well-being compared with children not engaged in the program. Girls in particular were helped.** Among child refugees in Uganda fleeing conflict in the Democratic Republic of Congo beginning August 2012, Child-Friendly Spaces (CFSs), implemented by World Vision Uganda and Save the Children, prevented a decline in children's social and emotional well-being and bolstered children's development. According to a house-by-house, randomized survey entailing interviews with caregivers to 633 refugee children in February 2013, a 73 percent majority of children age six to twelve attended CFSs, with 75 percent attendance by girls and 71 percent by boys. Particularly for girls, participation in CFS was found to increase developmental assets, such as positive values, social competencies, and empowerment. Furthermore, the psychosocial well-being of children attending CFS stabilized over time, and deteriorated for children not attending CFS.

How it works: Each of the 20 CFSs across the resettlement area consisted of a tent area for activities, latrines, a store, and playground equipment. Activities included literacy and numeracy, the English language, local dialects, traditional song and dance, art, storytelling, organized sports, and unstructured play. There was also time designated for peer-to-peer support and experience sharing, and some older children participated in vocational activities like dress making. Typically, the CFS offered a four-hour session for children ages six to twelve and a two-hour session for children ages thirteen to seventeen. The size of each CFS varied, ranging from 65 to 651 registered children.

Metzler, Janna, et al. 2013. *Evaluation of Child-Friendly Spaces: Uganda Field Study Summary Report*. London and New York: Save the Children, Columbia University, UNICEF, and World Vision.

- **In the war-affected villages of Afghanistan, interviews with community members showed that child-friendly spaces supported children's well-being, and in particular helped increase girls' ability to speak out about their needs.** The Child-Centered Spaces program, implemented by Child Fund Afghanistan in war zones of northern Afghanistan, reached almost 300 children, and was found to increase children's well-being and prompt girls to be more outspoken about their situations. This evidence was gathered through a series of semistructured interviews and focus group discussions between August 2003 and December 2004 in three of the villages.

How it works: Child-Centered Spaces, which is staffed by locals, provided nonformal education spaces that focused on normalizing and expressive activities to help children come to terms with their war experiences. This included a child-led village risk mapping process, which was presented by children through a role play. Tents with heating and 24-hour security for teachers and school supplies were also provided.

Loughry, Maryanne, Colin Macmullin, Carola Eyber, Behailu Abebe, Alastair Ager, Kathleen Kostelny, and Michael Wessells. 2005. *Assessing Afghan Children's Psychosocial Well-Being: A Multi-Modal Study of Intervention Outcomes*. Richmond: ChildFund International.

Kostelny, Kathleen. 2008. *Starting Up Child-Centered Spaces in Emergencies: A Field Manual*. Richmond: ChildFund International.

UNICEF and UNHCR—the UN's Leaders for Education in Emergencies

The United Nations Children's Fund (UNICEF) and the Office of the United Nations High Commissioner for Refugees (UNHCR) are the two leading UN agencies charged with delivering education in emergency contexts. UNICEF is the UN organization that leads on children's issues around the globe, with more than 100 country offices and multiple programs in developing countries to help support children's health and well-being, including deep expertise and programming in education. UNHCR is the UN organization that leads on the protection and care of refugees around the world. It carries out a wide range of activities, ranging from negotiating with governments, to setting up refugee camps, to delivering with its partners health, education, food, and shelter programs. Together, the two organizations are the most important UN players organizing the humanitarian community's response to children's needs in emergencies, including sustaining their education.

Back-to-School Campaigns

After an emergency ends and the effort of rebuilding begins, whether after a war or a disaster, one successful approach for ensuring education is prioritized is back-to-school campaigns. These are typically coordinated by governments and UNICEF education teams in the country, and are implemented with a wide range of partners. The focus is to rapidly restore schooling by providing the basics—supplies, teacher training, coordination, and community awareness. In many cases, the child-friendly spaces established during emergencies are expanded into formalized learning centers.

- **The Government of South Sudan's 2006 Go to School Initiative, supported by UNICEF, nearly doubled enrollment rates in South Sudan in less than one year.** By the end of 2008, 1.6 million children—though only 35 percent girls—were enrolled in school, up from merely 343,000 children enrolled during the civil war.

  How it works: Basic school supply kits for 1.6 million children were delivered, and training for 9,000 new teachers was implemented with a special emphasis on English language training and science, technology, engineering, and mathematics subjects. Public awareness campaigns and local events raised enthusiasm about education, urging communities to send children, especially girls, to school. Special provisions were made for child soldiers, and vocational classes were provided for adults who could not attend school during the conflict.

UNICEF. 2008. *South Sudan: Progress Report for UNICEF's Education in Emergencies and Post-Crisis Transition Programme.* Juba: UNICEF South Sudan.

- **After the typhoon Haiyan in 2013, the Philippines Department of Education and UNICEF supported 500,000 children in getting back to school through its Back-to-School Campaign.**

  How it works: The Back-to-School Campaign delivered supply kits and tent classrooms. The campaign also involved partners from a variety of sectors in order to provide displaced children with a healthy and protective environment for learning. The campaign also shares information about the location, timing, and operations of the makeshift learning spaces. The program's core elements are to give psychosocial support to teachers and care workers, as well as providing life skill programs for emergency-specific needs.

  UNICEF. 2014b. *Philippines Humanitarian Situation Report.* Manila: UNICEF Philippines.

Refugee Education: Strategies for Recognizing Student Learning

Girls and boys who are forced to flee their homes, crossing international borders alone or with their families, are some of the most vulnerable children in the world. Life as a refugee is not easy. More often than not, girls and boys who become refugees stay refugees for a very long time. Almost half of all refugees in the world face long-term or "protracted" displacement which, on average, lasts 25 years (UNHCR 2014). This means children may spend their entire school career as a refugee. The solution to where they live and make their home permanently after the war or crisis is over may be to return to the home country from which they fled, or it may be to integrate locally into the communities where they are living as refugees, or it may be to settle in a third country altogether.

According to the refugee education expert Sarah Dryden-Peterson, the education children receive during their displacement should not been seen as a stop-gap short-term solution, but rather "for most refugee children, the education received in exile is their one shot at education" (Dryden-Peterson 2011). Education in emergencies strategies are useful in a wide range of contexts, including when children have been forced to flee their homes. But there are a number of very specific concerns that apply to the schooling of refugee children; one of which is ensuring that the education they receive is recognized by the country or education system where they will ultimately end up or live.

The language of instruction, curriculum, teacher qualifications, and examination systems vary by country, and in any of these situations the schooling they gain may not be recognized by local educational institutions or employers, sometimes due to reasons as trivial as missing paperwork. In addition, technical challenges such as matching grade levels across different education systems and providing "bridge" programs to move between them can be difficult to provide (Kirk, 2009). Past examples show how poignant this problem is: In West Africa, due to outdated bureaucratic paperwork requirements, some Sierra Leonean refugee boys and girls who had been through primary and lower secondary school in refugee camps in the neighboring country of Guinea were, upon returning home to Sierra Leone, not allowed to continue to upper secondary school and placed back in the early grades of primary school.

In her comprehensive study on certifying refugee education, Jackie Kirk (2009) outlines solutions that have been proposed and implemented to ensure that refugee children's schooling is recognized wherever they may end up. Solutions include facilitating cross-border examinations, allowing access to host country schools and examinations for refugee students, and supporting refugee educators to develop local certification boards. She also recommends affected communities partner with NGOs and policymakers to tailor their education system and accreditation options to the specific context, depending on the length of displacement and needs of the community, and reviewing and revising the system as their situation changes. Tailoring the curriculum and language of instruction to both the students' country of origin as well as the country where they are living as a refugee can ease students' transitions at the end of displacement. Explicit policies that remove documentation or specific official paperwork as a barrier for school entry or progression, and technical support for implementing basic tests to place students, as well as grade conversion and syllabus comparison are solutions that Ministries of Education can implement.

Five Compelling Challenges for the Next Decade

Since the Millennium Development Goals were put forth—and even since the first edition of this book was published in 2004—there has been significant and impressive progress on girls' education. The number of girls not attending primary school has been virtually cut in half, and adolescent girls and women are completing more years of school than ever before. And yet, as we said earlier, the state of girls' education still should invoke more a sense of a lingering crisis that still needs to be conquered rather than a goal that has been met and deserves congrautlations.

As we also made clear earlier, we believe that the MDG of universal primary education by 2015 was simultaneously the world's most ambitious and pathetic goal. It is ambitious because in 2000, there were 100 million children out of school and progress seemed far away. But it was pathetic because no serious advocate or scholar ever thought that primary education was high enough of a global aspiration for educating girls or boys. And we know that the gains in access have not been met in terms of gains in learning and quality education, and that the gaps for girls' education are still strikingly high for girls impacted by war, disasters, or epidemics, as well as those who face multiple disadvantages—because they come from a large and poor family; because they live in a rural area; or because they face discrimination due to their ethnicity or a disability.

So now that we have reached 2015 and have seen both significant progress and yet a lingering crisis, what should be the focus going forward from 2015?

One must start by realizing that it is crucial to finish the job of universal access as we know tens of millions of girls are still denied even a basic education—sometimes due to being caught in hazardous child labor or cycles of conflict and violence or forced into early marriage. The lack of emphasis on secondary education and specific learning goals were not somehow missed or underappreciated in 2000. The focus on universal primary education was a product of prioritization and an understanding that you have to walk before you run—where walking meant first achieving a global commitment to the ideal that every child should be able to receive a basic education.

Yet, even as we finish that job, it is equally important that a new process of prioritization takes place in 2015 to guide those areas that should garner enhanced focus going forward. As discussed in chapter 1, we have chosen to place special attention on the following five: (1) learning and a high-quality education: (2) completing secondary education and adolescent girls; (3) helping girls to overcome violence and conflict; (4) school-to-work transitions; and (5) education to empower girls and women.

1. Quality Learning

Some who are skeptical about the movement toward universal education have expressed two criticisms—that advocates of universal education have been focused only on attendance and not learning and a high-quality education; and that it might have been better to move more slowly on universal access until there was more certainty that large inflows of children into schools would not strain efforts for high-quality learning. As discussed above, we do not agree with either of these contentions, for two reasons. First, serious education advocates have always sought not to just boost enrollment and attendance but also to ensure completion and effective learning. The reality is that too often it was easier for national policymakers to go without the revenues from fees than to carefully plan and pay for larger percentages of their youth to attend school. Second, no one in the United States or other wealthy countries would ever recommend that we allow half our children to be denied an education so that we can ensure there will be adequate resources for the other half to get a higher-quality education. Likewise, we would never take this position for children in other nations.

However, this does suggest that we must ensure that one of the five major future focuses is learning and a high-quality education. For this one area, we should point out that the same policies and interventions that are best for girls are also best for boys. In other words, well-trained teachers, teaching methods that work for students at all levels, a high-quality and accessible curriculum, and a focus on ensuring early basic reading and mathematics skills help provide a high-quality education to all children.

Nonetheless, considering the obstacles and biases against girls going to school in many parts of the world, ensuring a high-quality education may be even more important for making the case that for girls' education. In 2011, the Center for Universal Education called for a transformation of the existing global compact on education to a global compact on learning, one that would focus on ensuring all children are learning the skills they need to succeed in work and life. Now implementing this vision must be a top priority. (This Compact is discussed further in chapter 1 and just below.)

2. Reducing Violence Against Girls and Helping Girls Learn, Even in Conflicts and Emergencies

Unfortunately, the issue of violence that is directed against girls simply because they are seeking an education has become worse and worse in recent years. Although the near assassination of Malala and three of her fellow students and the kidnapping of nearly 300 schoolgirls in Nigeria have grabbed headlines and our hearts, there are more and more incidents of violence that never make the news but increasingly create a choice that no parent should ever face: Provide an education for your girl, or keep her out of harm's way.

To make this one of the five major global focuses, we first need to understand the four different categories of violence and emergencies that girls face and to understand the interventions that work best in each case:

- *Girls affected by humanitarian emergencies*: Ensuring education for girls affected by humanitarian emergencies—whether they be from war, natural disasters, or epidemics—has too often been ignored by the global community. Frequently, global responses focus on life saving measures like food and water without recognizing that education can be life saving and life-sustaining for girls and boys, particularly for their psychological and social wellbeing, We cannot give up on these children simply because they have the misfortune to be living in places where often poor governance, unrest, and disaster combine to overwhelm the coping capacity of families, communities, and governments.

- *Refugee girls*: Girls and boys who have been forced to flee their homes and nations are often among the worst-off children in the world. They face the traumas of humanitarian emergencies but do so in a foreign land with a foreign language and, at times, hostile host communities and governments. For many refugee girls and boys, education becomes a crucial intervention to sustain hope for a better life and to find ways to support their development, especially since they are frequently refugees for a significant portion of their childhoods.

- *Girls threatened and attacked because they go to school, even outside of war and conflict*: These are the girls like Malala and the girls kidnapped by Boko Haram who face attacks—from kidnapping to rape to dismemberment to murder—simply because they are seeking an education. These attacks on girls and girls' schooling, often employed as a tactic of terrorist groups, occur across a wide range of contexts, including in places that are not engulfed in war.

- *Girls subject to sexual violence in and around schools*: Aside from the dramatic cases of war, attacks on girls' education, and other violence, too many girls still face sexual abuse and exploitation in and around schools. Although the overwhelming numbers of teachers and adults involved in schools are honorable and committed, there must be zero tolerance for sexual abuse and exploitation in and around schools and a focus on specific policies to prevent such occurrences.

3. Secondary Education and Adolescent Girls

As mentioned above, the global community must now be clearly and unequivocally focused on enabling adolescents, including girls, to complete secondary education. This is not to suggest that we should deemphasize primary education; you cannot walk before you run, or reach secondary school if you have not attended and completed primary school. But future national education plans should be devised with universal secondary education in mind and should be judged by their strategies' effectiveness in reaching such goals. One cannot overestimate the importance or the challenge of this goal. There is no question that meeting it will require innovation, resources, and a commitment to teaching. Even in developing nations that have moved to free primary education, fees are still frequently charged for secondary school. And it will require more investment in teaching and teachers to ensure that they have the capacity to teach at higher levels to older students. In this section, we also add "adolescent girls," because in the push for secondary education for girls, we do not want to forget or leave behind those girls who have dropped out or never had the chance to start education along with the rest of those in their age group—

especially because of the increasing evidence base showing that alternative education paths for these girls are important.

4. Transitions from School to Work

Many poor parents who choose not to send their girls to school simply do not believe that education can provide an alternative economic path for their daughters. Thus, a greater focus on connecting secondary education to jobs not only provides the existing supply of educated girls with economic opportunities, but will inevitably create a positive cycle of demand for more and better education for girls. This must be one of the new major focuses for education for girls in the post-2015 era.

5. Empowering Girls to Lead

Today, even in 2015, one of the world's great moral crises is that so many women around the world, including in many developed nations, face discriminatory laws, domestic violence, economic barriers, and a lack of equal pay, job opportunities, and political representation. The push for girls' education must have a special emphasis and focus on empowering girls to overcome such barriers and to lead change for women. Yet, even when girls are successfully going to school and mastering their core subjects, they may be learning—from the stories in their textbooks or the statements of their teachers—that their place in the family and society is not in leadership roles. Too often we see curricula that portray women in a passive and discriminatory manner, a dearth of mentors, and an education system that places too little focus on the soft skills, sports participation, and leadership skills that are critical to success in jobs, to a more dignified family life, and to promoting political change. Education is empowering, but it will be more so if we start focusing on teaching empowerment and leadership skills to girls.

1 A High-Quality Education: Ensure That Girls are Truly Learning Both Hard and Soft Skills

We are facing a learning crisis around the globe, both in terms of "hard" skills like literacy and numeracy, and "soft" skills like communication, teamwork, and resilience. Improving the quality of education needs to be at the top of the agenda for improving girls' education.

Low learning levels due to a poor quality of schooling is one of the major challenges holding girls' education back. Although poor quality of schooling and low learning levels are problems that affect both girls and boys, we know that improving quality may be even more important for girls to succeed in their education and future lives, and that there are gender-specific quality issues that educators, academics, and advocates must be aware of. It is estimated that 250 million children around the globe are not meeting basic levels of proficiency in mathematics and reading, and 130 million of them have been in school for four years (UNESCO 2014c). These children are boys and girls, but because girls, especially marginalized girls, face higher barriers to getting into school, poor quality can compound the challenges they face.

Although the MDGs and the Education for All goals succeeded in mobilizing a wide range of actors committed to significantly expand access to schooling, there was far less progress in improving learning outcomes over this period. In 2000, the world's education ministers agreed to what essentially was a "global compact on education," whereby any developing country that devised a credible plan for expanding education to meet these global goals would not be held back for lack of financing, with developed countries agreeing to help where needed (Sperling, 2001b, 2008). A decade later, based on the mounting evidence of the crisis in the quality of learning for millions of schoolchildren around the globe, the Center for Universal Education at Brookings called for a Global Compact on Learning—putting improving quality at the center of the global education agenda (Perlman Robinson 2011). This proposal called for a wide range of actors—including governments, but also the philanthropic and business communities and civil society—to unite on a twin agenda of both bringing children to school and ensuring that they learn well while there. While education advocates have always understood the goal of universal education to be "access plus learning," putting a special focus on learning and quality education is essential for the next set of global goals on education and has been included in the discussions on the forthcoming Sustainable Development Goals. Realizing this Global Compact on Learning is essential to ensuring that girls as well as boys are able to make the most of their education and that reaching the doors of school does not turn into an empty promise for a better life.

Improving opportunities for high-quality learning will improve the educations of millions of girls, and will also reach millions of boys. Although both boys and girls suffer from a poor quality of schooling and low levels of proficiency, it remains a crucial challenge for girls specifically. Marginalized girls face greater opportunity costs for attending school, and if parents see they are not learning well they may be more likely to pull them out of school than their male peers. Additionally, many marginalized girls currently enter school late and leave early. Ensuring that the time they are able to spend in school is well spent and equips them with essential skills—such as knowing how to read, write, and count—can change their life course. Though the policies and interventions that will help improve girls' learning outcomes will most of the time also improve boys' learning, that is no reason to exclude them as drivers of improving girls' education.

- **Girls are less likely to be given the chance to enroll in school in the first place, and if schools are seen as not adding value to their lives and career prospects, then parents will be even less likely to send them to school.** The World Bank's *World Development Report 2012: Gender Equality and Development* explored many of the factors for why girls are still behind in schooling in many places, one of which is the perceived low return on a girl's education, meaning that many families do not see the value of educating their daughters, who will likely not work outside the home or even stay within their household following marriage. In Bangladesh, for example, when women's employment opportunities skyrocketed with the growth of the garment industry, female literacy became much more important for households, and girls' education grew so they could capitalize on the new opportunities.

  World Bank. 2012. *World Development Report 2012: Gender Equality and Development.* Washington: World Bank.

  Heath, Rachel, and Mushfiq Mobarak. 2012. *Supply and Demand Constraints on Educational Investment: Evidence from Garment Sector Jobs and the Female Stipend Program in Bangladesh.* Working Paper 2(4). New Haven, Conn.: Yale School of Management.

Unfortunately, the stakes can also be higher for girls attending school. In many countries, the poorest girls have the most responsibility at home for housework and caring for children. The opportunity cost for families to lose that help at home in order for girls and young women to attend school can be tremendous, and for many families is a hard decision. Even when girls are in school, they have less time at home to focus on assignments and homework and can easily fall behind due to their other responsibilities. All these factors mean that many girls will not attend a full cycle of primary and secondary schooling, and so it is crucial to ensure that the time they do spend in the classroom is worthwhile and they are learning real skills.

Millions of children around the globe are in school and not learning basic skills, meaning that we are in the midst of a "learning crisis." The ability to read and perform basic calculations is essential to participation in the modern world. The kinds of opportunities that being literate open up for people around the world in work, political participation, and community engagement are endless. And yet our main vehicle for imparting these skills to young people is failing millions of them. Millions of children who have been in school for years fail to read and comprehend a simple text or perform simple mathematical calculations.

As discussed in chapter 3, the majority of the 130 million children who are in school and not learning the basics live in less-developed countries, whose average learning levels are far behind the averages in developing countries.

- **The average student in poor countries performs on par with the worst 8 percent of students in rich countries.** One thorough study calculated that based on a handful of low- and middle-income countries that participated in international mathematics and reading assessments, the average student in a developing country got the same number of correct responses on the examination as the bottom 8 percent of students in rich countries in the most optimistic scenario, and the same number as the bottom 1 percent in the most pessimistic scenario.

    Crouch, L., and A. Gove. 2011. "Leaps Ahead or One Step At a Time? Skirting or Helping Engage the Debate." In *Policy Debates in Comparative, International and Development Education*, edited by J. N. Hawkins and W. J. Jacob. New York: Palgrave Macmillan.

- **Just 64 percent of students in low- and middle-income countries meet basic mathematics proficiency standards after four to six years of school.** According to data in the World Inequality Database on Education (WIDE), students in the most developed regions—in this case meaning Europe, Canada, the United States, Japan, Australia, and New Zealand—overwhelmingly meet the lowest benchmark for literacy and numeracy after four to six years of school, 100 percent and 97 percent, respectively. However, in developing regions and the rest of the world, just 84 percent meet minimum reading levels and 64 percent have basic mathematics proficiency (see figure 5.1).

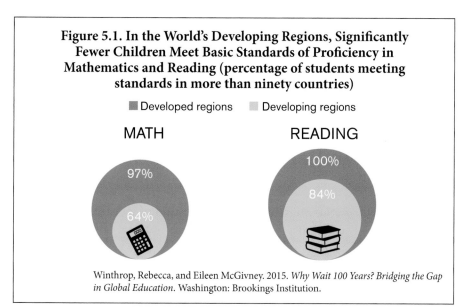

Figure 5.1. In the World's Developing Regions, Significantly Fewer Children Meet Basic Standards of Proficiency in Mathematics and Reading (percentage of students meeting standards in more than ninety countries)

Developed regions Developing regions

MATH

97%

64%

READING

100%

84%

Winthrop, Rebecca, and Eileen McGivney. 2015. *Why Wait 100 Years? Bridging the Gap in Global Education*. Washington: Brookings Institution.

The results are even more startling when looking at regional inequalities in learning where it is clear that the regions struggling the most at providing equal access to education for girls are also failing to meet basic learning levels. For example:

- **South and West Asia: Only 48 percent of girls and boys in school meet basic proficiency standards in reading, and only 28 percent in mathematics.**

- **Arab states: Only 59 percent of girls and boys in school meet basic proficiency standards in reading, and only 40 percent in mathematics.**

- **Sub-Saharan Africa: Only 67 percent of girls and boys in school meet basic proficiency standards in reading, and only 62 percent in mathematics.**

UNESCO. 2015b. "World Inequality Database on Education." http://www.education-inequalities.org/.

Winthrop, Rebecca, and Eileen McGivney. 2015. *Why Wait 100 Years? Bridging the Gap in Global Education*. Washington: Brookings Institution.

- **In India, a household assessment of all children living in rural areas found that whereas more than 95 percent of children are enrolled in**

school, less than half of all fifth-grade students can read at the second-grade level.

ASER (Annual Status of Education Report) Centre. 2015. *Annual Status of Education Report (Rural) 2014.* Provisional, January 13. http://img.asercentre.org.

- **Across Kenya, Tanzania, and Uganda, only 16 percent of third-grade students passed both the reading and mathematics examinations.**

Uwezo East Africa at Twaweza. 2014. *Are Our Children Learning? Literacy and Numeracy Across East Africa, 2013.* Nairobi: Hivos/Twaweza.

- **Perhaps the most startling finding of studies of learning outcomes in developing countries is that students are not improving over time.** The economist Lant Pritchett estimated the average gains on mathematics and science tests, using the results from the eight developing countries that participated in the Trends in International Mathematics and Science Study over multiple years. Looking at the progress over the years, the gains in science achievement among these countries have been so small that Pritchett estimates that if the rate of science learning in developing nations does not increase it will take 126 years for these countries to reach today's average level in the developed economies. For mathematics, the situation is dire because, on average, countries are actually regressing and performing worse over time, meaning that at current rates, they will never catch up.

Pritchett, Lant. 2014. *The Rebirth of Education: Schooling Ain't Learning.* Washington: Center for Global Development.

- **Annual household surveys of millions of students across Kenya, Tanzania, Uganda, India, and Pakistan show that girls' and boys' learning levels are not improving.** Two indigenous movements on learning— Pratham and Uwezo—conduct household surveys every year, and they have consistently found, in the words of Uwezo leaders, that "the learning needle has hardly moved. It is a constant reminder that many children continue to remain illiterate and innumerate."

ASER Centre. 2015. *Annual Status of Education Report (Rural) 2014.* Provisional, January 13. http://img.asercentre.org.

Uwezo East Africa at Twaweza. 2014. *Are Our Children Learning? Literacy and Numeracy Across East Africa, 2013.* Nairobi: Hivos/Twaweza.

Additionally, there are many important skills and competencies in addition to literacy and numeracy that all children need to cultivate to lead successful lives. Although literacy and numeracy and other fundamental skills are essential to survive in today's world, children also need a variety of other skills and abilities in order to succeed in a constantly changing workforce and increasingly connected world. Surveys of employers reveal that they struggle to fill many jobs due to candidates' lack of "soft" skills like communication. With the technological advances in today's economy and the ever-evolving nature of the green economy, knowledge economy, and service economy, more and more employers demand that workers have not only mastered foundational skills or specific technical skills for the job but are also able to adapt to changing demands, to innovate and be problem-solvers, to work in teams, and to be self-motivated, persistent, and confident. Additionally, being highly educated does not necessarily prepare youth to be good "global citizens" who possess knowledge of global issues and empathy toward others.

The evidence base about these other competencies is growing and experts are reaching a consensus on how best to measure and assess them, but this is an area that policymakers need to understand more and spend increasing effort addressing.

There is a growing consensus that what many have considered "soft" skills are actually some of the most crucial skills for girls' and boys' success in the twenty-first century. There are dozens of initiatives and frameworks—from school curricula, to NGOs, to labor market policies—that identify which non-academic competencies are important for children and adults. Although implementers, academics, and policymakers often use different terminology across the life cycle—such as twenty-first-century skills, social and emotional learning, or noncognitive skills—there is an ongoing effort to identify competencies that are a high priority for young children to young adults. Examples across the life cycle of competencies that researchers have identified as important frequently have common themes, such as communication, teamwork, and perseverance.

"Soft" skills help students succeed both in and outside the classroom. Multiple rigorous studies reviewing the literature on soft, or "noncognitive," skills, as well as dozens of interventions to foster these skills, make a strong outline for the case for focusing on these competencies in addition to IQ, or cognitive skills.

Examples of "Soft" Skills

Early Childhood Education
The child development experts Kathy Hirsh-Pasek and Roberta Golinkoff have developed the Six Cs, "a developmental model that outlines six critical skills for children":

- Collaboration
- Communication
- Content
- Critical thinking
- Creative innovation
- Confidence

> Hirsh-Pasek, Kathy, and Roberta Golinkoff. N.d. "Skills: The 6 Cs: Developing 21st-Century Skills." http://www.ultimateblockparty.com/download/the_6_Cs.pdf.

K–12 Education
The Partnership for 21st-Century Skills brought together multiple stakeholders—such as teachers, business leaders, and education experts—as well as doing a review of the literature and assessment frameworks, in order to design a framework for "twenty-first-century learning," or a vision for the most important skills for the new global economy, which has been used as a guiding framework for schools and practitioners. Among skills like information, media and technology skills, core subjects, and life and career skills, the framework includes "learning and innovation skills," what they deem the Four Cs:

- Critical thinking
- Communication
- Collaboration
- Creativity

> Partnership for 21st-Century Skills. 2011. *Framework for 21st Century Learning*. Washington: Partnership for 21st-Century Skills.

Workforce Development
Recently, as part of the USAID-funded "Workforce Connections" project, researchers at Child Trends conducted a rigorous, systematic review of 380 resources that examined the relationship between soft skills and key workforce outcomes. In consultations and focus groups with key stakeholders, these researchers have identified the top ten key soft skills for workforce success for youth between fifteen and twenty-nine years:

- Social skills
- Higher-order thinking skills (including problem solving, critical thinking, and decisionmaking)
- Self-control
- Positive self-concept
- Communication
- Hard work and dependability
- Self-motivation
- Teamwork
- Responsibility
- Positive attitude

> Lippman, Laura H., Renee Ryberg, Rachel Carney, and Kristin A. Moore. 2015. "Key 'Soft Skills' That Foster Youth Workforce Success: Toward a Consensus across Fields." Unpublished document, Child Trends Inc., Washington.

Across the Life Cycle

The Learning Metrics Task Force, a project cochaired by the UNESCO Institute of Statistics and the Center for Universal Education at Brookings, convened technical experts on measuring learning together with policy-makers and teacher organizations to begin to build a consensus on what learning outcomes are important for all children around the world, from early childhood through lower secondary education. The initiative had a particular eye to informing the global post-2015 education agenda and led a highly consultative process, with Ministers of Education or their representatives from 50 countries weighing in and a total of close to 2,000 people across 100 countries engaged in the process. The Task Force identified seven main domains of learning in which all children should have the opportunity to cultivate their skills:

- Physical well-being
- Social and emotional
- Culture and the arts
- Literacy and communication
- Learning approaches and cognition
- Numeracy and math
- Science and technology

Soft skills are an integral part of the framework and are represented in most of the seven domains, including competencies such as self-regulation, emphathy, resilience, cooperation, creativity, critical thinking, and flexibility.

> Learning Metrics Task Force. 2013. *Toward Universal Learning: What Every Child Should Learn*. Montreal and Washington: UNESCO Institute of Statistics and Center for Universal Education at Brookings.

- The Nobel Prize–winning economist James Heckman and his colleagues find that noncognitive skills are highly predictive of success in school in terms of grades, attendance, and completion and that these skills help improve academic skills, but the reverse is not necessarily true. "IQ tests and achievement tests do not adequately capture noncognitive skills, personality traits, goals, character, motivations, and preferences that are valued in the labor market, in school, and in many other domains. For many outcomes, their predictive power rivals or exceeds that of cognitive skills." Additionally, they find that high school graduates are much more successful in the labor market than GED recipients, who have proven to have the same cognitive ability but who lack many noncognitive competencies.

  Heckman, James J., Jora Stixrud, and Sergio Urzua. 2006. *The Effects of Cognitive and Noncognitive Abilities on Labor Market Outcomes and Social Behavior.* NBER Working Paper 12006. Cambridge, Mass.: National Bureau of Economic Research.

- Soft skills like personal efficacy have similar if not higher returns to hard skills such as mathematics: a 1 standard deviation increase in personal efficacy is associated with a 14 percent wage premium measured twenty years later. Studies from the United States suggest that once scores are standardized, a 1 standard deviation increase in mathematics performance can translate into a 12 percent increase in annual earnings, but personal efficacy translates into a higher percentage increase.

  Lazear, Edward P. 2003. "Teacher Incentives." *Swedish Economic Policy Review* 10: 179–214.

  Dunifon, Rachel, and Greg J. Duncan. 1998. "Long-Run Effects of Motivation on Labor-Market Success." *Social Psychology Quarterly* 61, no. 1: 33–48.

- Longitudinal data from nine countries show that social and emotional skills improve children's lives over the long term, including enabling them to become healthier adults who are less engaged in crime and other antisocial behavior. Evidence from the Education for Social Progress project at the Organization for Economic Cooperation and Development (OECD), including empirical analysis of longitudinal data tracking students over time in nine developed countries, shows that these skills play a very important role in the development of healthy societies as well as in the labor market, in conjunction with academic skills: "Raising levels of social and emotional skills—such as perseverance, self-esteem, and sociability—can in turn have a particularly strong effect on improving health-related outcomes and subjective well-being, as well as reducing anti-social behaviours. Results show that conscientiousness, sociability and emotional stability are among the important dimensions of social and emotional skills that affect children's future prospects. Social and emotional skills do not play a role in isolation, they interact with cognitive skills, cross-fertilise, and further enhance children's likelihood of achieving positive outcomes later in life."

OECD. 2015b. *Skills for Social Progress: The Power of Social and Emotional Skills.* Paris: OECD. http://dx.doi.org/10.1787/9789264226159-en.

There are proven methods for developing soft skills through child development programs, education systems, and workforce development programs. Both James Heckman and the research led by the economist Koji Miyamoto at the OECD have identified dozens of effective interventions and policies that can strengthen soft skills. Many effective interventions place a premium on individual relationships—from helping parents with their young children, to personalized learning in school, to mentorship programs for youth.

What Works to Improve Girls' and Boys' Learning in School

A number of strategies have been shown to be effective at improving the quality of education, and specifically the learning levels of girls and boys. Some of the most well established strategies have been previously reviewed in chapter 4 and are referenced here again, such as supporting good teachers and training teachers in student-centered teaching methods. Others—such as aligning the curriculum with student needs, harnessing creative local and global partnerships to improve learning, and focusing on soft-skills development—are promising areas that merit increased attention from policymakers.

We also recognize that a high-quality education, for girls especially, does not just mean getting high marks on mathematics or science examinations but also must fundamentally include messages about gender equality. What schools can do to support girls' empowerment is an important question, which we address directly in the last section of this chapter, "Education That Empowers Girls to Lead."

Hire Good Teachers Who Attend School and Engage Students

Good teachers and good teaching are essential ingredients for improving education quality for girls and boys. Across the developing world, one of the crucial first steps is making sure schools have enough good teachers. Teacher shortages are severe; UNESCO (2014c) estimates that 5.1 million more teachers are needed to achieve universal lower secondary education by 2030. Half of these teachers are needed in Sub-Saharan Africa, and an additional 1 million lower secondary school teachers are required in South and West Asia. Multiple studies have shown the benefits of having a good teacher on student learning; for example, students of good teachers have learning gains equivalent to one school year and students of weak teachers master less than half the expected content (Hanushek and Rivkin 2010, in King and Winthrop 2015).

In chapter 4, we discuss in detail the strategies for hiring good teachers who attend school and engage students. These strategies range from the careful crafting of entrance qualifications to providing incentives for teachers to attend and perform well, to working with parents to select local teachers from within the community—a strategy that has been shown to be especially effective for improving learning gains of students in rural India (Rawal and Kingdon 2010).

Can More Money Improve Education Quality?

Within education, there is a line of argument that holds that improving education quality, even in developing countries, has little to do with increasing the financial resources going into a school system and more to do with the strategies used with the resources available (Glewwe et al. 2011). However, recent studies have shown that in the most disadvantaged and under-resourced communities, financial resources—and more importantly the inputs that are purchased, such as textbooks, trained teachers, libraries, and science labs—matter a great deal. Providing inputs in these contexts can boost attendance and learning levels for all students, and especially for girls (Leon and Valdivia 2015; Michaelowa 2001; Room to Read 2015; Santhya, Zavier, and Jejeebhoy 2015; OECD 2013).

We suggest viewing school input interventions from the perspective of equalizing the distribution of resources across schools in a geographic area; for example, redistributing teachers from larger schools to smaller schools in the case of Operation Blackboard in India helped improve girls' primary school completion rate by 1.6 percentage points (Chin 2004). Ensuring schools have the basic resources to function—from books to teachers to blackboards—is important in most of the communities where girls are out of school or where they are in school but not learning well. Common sense dictates that you need both more inputs as well as a sound strategy for choosing and deploying the inputs to improve quality learning for marginalized girls in developing countries.

Improve How Teachers Teach

Providing training and coaching before teachers enter the classroom and while teachers are teaching is also a crucial and well studied strategy for improving student learning. In particular, teachers who are especially effective often practice teaching techniques that engage students in their own learning with, for example, interactive exercises. A comprehensive review of close to 500 studies on effective teaching practices in developing countries isolates a small set of teaching practices that highly effective teachers use and that play an important role in helping to improve children's learning (Westbrook et al. 2013). Again, this important strategy is discussed in depth in chapter 4—such as drawing on students' experiences and using materials beyond just the text book.

Align the School Curriculum with Students' Needs

The curricular gap, or the gap between what the curriculum expects students can do and what students actually can do, is a serious issue affecting the quality of learning for both girls and boys. Researchers argue that millions of students are being left behind while the curriculum has moved on (Pritchett and Beatty 2015).

- **In Pakistan, children in Punjab are three to four grade levels below the curriculum, meaning that if teachers are teaching the curriculum, they are using material three and four grade levels above the ability of their students.** For example, only 19 percent of third graders in Punjab could add fractions—the grade at which the Pakistani curriculum expects children to be able to add fractions. And in India's highest-achieving states, only one-third of students starting grade 3 were able to perform the cognitive tasks expected of them by the end of grade 5.

  Das, J. P. Pandey, and T. Zajonc. 2006. *Learning Levels and Gaps in Pakistan.* Policy Research Working Paper 4067. Washington: World Bank.

  Muralidharan, K., and Y. Zieleniak. 2014. "Cashing the Syllabus: Measuring Learning Trajectories in Developing Countries with Longitudinal Data and Item Response Theory." Working paper, University of California San Diego, San Diego.

  Pritchett, Lant, and Amanda Beatty. 2015. "Slow Down, You're Going Too Fast: Matching Curricula to Student Skill Levels." *International Journal of Educational Development* 40: 276–88.

- **In Kenya, providing textbooks only helped the best students, because for many students the textbooks were too advanced and in a language**

they did not know well. In an attempt to improve low student test scores in Kenya through the provision of textbooks, researchers found that, rather than raising average test scores, the intervention actually increased learning inequalities within schools by increasing the scores of the best students and having little or no effect on the rest of students. In this case, not only was curricular pace an issue, but students also could not use their textbooks effectively because they were written in English, which for most students was their third language.

Glewwe, Paul, Michael Kremer, and Sylvie Moulin. 2009. "Many Children Left Behind? Textbooks and Test Scores in Kenya." *American Economic Journal: Applied Economics* 1, no. 1: 112–35.

What these studies show us is that the curriculum, and thus teaching, is overly ambitious and caters to the strongest student, rather than the average student. According to Esther Duflo and colleagues (2011), this is because "a central challenge of educational systems in developing countries is that students are extremely diverse, and the curriculum is largely not adapted to new learners."

Accelerating the pace of student learning by paying special attention to weaker students and helping them catch up to the curricular pace has proven highly effective. Researchers and practitioners recommend tracking or remediation as ways to narrow the curricular gap, because both approaches "shift the curricular pace down a notch to better coincide with students' learning potential, or they accelerate the pace of student learning, usually through more targeted attention or tutoring, such that students can better keep up with curricular pace" (Pritchett and Beatty 2015, 285). While the studies below show the importance of remediation and customizing education to help children who have started at different levels to learn and to catch-up, the authors of this book stress the importance of not encouraging tracking that unnecessarily separates students, that works to stigmatize young people, or that intentionally or unintentionally signals to students that they have less potential or academic capacity than some of their peers.

- **In India, a randomized experiment showed that providing 2 hours a day of tutoring during school hours in basic literacy and mathematics to weak students improved their test scores by 0.40 standard deviation.** In India, a remedial education program called the Balsakhi

Program ("the Child's Friend"), run by the Indian organization Pratham and implemented in government schools, provided participating schools with a teacher (a *balsakhi*, a young woman recruited from the local community who has herself finished secondary school) to work with fifteen to twenty children in the third and fourth grades who have been identified as falling behind their peers. The *balsakhi* focused on remediating the children in basic literacy and numeracy skills—competencies they should have learned in the first and second grades—for two hours a day during school time. After the first year, the Balsakhi Program increased average test scores by 0.14 standard deviation, and after the second year by 0.28. Weaker students in the bottom third of the initial distribution gained the most—more than 0.40 standard deviation.

Banerjee, Abhijit V., Shawn Cole, Esther Duflo, and Leigh Linden. 2007. "Remedying Education: Evidence from Two Randomized Experiments in India." *Quarterly Journal of Economics* 122, no. 3: 1235–64.

- **A randomized evaluation in Kenya showed that organizing students by ability raised test scores by 0.14 standard deviation, with low-ability students improving the most.** In 2005, 121 primary schools with single first-grade classes in western Kenya split their single class into two sections, using funds received through a national program to hire an additional grade 1 teacher to teach the new section. Of these initial schools, 60 were randomly assigned to track low-ability students into the new grade 1 section. In these "tracking schools," where classrooms were organized by student ability, teachers were better able to teach to the level of their students. After 18 months, researchers found that tracking students raised the scores for all students, including those assigned to the lower-ability class. On average, test scores were 0.14 standard deviation higher in tracking schools than in nontracking schools. Students in the high-ability classes gained 0.19 standard deviation, whereas students in the lower-ability classes gained 0.16 standard deviation. Furthermore, tracking had persistent effects; one-year after tracking ended, those students in tracking schools improved their test scores by 0.16 standard deviation.

Duflo, Esther, Pascaline Dupas, and Michael Kremer. 2011. "Peer Effects, Teacher Incentives, and the Impact of Tracking: Evidence from a Randomized Evaluation in Kenya." *American Economic Review* 101, no. 5: 1739–74.

Harnessing Partnerships—from Local to Global—to Improve Learning

During the last decade, civil society movements within India, Pakistan, and East Africa have highlighted the learning crisis and called for greater attention from their governments. An important example of the power of communities is the citizen-led assessment movement—where literally thousands of community volunteers go door to door assessing what children know—that has helped get information about real learning levels of children in and out of schools into the hands of parents and community leaders. According to a 2015 evaluation of four citizen-led assessments:

> • "As governments and donors focused on increasing access in the wake of the Millennium Development Goals, the issue of learning received comparatively little concerted attention. Some organizations working in countries where access was rapidly increasing took notice of the fact that, while rising enrollment rates were being celebrated, there was little evidence of whether or not learning was taking place. One of the results of this realization was the emergence of the citizen-led assessment movement, initiated by Pratham in India in 2005. The movement is an attempt by civil-society organizations to gather evidence on learning and use it for two main purposes: first, to increase awareness of low learning outcomes and second, to stimulate actions that are intended to address the learning gap."
>
> Results for Development Institute. 2015. *Bringing Learning to Light: The Role of Citizen-Led Assessments in Shifting the Education Agenda*. Washington: Results for Development Institute.

Looking at two of the largest citizen-led assessment networks—the Annual Status of Education Reports (ASER) in India and Uwezo in Kenya, Tanzania, and Uganda—the evaluation found that the movement has played an important role in helping set the international education agenda to be more focused on learning outcomes, both by providing evidence of the learning crisis and by providing a low-cost model for assessing learning outcomes. At the national level, there is evidence that ASER and Uwezo have played a role at getting learning prioritized in national education plans, with their results being cited in government documents.

Other collective movements at the global level have played an important role in getting learning onto the education agenda. For example, the Learning

Metrics Task Force, discussed above in Examples of "Soft" Skills, is a collective effort whose "overarching objective . . . is to catalyze a shift in the global conversation on education from a focus on access to access *plus* learning." The task force consists of 30 member organizations and consulted more than 1,700 individuals in 118 countries to make concrete recommendations on what competencies all children should be learning, how to measure them, and how to implement better assessment and measurement to drive learning. The recommendations are now being taken up by 15 "learning champion" governments, which are working to integrate high-quality learning opportunities into local and national education systems and have influenced the development of the new sets of global goals on education (Results for Development Institute 2015; Center for Universal Education 2015).

Strategies for Cultivating Soft Skills

What are ways to ensure that girls and boys develop soft skills? This is an area where there is emerging research, but more needs to be done to fully explain the strategies that are most effective, especially for marginalized girls (Mansson and Farnsveden 2012). The student-centered learning methods outlined above are a good place to start, especially because these approaches emphasize the interpersonal and intrapersonal processes that are essential for developing noncognitive skills like communication, teamwork, and leadership.

Research, largely based in the United States, shows that to help children and youth develop soft-skills, a range of important things need to be considered:

- **First, the earlier the better.** Children build on soft skills developed from previous investments earlier in life. And those with higher levels of soft skills (e.g. self-confidence, perseverance) are likely to benefit more from later investment in hard skills (e.g., mathematics, science). Thus, skills gaps early in life persist and grow over a person's lifetime (Heckman, Stixrud, and Urzua 2006; OECD 2015b).

- **Second, hard and soft skills are not just acquired in the classroom, but are learned in the family and in the community as well.** This places a renewed importance on the role of parents and community engagement in the development of skills (Heckman, Stixrud, and Urzua 2006).

- **Third, early interventions, such as enriched child care centers and early childhood programs, can help children overcome initial**

disadvantages borne out of adverse home environments, not necessarily by boosting their IQ, but rather by boosting their soft skills (Heckman, Stixrud, and Urzua 2006; OECD 2015b).

- **Fourth, the window for developing soft skills continues into adolescence**, although the most successful adolescent-targeted interventions are not as effective as the most successful early childhood and primary

---

Kishoree Kontha—Girls' Soft-Skills Development in Bangladesh

Kishoree Kontha ("Adolescent Girls' Voices")—which was implemented by Save the Children and funded by the Nike Foundation—aimed to empower adolescent girls ages ten to nineteen years in rural Bangladesh with the soft skills and peer networks necessary to improve their education, economic, social well-being, and health outcomes. Using a peer education approach, participating girls attended five to six 2-hour peer-led sessions a week after school hours. Peer educators were girls thirteen through seventeen years old from the community who were selected by community adults and trained by program staff. These peers led sessions on information giving and skills building in areas like nutrition, sanitation, child rights, and violence against women. The peer educators used an array of learning methods, including role playing, games, questioning, lecturing, and discussion. Girls also participated in study circles in which academically successful girls helped younger girls with schoolwork. Nonliterate and semiliterate girls were mentored by other school-going girls. In addition, girls received learning materials to use in study circles to support their language and mathematics learning. But beyond learning opportunities, Kishoree Kontha also provided girls with recreational opportunities and social networking, which they typically do not experience at home or in school.

The girls who participated in Kishoree Kontha reported a mean 22 percent improvement in their soft skills and developmental assets, including peer support, empowerment, commitment to learning, sense of self-efficacy, communication skills, and positive identity. In practical terms, this meant that girls improved from having a "fair" level of soft skills and developmental assets to a "good" level after participating in the program for 6 months. Parents and community members also reported that girls in the program demonstrated more confidence, reported feeling more respected by their families and communities, and had enhanced commitments to be independent, to avoid early marriage and pregnancy, to continue schooling, and to contribute to family income.

Scales, Peter C., Peter L. Benson, Kathlee Fraher, Amy K. Syvertsen, Larry Desrhem, Raphael Makonnen, Shahana Nazneen, and Sarah Titus. 2013. "Building Developmental Assets to Empower Adolescent Girls in Rural Bangladesh: Evaluation of Project Kishoree Kontha." *Journal of Research on Adolescence* 23, no. 1: 171–84.

school programs. Nonetheless, workplace-based programs that include mentoring and guidance have been demonstrated to be quite effective (Kautz et al. 2014; OECD 2015b).

- **Fifth, a common feature of successful interventions in soft skills development is that they emulate the mentoring environments of successful families.** That is, they promote attachment through supportive relationships between parents, teachers, instructors, and the child, creating a safe and secure base from which to learn and explore (Kautz et al. 2014; OECD 2015b).

2 Protecting Education from Attack: Stopping the Growing Violence Against Girls

Unfortunately, the issue of violence directed against girls for seeking an education has risen to new heights in recent years. Although the near-assassination of Malala and three of her fellow students and the kidnapping of nearly 300 schoolgirls in Nigeria has grabbed headlines and our hearts, there are more and more incidents of violence that never make the news but increasingly create a choice no parent should ever face: education for your girl, or keeping her out of harm's way.

Violence against girls in educational settings takes different forms, all of them unacceptable. We believe that this second major challenge of addressing violence faced by girls in and around school must encompass all the contexts where this violence takes place: from wars to humanitarian emergencies to community-level attacks. Frequently, it is the less visible but equally unacceptable gender-based violence that takes place within the school community to which girls are subjected.

As seen in chapter 3, war and humanitarian emergencies can wreak havoc on children's lives, destroying their families and disrupting their communities. Sexual abuse and exploitation in and around schools is widespread and can undermine girls' ability to pursue their dreams. Fortunately, there are strategies that have been demonstrated to work both to sustain education amid emergencies and to make schools safe for girls.

To meet this second challenge—and to make good on the larger goal of universal secondary education for girls—the global community and the developing international governance mechanisms for education must make the issue of girls and boys in situations of violence, conflict, and emergencies a top focus. Fortunately there are promising strategies for helping to protect girls who find themselves in these most difficult situations. Here we review briefly some of the strategies discussed in-depth in prevous chapters and focus on other forms of education-related violence, particularly affecting girls, that policymakers and practitioners must do more to understand and address in order to fulfill the vision of all girls receiving a safe and high-quality education.

Sustaining Education in Emergencies

As discussed in detail in previous chapters, humanitarian crises destroy homes and uproot girls and boys in far too many countries around the world. Today 35 countries suffer from humanitarian crises, most of them caused by war and violence but some are also caused by natural disasters and health epidemics such as Ebola. A full one-third of the girls and boys who are out of school across the world are affected by humanitarian crises. Sustaining education amid crisis is important not only for ensuring all children can have an education—even if they live in some of the most difficult contexts in the world—but also because it provides a sense of hope amid despair. Numerous studies of children's physical and psychosocial well-being amid crises have showed that restoring education—even if it does not look like traditional schooling—is crucial for helping children adjust and adapt to their difficult surroundings (Loughry and Eyber 2003). Fortunately, practitioners have been developing strategies and guidance on how to sustain education amid crisis. These strategies are reviewed thoroughly in chapter 4 and highlight the importance of harnessing community initiative, quickly enrolling students in child-friendly spaces, and supporting back-to-school campaigns. These are several of the important strategies that help both children affected by humanitarian emergencies and children forced to flee their homes as refugees.

Protecting Girls from Education-Related Attacks

Together, political violence, along with school-related gender-based violence, have a direct impact on girls, their families, and their communities in traumatic ways. This section reviews the directions and lessons for protecting education from attack and stopping the growing violence against girls in (1) contexts of political violence, where girls are targeted simply because they participate in school, and (2) contexts where school-related gender-based violence adversely affects girls' lives and ability to get an education. The sensitive nature of these contexts makes information difficult to obtain, but there is a growing body of research that is documenting the extent of these problems and the strategies that are emerging as effective for addressing them.

A more recent growing phenomenon has been the explicit and growing attacks on education, particularly on girls' education. These are the girls like Malala and the girls kidnapped in Northern Nigeria by Boko Haram who face threats of violence simply for seeking an education. These threats can strike in a range of different contexts, including those countries that are not experiencing war or emergencies.

As discussed in chapter 3, students, teachers, and schools have been attacked in more than seventy countries. Girls in particular are often singled out. For example, 120,000 girls were forced to leave school in Pakistan after a violent campaign by the Taliban, girls' schools in Afghanistan have been violently attacked by gasing schools and bombing schoolgirls' buses, and in India and Colombia girls have been raped in school as part of sectarian political violence (GCPEA 2014b; Winthrop and McGivney 2014b).

These acts of violence also send the message to parents that schools are not safe places for their daughters. As a result, girls are the first to be withdrawn from school due to parents' fears for their girls' safety and security. Violence against girls is thus an urgent and crucial challenge to address in the next decade, not just because of girls' basic human right to a life of safety and security but also because violence affects their educational success, which, as we have seen from the evidence presented throughout this book, has far-reaching economic, social, and political effects for the women they will become and for the communities and nations where they live (OHCHR 2015).

Five years ago, the Global Coalition to Protect Education from Attack (GCPEA) emerged to address the growing issue of attacks on education. The GCPEA was launched with the on-going support of Qatar's Sheikha Moza bint Nasser, member of the UN Secretary-General's MDG Advocacy Group, and the Qatar Foundation, which, under Her Highness's leadership, has long focused on addressing attacks on education. The GCPEA's initiatives seek to strengthen the monitoring and reporting of attacks on schools and school personnel, and to promote effective programs and policies for the protection from and prevention of attacks on schools and universities, and also the military use of school structures during an armed conflict.

Strategies for protecting girls' education from attack may not look the same across contexts. To better explain these strategies, the GCPEA commissioned two recent reviews of practitioners' approaches. Christine Groneman's *Study on Field-Based Programmatic Measures to Protect Education from Attack* and Hannah Thompson's *The Role of Communities in Protection Education from Attack* provide useful insight to the growing body of information available about keeping girls and boys safe in these contexts (Groneman 2011; Thompson 2014). Together, their studies identify the below main strategies that are emerging as important.

School Safety Measures: Escorts, Guards, and Walls

- In Côte d'Ivoire, urban communities would send their children to and from school either in groups or with parental accompaniment as a strategy of prevention against attack. Following the 2010–11 crisis, this practice continued as an additional safety measure until successful negotiations between the school principal and commanding officers in the area assured parents and the community of the safety of their children and eliminated the need for group travel and escorts.

- In 2010, the governor of Yala, Thailand, changed security procedures so that members of security forces line the road to and from school to keep the route to school safe for both students and teachers.

- In Afghanistan, the Ministry of Education began an initiative to build boundary walls around all existing schools, with a priority for girls' schools. In 2011, a total of 8,327 school walls were constructed, and 1,796 more walls were planned. The ministry has also planned a program to build small residential houses for teachers at schools.

Avoid Giving the Impression That Schools Are Militarized

Practitioners' wisdom illuminates the pros and cons of assigning armed guards to schools in high-risk areas. Although this strategy may serve to physically protect students and teachers in some contexts, it may also give the impression that the school has been militarized, especially if the guards themselves are intended targets of violence, putting students and teachers at greater risk of attack. Assigning unarmed guards or escorts might help avoid the risks associated with schools appearing to be militarized, but these benefits must be carefully weighed on a case-by-case basis.

Groneman, Christine. 2011. *Study on Field-Based Programmatic Measures to Protect Education from Attack*. New York: Global Coalition to Protect Education from Attack.

Using Community Networks to Monitor Attacks and Send Early Warning Alerts

- In six schools in Zimbabwe, voluntary teacher–student–parent defense units have been formed to help monitor student participation in political camps at school and to remove militia camps from school grounds. Parents in these units also help warn teachers of imminent attack.

- In the Philippines, more than 3,500 local volunteers trained by the Mindanao People's Caucus formed the Bantay Cease-Fire Group to monitor and report violations against the cease-fire agreement between the Moro Islamic Liberation Front and the government, including incidences in which schools were attacked.

- As a way of mitigating violence during and after the 2011 crisis, communities in Côte d'Ivoire used mobile telephone communication to build communication trees and contribute to an early warning system. With mobile phone access pervasive across the country, student and parents used the short message service (SMS) to informally warn each other of attacks and to monitor each others' safety and well-being. Community members reported that during times when fighting had escalated, making it difficult to obtain phone credit, some network operators would provide free airtime to their customers.

Community Pressure for Safe Schools: Engage Community Leaders, Youth, and Teachers

- In the lower/middle Juba and middle/lower Shabelle regions of Somalia, Community Education Committees were successful in reducing the influence of al-Shabaab in schools when respected elders and religious leaders were encouraged to participate. Religious leaders risked their own safety to go on public radio and to visit schools to advocate against the recruitment of children by al-Shabaab forces.

- In cases across India, the Democratic Republic of Congo, the Occupied Palestinian Territories / Israel, Nepal, the Philippines, and Somalia, youth participation in girls' clubs, boys' clubs, community mobilization efforts, and other protection and advocacy activities has been crucial for creating protective school environments, for generating community-wide support for peace, and for raising awareness about child rights among military and political leaders.

Côte d'Ivoire—Lessons Learned on Protecting Education from Attacks

Case study research conducted by the GCPEA demonstrates the importance of careful planning and contextualization when members of the international community work with members of local communities toward protecting and continuing education for girls and boys. A set of lessons learned has emerged from this research:

- *Coordination:* Insufficient coordination among international and local actors can exacerbate tension, increase competition for community participation, or decrease the effectiveness of efforts to protect education and continue educational delivery.

- *Context analysis and mapping:* Efforts to protect education can be more effective if they build upon existing community strengths, resources, and opportunities. International actors should map current efforts and community engagement, key stakeholders, and relations of power in the community.

- *Awareness of local priorities* (including those of children): Initiatives should reflect the priorities and concerns of all groups, especially children directly and indirectly affected by conflict.

- *Create wider ownership:* Although the demand for education by parents is high during crises, cultivating community ownership of activities and initiatives is essential for sustaining education in emergencies.

- *Build in monitoring and evaluation and accountability measures:* Continuous monitoring and evaluation of programs are crucial not only for holding stakeholders accountable but also for building trusting relationships between community members and the external agencies involved in delivering educational programming.

- *Allow groups to self-organize:* Engaging marginalized groups, like children and mothers in contexts of emergencies, are often challenging. Efforts should be made to support informal clubs and groups in ways that empower the most vulnerable to participate.

Thompson, Hannah. 2014. *The Role of Communities in Protecting Education from Attack.* New York: Global Coalition to Protect Education from Attack.

- In the conflict areas in eastern Myanmar, where international actors are prohibited from visiting, protective activities are limited to local organizations and individual communities. For teachers in remote conflict-affected areas, this means that they are often isolated from support and resources. The Karen Teachers Working Group has responded by setting up a team of mobile teacher trainers who travel to these teachers and provide them with essential training and support.

- Following the 2002–3 crisis, the government of Côte d'Ivoire used financial incentives to redeploy teachers to their posts in the Center, North, and West regions. Community members saw this effort as protective because it allowed schools to remain open, decreasing the likelihood that the school would be used for military purposes.

Legal Reforms: Protecting Schools from Military Use

In addition to the practitioner and community strategies for reducing the attacks on education, international human rights actors, such as the organization Human Rights Watch, are working at the global level to strengthen the legal mechanisms protecting education. The human right *to* education, as well as the human rights *within* and *through* education are protected by almost every multilateral human rights treaty and by more than 140 national constitutions. There are even specific treaty provisions to ensure that refugees, asylum seekers, and stateless persons are not deprived of fundamental education in situations of armed conflict or occupation (OHCHR 2015). Yet despite these legal frameworks, there continue to be challenges in ensuring that their rights are not violated.

In 2010, the *Lucens Guidelines for Protecting Schools and Universities from Military Use during Armed Conflict* were drafted by a group of UN agencies and civil society organizations and later finalized in December 2014. The six guidelines reflect evidence of good practice already used by parties to armed conflict, and aim to "minimize the negative impact of an armed conflict on students' safety and education" by reducing "the use of schools and universities by parties to armed conflict in support of their military effort" (GCPEA 2014a, 2). The *Guidelines* are not legally binding, but they complement existing international humanitarian and human rights laws. They are intended to be used as a tool to raise awareness of the military use of schools among parties to armed conflict, and to facilitate discussion about issues of protection and education in conflict. The goal is to encourage a change in mentality toward the military use of schools (GCPEA n.d.)

In addition to the *Guidelines*, a Safe Schools Declaration was developed as an instrument whereby states can endorse and express their commitment to implement the *Guidelines* and express their political support for the protection and continuation of education in contexts of armed conflict. On May 29, 2015, thirty-seven states endorsed the Safe Schools Declaration, and the number is continuing to grow. (The declaration can be found at http://www.protectinged-ucation.org/sites/default/files/documents/safe_schools_declaration-final.pdf.)

A number of other national laws, court decisions, and military policies have also emerged to ensure greater protection for girls and boys from attacks against schools. For instance, in 2010, the commander-general of military forces in Colombia issued an order stating that it was a violation of the Principle of Distinction and the Principle of Precautions in Attacks to occupy schools, and that transgressions warranted disciplinary investigation (GCPEA 2015). And on May 25, 2011, the Cabinet of the Government of Nepal declared that all educational institutions in the country are Zones of Peace. Through the efforts of local NGOs, UNICEF, World Education, national stakeholders, and political groups (except the Medeshi armed groups) signed the national Schools as Zones of Peace Codes of Conduct, making strikes, protests, or other interference in schools a punishable offense. A key challenge of these efforts is that signing and respecting the codes are voluntary, making enforcement difficult (Groneman 2011).

Reporting Attacks on Education: The UN's Efforts to Achieve Better Accountability

In 2005, the United Nations ratified Security Council Resolution 1612, which established the UN Monitoring and Reporting Mechanism on Grave Violations against Children in Situations of Armed Conflict. And in 2011, UN Security Council Resolution 1998 made attacks against schools and hospitals a trigger for parties to a conflict to be listed in the annexes of the *UN Secretary-General's Annual Report on Children and Armed Conflict*. Once listed, parties to armed conflict can be referred to sanctions committees or to the International Criminal Court, although to date very few prosecutions of perpetrators have been documented (GCPEA 2014b). The military use of schools, however, is not a trigger for being listed because the military use of schools is not considered a violation of humanitarian law. Nonetheless, Resolution 1998 requires the Security Council to continue monitoring and reporting on military use of schools.

There are also several country-specific examples of local initiatives aiming to strengthen reporting of attacks on education. Again, in Nepal, the Schools as Zones of Peace initiative included local- and district-level reporting mechanisms for violations of the Codes of Conduct. Through these mechanisms, students, teachers, parents, or any other member of the community can report violations to School Management Committees, child rights groups, or political representatives and officials. In some cases, reporting of violations help support make-up school days; in other cases, apologies or reparations are given (Groneman 2011).

Addressing School-Related Gender-Based Violence

Outside the dramatic cases of war and attacks on education, too many girls still face gender-based violence in and around schools. This includes the range of explicit and implicit acts or threats of sexual, physical, or psychological violence girls and boys experience in and around schools. This type of violence often occurs quietly and in private and it affects large numbers of girls across many countries (Greene et al. 2013).

In chapter 4 we discussed in-depth some of the promising strategies for helping prevent gender-based violence from occurring in the first place and strategies for addressing incidents when they do occur. Important strategies include ensuring there are clear school safety and teacher conduct policies in place, gender-sensitivity training for teachers and students, and establishing safe spaces for girls within the school environment. One other emerging strategy that we discuss below is how to ensure boys and men are equal partners in the push for gender equality and for eliminating school-related gender-based violence.

Engage Boys and Men

There is a growing consensus about the need to engage men in the push for gender equity because definitions of masculinity are often what lead boys and men to view women as less than equal (Barker 2003; Buscher 2005; Ricardo et al. 2010; Van der Gaag 2011). Programs that engage boys and men in challenging these definitions of masculinity are therefore important in eliminating SRGBV against girls. Specifically, programs that are gender transformative—those that seek to transform gender roles and power dynamics in gender relations—are more likely to be effective than programs that are gender sensitive or gender neutral (Barker, Ricardo, and Nascimento 2007).

An emerging body of literature on engaging boys and men shows promising direction for interventions aimed at eliminating SRGBV. In a systematic review of fifty-seven interventions with men in the areas of GBV, sexual and reproductive health, and fatherhood, among others, researchers identified three good practices in engaging boys and men (Barker, Ricardo, and Nascimento 2007):

1. Group education
2. Community outreach, mobilization, and mass-media campaigns
3. Service-based programs

In terms of group education, the interventions that were most effective tended to include multiple sessions lasting 2 to 2.5 hours for 10 to 16 weeks, and built in time (a few days or a week) in between sessions for boys and men to reflect on or apply themes discussed in the sessions to real-life experiences (Barker, Ricardo, and Nascimento 2007). Just as girls' clubs with a well-trained facilitator can be an effective strategy for engaging girls in critical dialogue about healthy relationships, asserting their rights, attitudes toward gender and violence, or how to access social services, it appears that "boys' clubs" guided by trained facilitators also show promise as a space for engaging boys in critical dialogue about what it means to be a boy or a man, the connections between masculinity and violence against girls, and alternative nonviolent methods of communication, as well as what it means to be a victim of sexual, physical, or psychological GBV themselves (Parkes and Heslop 2013). Although, some research suggests that in contexts where mixed-gender clubs are appropriate, engaging girls and boys in these transformative discussions together can be more effective in promoting nonviolent norms of masculinity and less passive norms of femininity than engaging girls and boys or women and men separately (Peacock and Barker 2014; Reilly 2014).

The evidence also suggests that like girls' clubs, boys' clubs and similar group education interventions are not as effective in engendering changes in attitudes and behaviors related to GBV unless they are combined with other interventions like community outreach. In some cases, however, these other community-based interventions may be just as effective in reducing acts of violence as interventions through education.

- **Results from a quasi-experimental intervention in Ethiopia found that young men (between the ages of fifteen and twenty-four years) who participated in both interactive group education (GE) sessions and community engagement (CE) activities were twice as likely to show an increase in support for gender-equitable norms between baseline and endline measures compared with the control group.** However, the proportion of participants who reported incidences of intimate partner violence in the previous 6 months decreased similarly for both groups of men who received both group education and community engagement interventions (from 53 to 38 percent) and for men who received only the community engagement intervention (from 60 to 37 percent). The group education intervention took place over eight sessions, each for 2 to

3 hours long, conducted over four months at youth centers, and included activities like role playing, group discussions, and personal reflection. Groups were composed of about twenty participants and were facilitated by two to three peer educators. The community engagement intervention was conducted over 6 months and aimed to raise awareness and promote community dialogue on harmful norms by distributing monthly newsletters and leaflets, engaging in music and drama skits, holding monthly community workshops, and distributing condoms.

Pulerwitz, Julie, Lindsay Hughes, Manisha Mehta, Akiliu Kidanu, Fablo Verani, and Samuel Tewolde. 2015. "Changing Gender Norms and Reducing Intimate Partner Violence: Results from a Quasi-Experimental Intervention Study with Young Men in Ethiopia." *American Journal of Public Health* 105, no. 1: 132–37.

- **Plan International's Champions of Change (CoC) program helped male participants significantly improve their scores on the Gender Equitable Men Scale.** CoC is a part of Plan International's Because I Am a Girl Global Girls Innovation Program and is being implemented in four Latin American countries and Germany. It builds the capacity of male youth age fourteen to eighteen as peer educators for gender equality and girls' rights, and to engage other male and female youth in challenging harmful gender norms about masculinity in their schools and communities that discriminate against girls. An external evaluation of the program found that young men participating in the program showed more favorable attitudes toward sexual and reproductive rights and the use of violence.

May, Christina. N.d. *Evaluación del proyecto "Hombres jóvenes por la igualdad de género": El Salvador, Guatemala, República Dominicana, Honduras y Alemania*. Washington: Plan International.

Even though this is good evidence for participatory group education and youth engagement, it must be remembered that the challenge is sustaining these engagements within school systems facing structural deficits, resource constraints, and funding limitations, among other socioeconomic barriers that feed into SRGBV (Barker et al. 2012). More needs to be learned about the roles of boys and men as agents of change for gender equality. The good news is that more organizations are turning to this question. The "Engendering Men: Evidence on Routes to Gender Equality" (EMERGE) project, for example, is pooling together the research power of the Institute of Development Studies, Promundo-US, and the Sonke Gender Justice Network to build an open repository of evidence, lessons, and guidance for working with men (EMERGE 2015).

Instituto Promundo's Program H

Program H, which is named after the word *hombres* for *men* in Portuguese and Spanish, was launched by the Instituto Promundo in 2002 and is now in place in more than twenty-two countries. Although it was initially conceived in Brazil and then spread in Latin America, Program H has been adapted to local contexts around the world, including in India and parts of Sub-Saharan Africa. The program targets young men ages fifteen to twenty-four and aims to encourage critical reflection on rigid norms of masculinity. Program H involves a multifaceted approach that includes education, marketing campaigns, improved access to health clinic services, and evaluation using the GEM scale. Impact evaluations on a cohort of 750 men in Brazil using the GEM scale revealed a significant change in attitudes toward GBV, increased condom use, lower rates of sexually transmitted infections, fewer unplanned pregnancies, better use of government clinics, and improved partner negotiation skills in countries in Latin America and the Caribbean, as well as the Balkans, India, Tanzania, and Ethiopia. Young women interviewed in the study also confirmed improved gender attitudes on the part of their partners. Program H's success has led to its recognition by the World Bank, the United Nations Development Program, the United Nations Population Fund, UNICEF, and the World Health Organization. Today, Program M (for *mulher* or *woman* in Spanish and Portuguese) is also in place, working to empower women to gain a sense of agency and control over their lives.

Barker, Gary. 2003. "How Do We Know If Men Have Changed? Promoting and Measuring Attitude Change with Young Men: Lessons from Program H in Latin America." In *Expert Group Meeting on the Role of Men and Boys in Achieving Gender Equality*. Brasília: United Nations. http://www.un.org/womenwatch/daw/egm/men-boys2003/OP2-Barker.pdf.

Barker, Gary. 2006. "Engaging Boys and Men to Empower Girls: Reflections from Practice and Evidence of Impact." Document EGM/DVGC/2006/EP3, United Nations, New York. http://www.un.org/womenwatch/daw/egm/elim-disc-viol-girlchild/ExpertPapers/EP.3%20%20%20Barker.pdf.

Barker, Gary, Ravi Verma, John Crownover, Marcio Segundo, Vanessa Fonseca, Juan M. Contreras, Brian Heilman, and Peter Pawlak. 2012. "Boys and Education in the Global South: Emerging Vulnerabilities and New Opportunities for Promoting Changes in Gender Norms." *Thymos* 6, nos. 1–2: 137–50.

Nascimento, Marcos. 2006. "Working with Young Men to Promote Gender Equality: An Experience in Brazil and Latin America." Eldis. http://www.eldis.org/fulltext/working-with-young-men-Jan2006.pdf.

Ricardo, Christine, Marcos Nascimento, Vanessa Fonseca, and Marcio Segundo. 2010. *Program H and Program M: Engaging Young Men and Empowering Young Women to Promote Gender Equality and Health*. PAHO / Best Practices in Gender and Health. Washington: Pan American Health Organization and Promundo. http://promundo.org.br/wp-content/uploads/2014/12/Program-H-and-Program-M-Evaluation.pdf.

3 Secondary Education and Adolescent Girls

The third challenge for the next decade is ensuring that adolescent girls do not have their learning opportunities cut short. For millions of girls around the world, their dream is to continue with their education beyond primary level and through a full course of schooling. Secondary education provides high returns and an important pathway to a better future. Girls around the world are not lacking in ambition, rather political leadership and funding priorities must be aligned to meet their aspirations. As discussed in deetail in chapter 4, at times this will include ensuring girls have strong beginnings through quality early childhood development and successful early primary grades. Girls can only make it to secondary school if they successfully finish primary school. At other times, the transition from primary to lower secondary and beyond must be the focus of attention. This transition usually coincides with the time girls are maturing into adolescence and facing a host of life changes both physically and socially.

> "We know that if you get girls into schools and keep them there, you can change the course of a nation."
>
> *Her Majesty Queen Rania Al-Abdullah of Jordan, 2007*

Additionally, the push to ensure a full course of schooling for girls, we do not want to forget the adolescent girls for whom the best solution is not formal secondary school but an alternative route to learning and enrichment. Some of the most marginalized adolescent girls are those who have never been to school, have been forced into child labor, or trafficked, and for whom sitting with younger children in a primary classroom may not be feasible, desirable, or allowed by school regulations. The education community should not give up on these girls. These adolescent girls have a right, like all other girls, to learn, grow, and develop to their full potential.

The Goal of Universal Secondary Education for Girls

As mentioned in chapter 1, the Millennium Development Goals' ambition for universal primary education was simultaneously the world's most ambitious and pathetic goal (Sperling 2006b). It was ambitious because reaching this goal in just fifteen years—or even making the substantial progress that has been made so far—required a momentous global effort. And yet it was also pathetic, because even when we had to speak to groups of children about the MDGs, most of us were left speechless when a child asked, "why only primary education?" There is no good answer, other than a lack of will and resources. Certainly, as we observe the pace of technological change and globalization's impact in even developing nations, the question of why the global community should aspire to only primary education for girls is even more striking. Although honorable policymakers and experts may disagree on exactly how many years beyond primary school should constitute universal secondary education, looking forward from 2015, there is now a growing consensus that the aspiration must be nothing less than a meaningful and universal full course of schooling from early childhood through secondary education for all girls and boys. This vision was reflected simply, yet so powerfully by a student herself. In her Nobel Prize acceptance speech Malala argued:

> "The world can no longer accept that basic education is enough. Why do leaders accept that for children in developing countries, only basic literacy is sufficient, when their own children do homework in Algebra, Mathematics, Science and Physics? Leaders must seize this opportunity to guarantee a free, high-quality, primary *and* secondary education for every child. Some will say this is impractical, or too expensive, or too hard. Or maybe even impossible. But it is time the world thinks bigger."

The fact is that though much of the policy focus during the last couple of decades has been on what works to attain access and a high quality basic education, many of the seminal studies on returns to education found their greatest weight in the impact of secondary education, especially for girls (Colclough et al. 2009; Patrinos 2008; Psacharopoulos and Patrinos 2004; UNESCO 2012b).

- **Impact of secondary education on wages**: Many of the seminal studies documenting the impact of girls' education on growth involved secondary education. It was secondary education for girls where the Yale University economist Paul Shultz found especially larger returns of 15 to 25 percent for investment in girls' education as opposed to boys' education.

  Schultz, T. Paul. 2002. "Why Governments Should Invest More to Educate Girls." *World Development* 30, no. 2: 207–25.

"Returns to Women's Schooling." In *Women's Education in Developing Countries: Barriers, Benefits, and Policy*, edited by Elizabeth King and M. Anne Hill. Baltimore: Johns Hopkins University Press.

Schultz, T. Paul. 1992. "Investments in Schooling and Health of Women and Men: Quantities and Returns." Paper prepared for Conference on Women's Human Capital and Development, May, Bellagio, Italy.

Schultz, T. Paul. 1995. *Investment in Women's Human Capital.* Chicago: University of Chicago Press.

- **Impact of girls' secondary education on national income**: In their seminal 100-country study linking economic growth to national income growth, David Dollar and Roberta Gatti found that it was increasing the share of women with *secondary education* by 1 percentage point that boosted annual per capita income growth by 0.3 percentage point, on average.

  Dollar, David, and Roberta Gatti. 1999. *Gender Inequality, Income, and Growth: Are Good Times Good for Women?* Working Paper 1 for *Policy Research Report on Gender and Development*. Washington: World Bank.

- **Impact of girls' secondary education on creating smaller, more sustainable families**: Another important early study, written by Laura Raney and K. Subbarao, looking at women in sixty-five low- and middle-income countries found that it was doubling the proportion of women *with a secondary education* that would reduce average fertility rates from 5.3 to 3.9 children per woman. This study of secondary education led the authors to conclude that "the expansion of *female secondary education* may be the best single policy for achieving substantial reductions in fertility" (emphasis added).

  Subbarao, K., and Laura Raney. 1995. "Social Gains from Female Education." *Economic Development and Cultural Change* 44, no. 1: 105–28.

- **Impact of secondary education and BRAC's conditional cash transfers:** The largest and best-known scholarship program for girls in low-income countries is Bangladesh's national program for stipends for girls in *secondary school* in rural areas. The program began in 1982 through the Bangladesh Rural Action Committee (BRAC) program; it lifted girls' enrollment to almost double the national average. BRAC was first scaled up by the national government to cover one-fourth of all administrative districts. During the first five years that the program ran in pilot areas, girls' enrollment in grades 6–10 rose from 27 to 44 percent, almost double the national average. Under popular pressure, in 1992 the Bangladesh government eliminated girls' tuition and extended the stipend program to all rural areas nationwide. Girls' and boys' enrollment climbed to 55–60 percent, but girls' enrollment climbed faster than boys'.

World Bank. 2001. *Engendering Development through Gender Equality in Rights, Resources, and Voice.* World Bank Policy Research Report. New York: Oxford University Press.

Khandkher, S., and Mark Pitt. 2003. "Subsidy to Promote Girls' Secondary Education: The Female Stipend Program in Bangladesh." Washington: World Bank.

- **More recent evidence further demonstrates the high returns from secondary education for girls**: Based on an analysis of forty-six of the world's poorest countries, UNESCO found that if an additional 75 percent of fifteen-year-olds in developing countries reached the lowest benchmark for mathematics on the OECD's Program for International Student Assessment, 104 million more people who currently live on less than $1.25 per day would be lifted out of extreme poverty. Long-run economic growth would dramatically increase by 2.1 percentage points above baseline trends. This means that for every $1 invested in education, between $10 and $15 would be generated through an economic growth premium over a working lifetime of eighteen to twenty-two years.

- **Secondary education for girls and inequality:** Secondary education is a tipping point in terms of reproducing or transforming inequalities. According to UNESCO, secondary education has a dual function: "providing skills for early employment for some, selecting and preparing others for further education, based on their interests and academic ability. If disadvantaged youth are to have similar chances as youth from rich backgrounds to gain access to good jobs on the basis of merit and not privilege, secondary education has to be made more equitable and more inclusive, offering the widest possible range of opportunities in order to meet young people's differing abilities, interests, and backgrounds."

UNESCO. 2012b. *Youth and Skills: Putting Education to Work—EFA Global Monitoring Report 2012.* Paris: UNESCO, 203-4, 229.

- **National experiments in Nigeria, Tanzania, and Turkey have shown clear evidence of benefits from girls' secondary education**: In an endline analysis of a special initiative between ActionAid and local NGOs in Nigeria and Tanzania to transform the education of girls, researchers found that mean girls' empowerment index in both countries is significantly higher for girls at the junior secondary level than at the primary level. The researchers argue that "this gives strong support to arguments to extend global and national policy demands relating to the period girls remain in formal schooling to at least nine years, as it indicates that for girls living in poverty those who are in junior secondary school are more knowledgeable about their rights, risks associated with HIV and more confident to challenge gender-based violence than girls from the same contexts who have only primary schooling."

> Unterhalter, Elaine, and Jo Heslop. 2012. *Transforming Education for Girls in Nigeria and Tanzania: A Cross-Country Analysis of Endline Research Studies.* Washington: ActionAid, 8.

- **In Turkey, where in 1997 a law extended the duration of compulsory schooling from five to eight years, not only were girls able to complete more schooling, but also the positive spillover effects included a substantial delay in the age of marriage and first birth.** The probability of marriage by the age of sixteen fell by 44 percent, and the probability of first birth fell by 36 percent. More significantly, these effects of the new compulsory schooling policy on marriage and first birth persist more than a year after most girls complete the new compulsory schooling, suggesting that girls are benefiting from the investment in their human capital in some way that leads them to delay marriage even after they have completed school. More research is needed, however, to understand why girls or their families are choosing to delay marriage.

> Tayfur, Meltem Dayioglu, Murat G. Kirdar, and Ismet Koc. 2011. *The Effect of Compulsory Schooling Laws on Teenage Marriage and Births in Turkey.* IZA Discussion Paper 5887. Bonn: Institute for the Study of Labor. http://ftp.iza.org/dp5887.pdf.

Walk before you run, but aim to run: The new goal of universal secondary education for girls and boys is no way meant to deemphasize primary education or the importance of early childhood development; it is clear that a high-quality pre-primary and primary education has a positive impact on economic growth and health and helps children experience childhood. And what is more, you cannot walk before you run, or reach secondary school if you have not attended and completed primary school.

There is no question that this will require innovation, resources, and careful planning. Even in developing nations that have moved to free primary education, fees are still often charged for secondary school. It will also require more investment in teaching and teachers to ensure they have the capacity to teach at higher levels to older students. This means that national policymakers must commit to better teacher recruitment, teacher training, and teaching and learning resources. To achieve this, policymakers and practitioners need additional studies directed not just at the benefits of secondary education for girls but also at the precise interventions that are most effective in encouraging both quality and completion in secondary schools for girls. Both policymakers and academics also need to focus on policy solutions to girl's secondary education, from teacher policies, to the most effective conditional cash transfers or stipends to ultimately free and compulsory secondary education. This must be at the top of the post-2015 global education agenda, especially for girls.

The Case for Investing in Basic Education plus Upper Secondary Education

While perhaps commons sense, there are several important reasons for continuing to invest in basic education while at the same time expanding to secondary. Several economists put forward a clear argument for why we should continue investing in a high-quality basic education *in addition to* increasing investment in secondary education:

1. A high-quality primary education is a necessary first step for girls to access higher education opportunities.

2. A high-quality primary education is a girl's right.

3. Estimates of returns to education are based primarily using wages; however, wage-earning workers constitute a small fraction of the total workforce in many developing countries. Research shows that women occupy most of the informal labor market; for them, returns to basic education might be greater.

4. Basic education has many positive nonmarket spillover effects whose monetary impact is hard to define, including reductions in fertility and mortality, empowerment, lower crime, and democratic participation.

Colclough, C., G. Kingdon, and H. A. Patrinos. 2009. *The Pattern of Returns to Education and Its Implications*. Policy Brief 4. Cambridge: Research Consortium on Educational Outcomes and Poverty.

Strategies for Out-of-School and Marginalized Adolescent Girls

This section adds "adolescent girls" because in the push for secondary education for girls, we do not want to forget or leave behind those girls who have dropped out, been forced into child labor, trafficked, suffer from disabilities, or never had the chance to start an education with their age group—especially as there are promising strategies that have been shown to provide alternative paths for such adolescent girls.

"I dream for a world which is free of child labour, a world in which every child goes to school. A world in which every child gets his rights."

Kailash Satyarthi, Indian child rights activist, founder of Bachpan Bachao Andolan, and Nobel Peace Prize Laureate

---

What Do We Know About Schooling and Girl Child Labor?

One hundred sixty eight million children around the world are forced into child labor, 85 million of whom are in hazardous work (ILO-IPEC 2013). The International Labor Organization's (ILO's) International Program for the Elimination of Child Labor defines child labor as "work that deprives children of their childhood, their potential and their dignity, and that is harmful to physical and mental development." It may interfere with their schooling in three ways: by depriving them of the opportunity to attend school, by obliging them to leave school prematurely, or by requiring them to combine school and work. Included in this definition are the worst forms of child labor, known as hazardous work—including things that constitute modern day slavery like trafficking, child prostitution, and bondage—where the nature of or the conditions in which the work is carried out jeopardize the child's physical, mental, or moral well-being (ILO 2015).

Girls are particularly vulnerable because their work is often hidden, undervalued, and unpaid; the ILO estimates that more than 75 percent of girl child laborers are unpaid family members, compared with 64 percent of boy child laborers (Diallo, Etienne, and Mehran 2013). Combined with the expectation that they perform household chores in their own home, girl child laborers face a double burden that further interferes with their schooling. Surveys indicate that 10 percent of girls age five to fourteen years perform household chores for 28 hours or more per week—

twice as high as the percentage of boys. These girls' attendance rate was 25 percent lower than that of girls who perform household chores for less than 14 hours a week, showing the difficulty of combining education with long hours of work (ILO 2009). The ILO's resource kit and SCREAM (Supporting Children's Rights through Education, the Arts, and the Media) Stop Child Labor Pack offer policymakers, practitioners, and educators in both formal and nonformal education settings ways to harness education policy to mitigate against the causes and consequences of child labor, especially for girls (IPEC 2009).

For girls in the worst forms of hazardous labor, especially child trafficking, efforts must not only be made to rescue victims, but also to provide them with rehabilitation and counseling services and the educational opportunities needed to reintegrate into their communities and to go from victim to survivor to leader. In the case of child sex trafficking, it is critical to ensure that public officials see the children as victims of rape by adults and not as criminals shut out from the health, education, and public services they need to start a new path (Abner et al. 2013). A number of organizations, programs, and initiatives work to combat child trafficking, either working directly with victims or by educating communities on how to identify and prevent child trafficking and other forms of child labor, including World Education's Combating Child Trafficking through Education project in Benin and its Brighter Futures Program in Nepal, as well as the ILO's International Training Center, and the UN Global Initiative to Fight Human Trafficking.

Return-to-School Policies

- **For schoolgirls who become pregnant, changes in school policies that allow them to return to school after childbirth is a policy mechanism that should be pursued to ensure that marginalized and vulnerable girls can complete secondary school.** Although we do not know how many girls who become pregnant while enrolled at school have actually taken advantage of these policies, we do know that negative social attitudes toward schoolgirl pregnancy have influenced current policies that either expel schoolgirls who become pregnant or discourage her from returning. A survey conducted by the Forum for African Women Educationalists in Zambia shows that a strategic combination of communication activities, legislative change, and local training for teachers and students can change social attitudes toward school reentry. FAWE found that though 69 percent of teachers were against school reentry for pregnant girls in 2001, 84 percent expressed a positive attitude after receiving training in 2004. Parental opposition to reentry also decreased, from 53 to 25 percent.

UNESCO. 2012b. *Youth and Skills: Putting Education to Work—EFA Global Monitoring Report 2012.* Paris: UNESCO.

- **A study that examined national policies on pregnancy in education systems in Africa concludes that expulsion policies symbolize overt violence against girls, while continuation policies provide the most opportunity for gender equity.** However, these policies need to explicitly challenge societal beliefs, values, and attitudes about pregnancy rituals involved after childbirth, and other traditional motherhood ideologies that could disable girls' mothers and perpetuate subtle forms of violence against them.

  Chilisa, Bagele. 2002. "National Policies on Pregnancy in Education Systems in Sub-Saharan Africa: The Case of Botswana. *Gender and Education* 14, no. 1: 21–35.

An Inclusive Education for Girls with Disabilities

Globally there are between 93 million and 150 million children with long-term physical, mental, intellectual, or sensory impairments; the majority are girls (UNICEF 2005; WHO 2011). Children with disabilities are some of society's most marginalized, invisible, and excluded groups, facing discrimination, stigmatization, neglect, and abuse; overlooked by policy and legislation; and barred from realizing their rights to education, healthcare, and sometimes even survival. Poverty, social isolation, and humanitarian emergencies further exacerbate their vulnerability and prevent them from accessing adequate social services and support (UNICEF 2013). A thirty-country study by Plan International (2013b) estimates that children with disabilities are 10 times less likely to attend school than their peers without disabilities. When they do attend, their level of schooling is below that of their peers.

Girls with disabilities—discriminated on the basis of their gender and ability—face even more obstacles and barriers to entering, staying in, and completing school. This translates into lower levels of literacy, greater barriers in finding and retaining employment, and severely limited opportunities to achieve their full potential and to develop the skills and competencies needed for a successful and productive adulthood (Walker 2013). Efforts to reach out-of-school and marginalized adolescent girls must include girls with disabilities.

The *2006 UN Convention on the Rights of Persons with Disabilities* established inclusive education as the key mechanism to deliver the right to education for girls and boys with disabilities. Inclusive education systems benefit all children by removing physical and educational barriers so that *all* children, regardless of ability, can access a high-quality education. Providing an inclusive education involves more than just integrating disabled boys and girls in schools and expecting the child to adapt to the system. Rather, inclusive education involves disabled children learning alongside their non-disabled peers and teachers using teaching methods and materials that are gender-sensitive, empower learners, celebrate diversity, combat discrimination, and promote more inclusive societies. In short, inclusive education ensures that the education system adapts to the child by transforming the cultures, policies, and practices of schools and communities to accommodate the differing needs of girls and boys with disabilities (Walker 2013; Schuelka and Johnstone 2011). It is based on the conviction that it is the responsibility of the regular education system to education all children (UNESCO 2005).

Nonformal Schooling

If barriers exist for girls to transition smoothly from primary to secondary education, then even more barriers exist that prevent girls who have fallen out of the education pipeline from returning to school. In the Population Council's detailed review of interventions to support adolescent girls, Cynthia Lloyd (2009, 10) explains that adolescent girls face particular hurdles because "the formal schooling system is designed to follow a set sequence of curricular material regardless of age, those who start late can find themselves sharing a classroom with younger children, a situation that often leads to early dropout, particularly for girls." Nonformal learning opportunities, including complementary remedial or accelerated learning programs and "second chance" alternative youth literacy or livelihood training, have been developed to address the misalignment between the learning trajectory of education systems and the developmental trajectory of youth in many developing countries.

Lloyd (2009) defines four key features that distinguish nonformal schools from formal schools: (1) They use a nonstandard curriculum, which often gives these educational platforms the freedom to test out alternative pedagogies and learning materials. (2) They follow a flexible grading system (rather than a set number of grades). And (3) they have a flexible calendar or hours, enabling those girls who either have missed out on entering school at the appropriate age or whose economic circumstances have prevented them from participating at the right pace to catch up and reenter the formal system at a later time. (4) Finally, they are not necessarily registered, licensed, or accredited, which can mean that schools are unencumbered by the structural barriers of standardization and regulation that make formal schooling inaccessible to marginalized populations. But it also means that students who complete these programs may have difficulty gaining entry to higher levels of education or obtaining jobs from employers who are unfamiliar with their program.

Although there has not been much empirical research investigating the impact of nonformal schooling on learning or identifying which components are effective in helping girls return to formal schooling (with some exceptions, like Gee 2015), we know that these opportunities are often the only educational pathway for marginalized and disadvantaged girls. Nonformal and second chance schooling are especially critical, considering that basic education is not always sufficient in preparing youth with the hard and soft skills needed for a successful, productive, and healthy adulthood.

Biruh Tesfa—Second Chance Schooling in Ethiopia

Established in 2006, Biruh Tesfa, or "bright future" in Amharic, aimed to deliver second chance schooling to out-of-school girls in the poorest urban areas of Ethiopia. By combining basic literacy training and life skills as well as wellness checkups delivered by female mentors in girls-only safe spaces (segmented by age), Biruh Tesfa illustrates how girls can be reconnected to educational pathways to better health and educational outcomes through government-implemented nonformal education programs. Run by the Ethiopia Ministry of Women, Children, and Youth Affairs in partnership with regional bureaus in program cities, safe spaces groups meet five days per week in school classrooms for 2 hours in the late afternoon to accommodate hours that girls are likely to be working in domestic service. Using the Ethiopia's Ministry of Education nonformal education curriculum, girls receive nonformal schooling for four days of the week, and on the fifth day receive life skills training on topics like communication, financial literacy, hygiene and menstruation, and violence. Girls participating in Biruh Tesfa also receive school materials, basic clothing, and sanitary napkins worth about $42.

Formal external evaluations of the program show that participation in formal schooling increased dramatically, by 38 percent. However, this increase was similar between experimental and control groups, which the researchers explain might be a result of a school reentry campaign targeted at out-of-school children by the Ministry of Education launched at about the same time as the Biruh Tesfa program. Nonetheless, in communities where Biruh Tesfa was implemented, attendance in nonformal schooling increased significantly, from 6 to 49 percent, compared with an increase from 5 to 12 percent in control communities, which the researchers conclude is due to the program, because 86 percent of those who reported attendance in nonformal education were participants in Biruh Tesfa.

Because the program was implemented at the same time as a nationwide government education campaign, it is difficult to determine whether gains made by students should be attributed to the program alone or to the overall improvement in values toward girls' education. Controlling for the government's education campaign, researchers attempt to estimate the effect of Biruh Tesfa by focusing on the learning outcomes of girls who had never been in the formal schooling system, in both the baseline and endline studies. With these controls in place, signs of improved test scores suggest that programs like Biruh Tesfa are a promising mechanism for delivering nonformal education to out-of-school girls. For example, girls in the experimental group who had never been to formal school but participated in Biruh Tesfa increased their mean numeracy score from 2.6 to 3.5 (out of a maximum of 9.0, $p < 0.001$), though similar improvements were not observed for girls in the control group who had never been to formal school at endline measurements.

In 2013, the program was expanded beyond Addis Ababa to twenty low-income areas on the outskirts of the city that have emerged due to Ethiopia's rapid urbanization. Powering Up Biruh Tesfa now reaches more than 3,000 young adolescent girls, 41 percent of whom are child domestic workers. The expanded model also includes a health voucher program to subsidize the cost of basic health services and medications at twelve participating public and private partner clinics. Girls can request a health voucher from their mentors, who also offer to accompany the girls. During the first six months of the expanded program, 487 health vouchers were issued to 320 participants, of whom 70 percent had never visited a health facility before.

Erulkar, A., A. Ferede, W. Girma, and W. Ambelu. 2013. "Valuation of 'Biruh Tesfa' (Bright Future) HIV Prevention Program for Vulnerable Girls in Ethiopia." *Vulnerable Child and Youth Studies* 8, no. 2: 182–92.

Erulkar, Annabel, and Girmay Medhin. 2014. *Evaluation of Health and Education Impacts of a Girls' Safe Spaces Program in Addis Ababa, Ethiopia.* Addis Ababa: Population Council.

Tostan—Nonformal Education in West and East Africa

Founded in 1991 as an NGO grounded in the principles of community-led development, Tostan's Community Empowerment Program provides a model of nonformal education for girls, many with no or very little education. Although not specifically targeted at girls, its adolescent and adult curricula have had an empowering effect on girls and women, who for many learn to speak up in class and community meetings for the first time about issues that influence their own futures and the well-being of their children, families, and communities. Classes are taught by facilitators who are from the same ethnic background as participants, and who draw upon participants' values and experiences. With the goals of "breaking through" and "spreading and sharing"—what Tostan means in Wolof, the most widely spoken African language in Senegal—facilitators discuss with participants issues of democracy, accountability, or conflict management, for example, with the aim of breaking through to new understandings of their situations that lead them to undertake social change that results in more socially and gender equitable practices.

Combining human rights education and participatory classroom activities, the curriculum has two complementary phases. During the first phase, called Kobi—a Mandinka word meaning "to prepare the field for planting"—classes focus on discussions on human rights to health and education, which are taught orally because most program participants cannot read or write. The interactive pedagogical approach motivates participants to examine their own values, beliefs, and norms about controversial issues affecting girls, for example, female genital cutting and early marriage. These particular discussions encouraged communities to critically engage with what it means for their daughters to have the right to bodily integrity or the right to education, and have led to community-wide efforts to abandon harmful practices like female genital mutilation/cutting and early marriage in thousands of communities across the region. During the second phase, called Aawde—a Fulani word meaning "to plant the seed"—classes shift to literacy and numeracy lessons to teach participants how to read and write in their own language, as well as small-project management training with the aim of economically empowering participants and communities.

Qualitative evaluations of Tostan's nonformal education programs indicate promising gains in women's knowledge of their rights, health and hygiene, and mathematics, for example, as well as in their confidence in their abilities and leadership aspirations. Data also indicate optimistic gains in the development of income-generating activities that improve living conditions in villages and in community support for girls' education. Since its beginnings in Senegal, the program is now being taught in twenty-two African languages in remote regions in eight countries in West and East Africa.

Kothari, Brij. 2014. "Better Late Than Never." In *Education and Skills 2.0: New Targets and Innovative Approaches*, edited by World Economic Forum. Geneva: World Economic Forum.

Nafissatou, J. Diop, Amadou Moreau, and Helene Benga. 2008. *Evaluation of the Long-Term Impact of the TOSTAN Programme on the Abandonment of FGM/C and Early Marriage: Results from a Qualitative Study in Senegal.* Dakar: Population Council. http://www.popcouncil.org/uploads/pdfs/frontiers/FR_FinalReports/Senegal_TOSTAN_EarlyMarriage.pdf.

Harness Technology to Maximize Learning Opportunities

For those who drop out of school before achieving functional literacy and for those girls whose schooling is interrupted, the innovative interventions briefly described here, which take advantage of basic technology as well as information and communications technology (ICT), appear to be promising not just for improving functional literacy but also for helping to sustain gains made by incorporating literacy and numeracy into girls' and boys' everyday lives.

Evidence about the usefulness of mobile technology to enhance educational quality and improve educational access for marginalized girls is only just beginning to emerge (see, e.g., the recent landscape reviews of mobile education for reading, numeracy, and youth workforce development commissioned by the Education Alliance: Wagner 2014; Spencer-Smith and Roberts 2014; and Raftree 2015). Already, we are starting to see promising evidence that suggests access to technology not only can help reach hard-to-reach girls and women, but that gains in literacy and numeracy through mobile learning could also signal significant increases in girls' and women's autonomy in their villages, their ability to participate in income-generating activities, and thus their interhousehold bargaining power (UNESCO 2015a). And, with their digital literacy and ICT skills, girls and women would have increased access to new social networks and to new opportunities in the public sphere, as well as to online information about education or business services (Cummings and O'Neil 2015).

- **Mobile telephones help girls catch up on missed schooling in Kenya.** In Kenya, mobile phones appear to be a promising tool to help mediate interrupted school attendance for adolescent girls by providing learners with access to missed lessons or to current information when textbooks are scarce, outdated, or irrelevant. In this particular case study, girls' self-directed educational use of mobile phones was due to traditional means of mediating school interruption, like seeking the assistance of a friend or studying on one's own, were not feasible for girls in contexts where walking to a friend's home in the evening is not safe or acceptable or when accessing information on what was learned during the school day is difficult. Findings suggest that mobile use for learning helps empower girl learners by facilitating educational opportunities that would otherwise be unobtainable. Furthermore, accessing information through the Internet via mobile phones is easier and sometimes cheaper than accessing information via the Internet from an unreliable Internet connection through a

Technology and Education

Although technology enthusiasts have long advocated the integration of technology in education in developing countries, the rapid expansion of ICT has recently caught the attention of educationalists seeking to identify innovative and inexpensive ways to advance literacy and numeracy for some of the world's most disadvantaged girls and boys, and women and men:

- *e-Learning*: Electronic learning, often a form of distance education, typically includes delivering a course, program, or training via the computer and the Internet. Its processes of information delivery, learning objectives, and methods of assessment are similar to those of a traditional classroom, albeit conducted online.

- *m-Learning*: Mobile learning refers to mobile education through the use of mobile technologies like mobile phones, tablets, and other handheld electronic devices. It is defined by the mobility of the learner, where learning takes place across a variety of contexts, information is accessed at the moment it is needed, and information is often applied immediately.

Educationalists have also leveraged existing technology, like radio and television, to support student learning and classroom instruction by delivering supplemental material to marginalized communities. These initiatives have typically taken the form of separate educational stations or channels that broadcast round-the-clock educational programming, to prerecorded programming that teachers can use in the classroom, to infusing literacy components into existing broadcast entertainment.

Winthrop, Rebecca, and Marshall S. Smith. 2012. *A New Face of Education: Bringing Technology into the Classroom in the Developing World*. Brooke Shearer Working Paper Series. Washington: Brookings Institution.

computer at school—which one must first receive permission to use—or from textbooks available in the school library—which they may not have priority to use depending on their status at school.

Zelezny-Green, Ronda. 2014. "She Called, She Googled, She Knew: Girls' Secondary Education, Interrupted School Attendance, and Educational Use of Mobile Phones in Nairobi." *Gender and Development* 22, no. 1: 63–74..

- **Learning by mobile phones helped boost girls and women's literacy in rural Senegal.** The Jokko Initiative is part of Tostan's Community Empowerment Program, which includes a new 150-hour Mobile Phone Literacy for Empowerment module. The pilot initiative in fifteen villages attempts to improve literacy and numeracy outcomes by adding an SMS Community Forum to the mobile phone literacy course. Community members can use this forum to send free SMS text messages to other members to practice their literacy and numeracy skills. The initiative was also designed to promote social interaction and empowerment among girls and women. Based on follow-up surveys conducted after the pilot study, it appears that the SMS Community Forum helped significantly improve the literacy and numeracy of participants with a combined literacy/numeracy score of 16.85, compared with a combined score of 14.85 for the five control villages that did not have access to the forums ($p <$ 0.02). Moreover, the initiative had large effects on girls and women, who reversed the illiteracy trends in their villages, lifting a majority of their scores from none to low literacy to medium to high literacy.

Beltramo, Theresa, and David Levine. 2012. *Do SMS Text Messaging and SMS Community Forums Improve Outcomes of Adult and Adolescent Literacy Programs? Evidence from the Jokko Initiative in Senegal.* CEGA Working Paper 15. Berkeley: Center for Effective Global Action at University of California

Planet Read—Using TV Subtitles to Boost Literacy for Millions in India

In Gujarat State of India, where Bollywood film-based entertainment and television command an overwhelming share of media consumption for the average household, same-language subtitling (SLS) has proven to be a simple strategy for infusing reading practice into day-to-day entertainment. By subtitling audiovisual content word-for-word of film song lyrics, and designing the color of subtitles to change in perfect timing with the songs, a neoliterate person can identify the individual word being sung.

The idea behind SLS interventions, as explained by Brij Kothari, the primary researcher behind the use of SLS on mainstream television for mass literacy in India, is this: "For whatever reason, if a child drops out of school, say before becoming functionally literate, inescapable reading practice would still continue as a by-product of entertainment. Those in their youth and adulthood who did not attain functional literacy but still have cognitive traces of letter familiarity—perhaps dormant through disuse—can be expected to experience a revival through exposure, effortless reinforcement and steady improvement of literacy skills" (Kothari 2014, 54). Kothari's research demonstrates that integrating reading into everyday entertainment in India—especially when combined with schooling, formal or nonformal—can be an effective and highly cost-effective pathway for increasing the number of neoliterate or partially literate children, adolescents, and adults to continue to practice, maintain, and improve their reading skills to a higher functioning level. Kothari estimates that the cost of subtitling one 30-minute program of songs per week is approximately $23,000. Thus, the cost of giving 325 million neoliterates in Gujarat half an hour of reading practice through SLS on television equals $0.0066 per person per year, compared with the $0.75 per person per year spent on postliteracy or continuing education centers that reach about 2.4 percent of Gujarat's neoliterate population.

For 6 months in 1999, the first randomized control study of the impact of SLS on literacy was conducted with three groups of children in the State of Gujarat in a government-run public school serving low-income children. The children were primarily children of migrants from the states of Madhya Pradesh, Rajasthan, and rural Gujarat who now lived in nearby slums and generally work as laborers, hawkers, or small traders. The school progressed children automatically from grade to grade regardless of scores on examinations, meaning that it is not uncommon to find children in grades 4 and 5 who are functionally illiterate. In the study, the Subtitle group was regularly exposed to 30 minutes of film songs with SLS, the Without Subtitle group saw the songs without subtitles, and the control group saw nothing. After three months of the intervention, the Subtitle group was found to have higher decoding skills, or the ability to convert text into sound, than the Without Subtitle and control groups. Notably, girls in the Subtitle group improved the most out of all participants.

In a follow-up study conducted by the Nielsen-ORG Center for Social Research, findings show that exposure to 30 minutes of SLS per week in parallel with five years of schooling increased the functional literacy rate of rural children from 25 percent to 56 percent. Moreover, 25 percent of the control group remained illiterate, even after five years of schooling; whereas only 12 percent of the treatment group remained illiterate. Taken together, exposure to SLS more than doubled the percentage of children who became good readers and halved the percentage of children who remained illiterate, demonstrating that children who acquire reading skills in school and practice reading at home are able to maintain and improve their literacy skills. This has tremendous implications for marginalized girls whose formal schooling may be interrupted and/or of low quality.

Kothari, Brij. 2014. "Better Late Than Never." In *Education and Skills 2.0: New Targets and Innovative Approaches*, edited by World Economic Forum. Geneva: World Economic Forum.

Kothari, Brij, Avinash Pandey, and Amita R. Chudgar. 2004. "Reading Out of the "Idiot Box": Same-Language Subtitling on Television in India." *Information Technologies and International Development* 2, no. 1: 23–44.

Kothari, Brij, Joe Takeda, Ashok Joshi, and Avinash Pandey. 2002. *Same Language Subtitling: A Butterfly for Literacy?* Working Paper 2001-07-02. Ahmedabad: Indian Institute of Management.

Planet Read. N.d. "Same-Language Subtitling (SLS) Project: Some Key Research Findings." Unpublished project document. http://www.planetread.org/pdf/Research%20Summary_SLS.

Successful Transitions: Bridges from School to Work

The fourth challenge for the next decade is building girls stronger bridges from school to work. This means focusing not only on girls' successful transitions to work and livelihood after leaving school but also improving her employment outcomes, including wages and the nature of her work. Although, as documented in chapters 2 and 3, there are enormous health and family gains from girls and future mothers being educated, ensuring that girls and women have the opportunity to turn their skills into jobs that produce income for themselves and their families is critical for addressing poverty and women's empowerment and for showing those who doubt the benefit of educating girls the tangible economic benefits that it can bring. Certainly, education is only one piece of the puzzle; even girls who complete secondary education can face job challenges in developing nations when there are significant shortages of job openings and where gender discrimination and labor market segmentation by gender severely limits job opportunities across-the-board, but especially for women. Yet, these barriers are all the more reason that the emphasis on girls' education needs to focus on how to build better pathways and bridges to the job market through access to high-quality learning opportunities, apprenticeships, entrepreneurial education, job training, and career counseling, and, where needed, appropriate forms of special efforts and affirmative action to help women overcome gender discrimination in the workplace.

Stronger Bridges to Work Improve Perceived Rates of Return and Thus Investment in Girls' Education

One problem that academics and practitioners have worked to solve is the misperception by both parents and policymakers that educating girls, especially at the secondary level, will have high opportunity costs but low returns. Two specific interventions in Madagascar and India showed that using information to demonstrate the degree that education could create job opportunities for women positively influenced the decision to invest in education for girls, including by girls themselves.

- **Changing Perceptions on the Returns to Education in Madagascar**: In Madagascar, for example, an intervention that provided parents and students with statistics on the average earnings associated with each additional level of education dramatically improved perceptions of the returns to education. This shift in perceived returns not only translated into increased investments by parents in their children's education, but also improved average test scores of students by 0.2 standard deviation and improved attendance by 3.5 percentage points, compared with the control group. Of note is that for those in the intervention group whose initial perceived returns were below the statistics (those whose perceptions changed the most due to the intervention), test scores improved even more, by 0.37 standard deviation.

Nguyen, Trang. 2008. "Information, Role Models and Perceived Returns to Education: Experimental Evidence from Madagascar." Abdul Latif Jameel Poverty Action Lab, Cambridge, Mass. http://www.povertyactionlab.org/doc/information-role-models-and-perceived-returns-education.

- **Business Process Outsourcing recruiting services in India:** Similarly, an experiment in India provided three years of Business Process Outsourcing recruiting services to girls age fifteen to twenty-one in randomly selected rural villages, where there was limited awareness of the recent rapid expansion of jobs in this field or knowledge about how to access them. The jobs generally had high educational requirements, were well-paid, and preferred female employees. By connecting women to recruiters (the jobs were not guaranteed), the intervention was designed to change awareness of the returns to human capital investment. As expected, the cohort of fifteen- to twenty-one-year-old women was significantly more likely to enroll in computer or English language courses. Moreover, they were more likely to enroll in private, for-fee training institutes, demonstrating their willingness to invest in career-building skills when employment opportunities are made available. The intervention also saw significant spillover effects; women in the fifteen- to twenty-one-year-old cohort, the peak age range for marriage and initiation of childbearing in rural India, were 5 to 6 percentage points less likely to get married or to have given birth during the three-year period of the intervention. In addition, girls age five to fifteen in treatment villages were 3 to 5 percentage points more likely to be in school as well, and to have a higher Body Mass Index, reflecting greater investment made in their education, health, and nutrition as well.

Jensen, Robert T. 2010. *Economic Opportunities and Gender Differences in Human Capital: Experimental Evidence for India.* NBER Working Paper 16021. Cambridge, Mass.: National Bureau of Economic Research.

Jensen, Robert T. 2012. "Do Labor Market Opportunities Affect Young Women's Work and Family Decisions? Experimental Evidence from India." *Quarterly Journal of Economics* 127, no. 2: 753–92.

- **New local technology jobs created more demand for education for girls:** In another study in India, researchers found that the introduction of Information Technology Enabled Services (ITES) firms to a town increased school enrollment, especially in English-language schools, in the following year between 4 and 7 percent, an effect that is comparable to other interventions designed to increase school enrollment like cash transfers. Researchers also found that the introduction of ITES firms caused 26 percent of out-of-school children to enroll in school. The effects were similar for girls and boys, which the researchers explained was due to the fact that these particular firms did not display a preference for female labor.

  Oster, Emily, and M. Bryce Millet. 2010. "Do IT Service Centers Promote School Enrollment? Evidence from India." *Journal of Development Economics* 104: 123–35.

These examples illustrate how both the supply of jobs—and the perceived impact that the education of girls would have on achieving jobs—intersects with the demand side for girls' education, and how interventions aimed at supporting girls' transitions to the workforce should pay attention to both. Here, providing information that improves perceived expected returns to education (especially secondary education) not only provides parents with extra incentives to invest in their children's education but also may help raise the aspirations and motivations of youth to continue schooling and to study hard, as demonstrated above by students' improved attendance and test scores. At the same time, the expansion of economic opportunities for women can have significant effects; higher demand for female labor and the prospects of higher returns can contribute to higher investment in girls' education (Jensen 2010).

Align Curricula with the World of Work

Although aligning curricula and credentials with existing and future job openings is a hot-button labor market issue in advanced economies like the United States, aligning curricula with the world of work may be even more essential for rural girls and women in developing nations, where too often formal education can be irrelevant to the needs of a rural economy. Moreover, the quality of education in rural areas tends to be challenged by poor infrastructure, inadequate resources, and a lack of qualified teachers; and employment prospects for rural women tend to be in unstable, low-wage jobs. Thus, rural women start from a position of disadvantage, even if they are able to continue to and complete secondary school (UNESCO 2012b).

For youth in urban areas, aligning curricula with the world of work means recognizing that many youth are employed in the informal sector—often by a small- or medium-sized family—or in microenterprises that range from subsistence activities to street vending, from handicrafts or garment-making to waste-picking. However, this does not reduce the demand for education; on the contrary, studies have shown that education can enhance earnings in the informal sector and that skills training is particularly important. For an urban woman, however, discriminatory social norms and cultural barriers may limit their access to work-related learning opportunities, keeping her just out of reach of seeing the returns to her schooling (UNESCO 2012b).

Interventions attempting to address the challenges of curricular irrelevance and linkages between schooling and work have largely been the focus of the youth workforce development community. However, these initiatives tend to target adolescent youth or young adults who have left school or who are in upper secondary school and have already been separated into academic or vocational streams. More work is still needed to identify ways to improve the quality of education, including the relevance of curricula and the development of twenty-first-century skills, including the ability to innovate (ILO 2013), much earlier in primary and lower secondary school.

Although the nature of tomorrow's labor market is unpredictable, policymakers and practitioners still need to be forward looking and help prepare girls and boys. Reallocating aid for skills development or engaging public and private sector actors in curricular reform are possible ways of realigning curricula and the world of work in earlier levels of school. For upper secondary school, strategies might include diversifying curricula to cater to a wider range of interests, abilities, and future economies (e.g., the green economy); engaging alternative providers of training (e.g., in agribusiness or small-business development for rural or low-growth areas); offering more work-based learning opportunities like apprenticeships and internships; and creating stronger linkages with the informal sector (IEG 2013; UNESCO 2012b). These strategies and others remain to be investigated, especially their impact on marginalized girls' transitions to the workforce.

Technical Training, On-the-Job Training, and Apprenticeships

Studies point to the positive impact of technical and vocational training on girls and women: marked improvement in employment and earnings, as well as in noneconomic outcomes like delayed pregnancy, fewer numbers of desired children, increased educational and career aspirations, and increased social empowerment, such as decisionmaking, self-confidence, and technical skills and capabilities (see, e.g., Aslam and Rawal 2013). Yet, though the literature points more definitively to positive employment outcomes for men who participate in practical, work-related education pathways like internships, job-shadowing, and on-the-job training (OECD 2015b), the literature is more mixed for women. This implies that both policy and academic work needs to be done to ensure that some of the most promising pathways from school to work are indeed working for young women as well as men:

- **Classroom and on-the-job training are effective in helping disadvantaged Colombian youth find work**: The Jóvenes en Acción (Youth in Action) program in Colombia provided disadvantaged youth between eighteen and twenty-five years who were either unemployed or working informally with three months of classroom training and three months of on-the-job training. Classroom training was provided by private training institutions, and on-the-job training was provided by legally registered companies, all of which had to participate in a bidding process to be able to participate. Companies also provided unpaid internships to participants. Jóvenes en Acción provided cash transfers of $2.20 per day to male and female participants without young children to cover transportation and lunch. Female participants with children under seven years of age were given transfers of $3.00 to cover transportation, lunch, and child care expenses. All transfers were conditional upon participating in the program. During its four years of implementation (2001–5), Jóvenes en Acción reached more than 80,000 youth. Women who were randomly selected for training experienced strong positive program effects: specifically, their probability of being in paid employment rose by 7 percent, the number of hours worked per week increased by almost 3 hours, and their wages increased by nearly 20 percent. The impact on employment formality improved significantly for both trained women and men: Women's likelihood of holding a formal contract increased by 8 percent, and their likelihood of being in formal employment increased by 7 percent, compared with increases of 6 percent and 5 percent for men, respectively. Finally, women's formal wages increased 33 percent, compared with 23 percent for men.

Attanasio, Orazio, Adriana Kugler, and Costas Meghir. 2011. "Subsidizing Vocational Training for Disadvantaged Youth in Colombia: Evidence from a Randomized Trial." *American Economic Journal: Applied Economics* 3: 188–220.

- **Technical training and life skills program boosted employment for Liberian young women by 47 percent:** Similarly, in Liberia, the Economic Empowerment of Adolescent Girls and Young Women (EPAG) project had positive outcomes for women between sixteen and twenty-seven years. Launched by the Liberian Ministry of Gender and Development in 2009, EPAG combined six months of classroom-based technical and life skills training, with a focus on skills with high market demand, followed by six months of follow-up support to facilitate participants' transition to productive work, whether in wage employment or self-employment. Compared with a control group of nonparticipants, EPAG participants increased employment by 47 percent and earnings by 80 percent, and showed improvements in various empowerment measures (e.g., access to and control over money). For example, EPAG participants had an average savings of $35 more than the control group. Moreover, 80 percent of EPAG graduates who were engaged in income-generating activities reported that they controlled the money they earned, an increase of 8 percentage points from earlier measurements.

Adoho, Franck, Shubha Chakravarty, Dala T. Korkoya, Mattias Lundberg, and Afia Tasneem. 2014. *Impact of an Adolescent Girls' Employment Program: The EPAG Project in Liberia.* Washington: World Bank Africa Region Poverty Reduction and Economic Management Unit.

- **An example of how apprenticeships must be made more effective for young women: Malawi case study**. In Malawi, a program designed to provide apprenticeships rather than classroom-based training had less positive effects on women's employment outcomes. Targeting a wider age range (fifteen to twenty-four years), the program assigned 1,900 youth from twenty-eight districts to be apprentices to master craftspeople in their areas of interest. Results from the treatment group (those who entered the program four months earlier) saw similar gains in self-reported skills between trained women and men. However, beyond that, the program appeared to benefit men more; men spent more time in training and continued to invest in their human capital development after completing the program, with, on average, 11 extra hours in further skills development in the month after training. And men were three times as likely to receive a paid job offer from the master craftsperson following the training period. Women, however, did not experience a similar treatment effect. Researchers did, however, observe other benefits for female trainees. For example, women in the treatment group were 7 percentage points less likely to have given birth in the past year, a significant decrease compared with the members of the control group, of whom 19 percent had given birth.

- **Financial support for women and lower costs could improve apprenticeships**: The study conducted on the apprenticeship program in Malawi found that participation in the program was more costly for women than for men, and that the stipends provided for the participants were not sufficient. Women were more likely to draw from their savings to participate, sometimes as much as $38, which is a substantial amount for this population. This and other constraints led to women's poorer attendance and greater risk of dropping out, and may partially explain why master craftspeople treated male trainees better during training. For example, researchers found that male trainees were likely to receive financial support from their master craftsperson during training. Experiences like this may explain females' lower levels of subjective satisfaction and participation. In addition, the distance to training facilities was a significant constraint for women. Whether a woman had friends of family close to the training center was a strong predictor of whether she would complete her training. Women were more likely to drop out of the program due to illness or injury, along with family obligations or marriage. This may suggest that stronger financial and personal support can be important for achieving the full benefit of such programs.

Cho, Yoonyoung, Davie Kalomba, Ahmed M. Mobarak, and Victor Orozco. 2013. *Gender Differences in the Effects of Vocational Training: Constraints on Women and Drop-Out Behavior.* Discussion Paper 7408. Bonn: IZA–Institute for the Study of Labor.

Entrepreneurial Training and Education

Intense but flexible business certificate or entrepreneurial skill programs can offer significant opportunities for young women to expand their skills into income-producing business activities. Women who successfully run their own business are not dependent on male superiors or necessarily held back by discriminatory hiring practices or gender job segmentation:

- **Goldman Sachs's 10,000 Women initiative helps women become successful entrepreneurs**: The Goldman Sachs 10,000 Women initiative combines an intense but short-term business and management education for women running existing businesses who lack even a basic business education. The program gives an intense education in business basics from accounting to marketing while working with women on their specific business plans. Working in partnership with business schools in both developed and developing nations, the program offers a business certificate program as well as the opportunity for access to capital in programs in such nations as Afghanistan, Rwanda, Egypt, and India. Overall, the Goldman Sachs 10,000 Women initiative is a campaign to foster economic growth by providing women entrepreneurs around the world with a business and management education and access to capital. Through a network of 100 academic, nonprofit, and bank partners, the initiative has reached women across fifty-six countries. It recently created a partnership with the International Finance Corporation to provide a $600 million finance facility for such women entrepreneurs. An independent impact assessment of 10,000 Women by Babson College found that 18 months after graduation, 69 percent of surveyed graduates have grown their company's revenues, 58 percent have added jobs, and 90 percent have mentored other women in their communities.

  Babson College. 2014. "Investing in the Power of Women: Progress Report on the Goldman Sachs 10,000 Women Initiative." http://www.goldmansachs.com/citizenship/10000women/news-and-events/10kw-progress-report/progress-report-full.pdf.

Demand-Side Interventions, from Recruiting to Wage Subsidies

Studies from Europe suggest that training programs for youth can yield more positive employment outcomes when combined with demand-side interventions like the provision of wage subsidies or vouchers for employers, as well as services focused on better job matching (e.g., career counseling) (Kluve 2010).

With respect to demand-side interventions in developing nations, the case of Jóvenes en Acción in Colombia illustrates that job placement rates are higher if training programs can secure commitments from participating companies to hire a trainee (Attanasio, Kugler, and Meghir 2011; Fewer, Ramos, and Dunning 2013). And the case of Business Process Outsourcing recruiting in India, described above, demonstrates that creating pathways to work not only affect the educational decisions of parents and the educational attainment of upcoming generations of girls, but also has immediate employment effects for women who can directly take advantage of recruiting services. In developing economies, policymakers and academics need to keep in mind that though generally promising job strategies like wage vouchers are important, they alone may not address underlying barriers to female employment (see, e.g., Groh et al. 2012) and, therefore, may need to be combined with strategies targeted to the specific barriers faced by women seeking to join the workforce.

A Gender Framework for Youth Workforce Development

As part of the International Youth Foundation's (IYF's) gender framework developed under the USAID Youth:Work Leader with Associates Award, IYF and its partners developed a list of issues to keep in mind when designing and implementing programs aimed at improving girls' (and boys') transitions to the workforce, including:

1. **Participant selection**: How do programs ensure that females/males have equal access to training opportunities? What are the barriers to females'/males' participation, and how can they be addressed? Are program selection policies and processes fair and gender sensitive?

2. **Vocational/technical training**: Are there differences in male/female training enrollment? If so, does this vary with the type of training? What factors may exacerbate this imbalance? Is there equal access to technology? How can curricula be adapted to reduce or eliminate sex-role stereotypes?

3. **Teachers/trainers/facilitators:** Does teacher training address gender issues? Are teaching/training pedagogies and methodologies gender responsive? Are there both female and male facilitators/trainers? Are there any issues of sexual harassment, exploitation, or violence during training?

4. **Environmental constraints:** Is the timing of training and internships conducive to female/male participation? Are there transportation issues that impede students' enrollment and participation? Health or safety issues? Child care issues? Family/household issues? Scheduling issues? How can the program and/or its partners address or mitigate these issues?

5. **Job placement support**: Do females and males receive the same career guidance and other support services? Do both gender groups have access to mentoring support? Are females' and males' support needs considered equally? Are there differences in internship placement rates and types between females and males? Differences in their treatment by internship organizations? In their internship performance? In the perceptions of employers toward female and male interns?

6. **Employment:** Are there differences in job placement between female and male participants? In their wages in formal sector jobs? In the quality, status, and security of their jobs? In their treatment by employers? In their job performance? In the perceptions and expectations of employers toward female and male employees? In the number of females and males working in the informal sector? Do females and males have the same opportunities for advancement? Are females/males working in hazardous conditions or experiencing exploitation, threats, sexual harassment, abuse, or violence? Do female/male entrepreneurs have the same access to credit and business support services?

5 Education That Empowers Girls to Lead

Even today, in 2015, one of the world's great moral crises is the degree to which women face discriminatory laws, domestic violence, economic barriers, a lack of equal pay and job opportunities, and unequal political representation around the world, including in many developed nations. The push for girls' education must have a special emphasis and focus on empowering girls to overcome such barriers and to lead change for women.

> "When we switch from thinking about schooling improving learning outcomes for girls to school improving life outcomes for girls, we realize we must teach gender equality just like any other subject in the curriculum."
>
> *Urvashi Sahni, Founder of the Study Hall Foundation, India*

However, even when girls are successfully completing school, some curricula portray women in a passive and discriminatory manner, there is a dearth of mentors, and education often places too little focus on the soft skills, sports participation, and leadership skills that are critical to success in jobs, to a more dignified family life, and to promoting political change. Education is empowering, but in the words of Urvashi Sahni, a girls' education advocate in India, it will be more so when gender equality is taught like mathematics, science, and other important subjects.

As illustrated in chapter 2, we know that education empowers a woman in many ways, especially her capacity to control and make decisions about her own life. But just how does education do this? An emerging school of thought suggests that the skills girls acquire in school create "pathways" to better employment outcomes, health outcomes, and the like, by socializing girls with specific kinds of literacies and competencies necessary to operate in these spheres. In other words, the benefit of increased schooling is not just the economic returns that come from increased status of education or higher wage earnings, but also the fact that girls actually learn how to communicate, negotiate, and engage a bureaucratic world. This goes beyond merely a girl's ability to read print messages or to understand oral instructions about medical care, for example, or to calculate her expected wages or the discounted price of a food staple. Rather, this entails her ability to understand the general forms and norms of interrogation and explanation that are expected in bureaucratic settings and that, under some circumstances, can mean the difference between gaining or being denied valuable resources for her and her family (LeVine, LeVine, and Schnell 2001; see also Aslam and Kingdon 2012).

Defining Women's Empowerment

Jo Rowlands' definition of empowerment is widely used by gender specialists—academics and practitioners alike—and has informed many of today's definitions of women's empowerment. Rowlands defines empowerment as having four dimensions:

- "Power within": belief in self-worth, self-respect, and self-acceptance;

- "Power to": the ability to make choices and influence others;

- "Power over": the ability to control others; and

- "Power with": acting with others to challenge discriminatory structures.

Rowlands, J. 1997. *Questioning Empowerment: Working with Women in Honduras*. Oxford: Oxfam.

The evidence indicates that girls who spend more years in school know in advance and are more proficient at these everyday literacies. Combined with what we know about soft skills, this literacy-as-pathway framework places an even greater sense of urgency on the need for policymakers, practitioners, and academics to pursue strategies that promote women's empowerment through a *high-quality* education.

But what is a high-quality education? Over the years, education experts have defined a high-quality education through three main dimensions.

1. A focus on *inputs*, such as textbooks, the distribution of flipcharts or computers in the classroom, hiring more teachers to reduce the student/teacher ratio, or constructing latrines and water wells. These inputs are of course cruial for under-resourced schools as discussed above in Can More Money Improve Education Quality?

2. A focus on *learning outcomes*, such as students' ability to master educational content. This is often tracked through some form of student learning assessment and with a heavy emphasis on mastering foundational skills like literacy and numeracy. As discussed above this is both critical and missing for so many girls and boys.

3. A focus on *social learning outcomes*, which include things such as young people's beliefs about themselves and others, attitudes toward gender equality and gender-based violence, and their ability to communicate effectively with others.

This third dimension is not as widely used as the first two but is very important for understanding the full ways in which education can empower girls and women. Afterall, a girl could be taught in a well resourced classroom and excel in core subjects and still learn and believe that she is less valued in society than her male peers. Paying special attention to social learning outcomes means focusing on educational processes inside the classroom as well as outside in the school and community environments. Most important, it means that gender equality is built into definitions and measurements of educational quality.

Understanding quality through all three dimensions is an approach we support and it is an approach that can capture girls and women's empowerment. The academic community has been developing frameworks for this for some time, grounded in concepts of human rights and social justice (cf. Aikman and Rao 2012; Aikman and Unterhalter 2012; Alexander 2015; Miske and DeJaeghere 2013).

Within this framework of a high-quality education, we can focus on ensuring girls leave school equipped with the power within, power to, power over, and power with. Although this is not an area that lends itself as easily to crisp, crystal clear measurement, there are nonetheless significant studies and case studies that offer insights and promising methods to creating educational pathways and to promoting gender equality and empowerment through education (see e.g., Fuhriman et al. 2006). Although this is an area where more research can be helpful, we highlight here a few areas from which to learn and build on:

- Textbooks and learning materials reflect gender equality.

- Teachers demonstrate and teach gender equality.

- Provide girls with female mentors and role models.

- Strengthen girls' negotiation and decisionmaking skills.

- Give all girls the skills to work.

- Provide avenues for developing girls' leadership skills.

- Empower girls through sports and extracurricular activities.

Textbooks and Learning Materials Reflect Gender Equality

Textbooks and curricula matter not only for learning new information but also for what perceptions they create about women and their roles. Rae Blumberg (2007) notes that research shows students spend as much as 80 to 95 percent of classroom time using textbooks, and that teachers draw a majority of their instructional decisions based on textbooks (Sadker and Zittleman 2007). Thus, one cannot overestimate the negative impact of the fact that study after study shows significant gender bias in textbooks, with women greatly underrepresented and both women and men depicted in gender-stereotyped ways. Blumberg and others warn that this "hidden curriculum" constrains girls' and boys' visions of who they are and who they can become, laying the foundations upon which gender inequality in education and gender hierarchies in society are built and reinforced (Blumberg 2007, 4; see also Stromquist, Lee, and Brock-Utne 1998). The effects are experienced immediately in school when girls are led away from mathematics and science and into gender-stereotyped courses of study, and later when they leave school and are either held behind glass doors our under glass ceilings in the labor market.

What is the Hidden Curriculum?

The "hidden curriculum" refers to the often-invisible or unspoken messages communicated to students via textbooks, teachers, and school rules and norms, and even school structures and procedures. These messages may differ from what is being explicitly taught by the official curriculum, but they are equally influential in shaping students' attitudes and beliefs about themselves and the world.

- **Gender messages in Pakistani curriculum:** For example, in Pakistan, a recent gender analysis of public school textbooks found that illustrations and depictions of women and men continue to perpetuate dominant gender stereotypes and gender norms, "fixing" the idea that men dominate Pakistani society. Men were far more likely to be represented in positions of authority and power—such as judges, police and army officers, business executives, and independent farmers—whereas images of less prestigious occupations were populated by women.

  Ullah, Hazir, and Christine Skelton. 2013. "Gender Representation in the Public Sector Schools Textbooks of Pakistan." *Educational Studies* 39, no. 2: 183–94.

- **Gender messages in Jordanian curriculum:** Similarly, a gender analysis of the Jordanian national curriculum illustrates that not only are textbooks highly gender biased in the explicit images and languages used, but the hidden ideological messages embedded throughout also convey a particularly disempowering desirability for women to remain in the home and legitimize the role of education as preparing girls for the marriage market rather than the labor market.

  Abu Jaber, Mayyada. 2014. *Breaking Through Glass Doors: A Gender Analysis of Womenomics in the Jordanian National Curriculum.* Working Papers from the 2014 Echidna Global Scholars. Washington: Brookings Institution.

To date, the literature on gender and textbooks has been dominated by studies that illustrate how curricular materials are gender biased, rather than evaluating the impact of attempts to gender sensitize them (Blumberg 2015; Camfed 2012). But what we have learned from practitioner wisdom is that when schools pay attention to whether their curricula and teaching materials not only reflect principles of gender equality but also explicitly teach issues of gender equality, girls gain tremendously.

Prerna and the Study Hall Educational Foundation

The Prerna Girls School, which was established in 2003 and is run by the NGO named the Study Hall Educational Foundation, has had an impact on the lives of more than 5,000 of the most disadvantaged girls and their families from the lowest castes and poorest slums of Gomtinagar in Luchnow, India. An all-girls school, Prerna (its name means "inspiration") provides a model of what a focus on gender equality in its school inputs, outcomes, content, and processes can do to improve the quality of education for marginalized girls, especially their development of soft skills necessary for success in life. The school meets in the afternoon to accommodate the needs of girls whose economic circumstances require that they work. Every child is given a snack every day, which helps boost attendance, and regular health checkups are conducted free of cost for students. Teachers are engaging and interactive, and use activity-based learning approaches. What makes Prerna's curricular approach unique is its incorporation of critical dialogues throughout its lessons, creating a space where girls can think about issues of gender equality and talk through and understand the oppression they face every day. In other words, gender equality is built into its curriculum and taught like other subjects with the goal of developing girls' ability to challenge and resist discrimination while rising above it. The curriculum is enriched with an emphasis on English fluency, and it includes theater, workshops, creative writing, sports, yoga, martial arts, music, art, and painting; its relevance is enhanced with gender studies content and an explicit empowerment objective. Computer and vocational training are also provided to equip girls with skills that enable them to participate in a broader range of income-generating activities other than domestic work.

The results have been impressive in retention, graduation, academic performance, and job transitions. Prerna students outperform national and state averages on indicators of attendance, completion, and language and mathematics achievement. A total of 90 percent of Prerna's six cohorts of students have completed grade 10, compared with the national average of 39 percent. And of those who complete grade 10, 88 percent go on to tertiary education. Its empowerment curriculum and use of critical dialogue have been so successful that 106 public schools in India have now incorporated Prerna's approach to girls' education.

Sahni, Urvashi. 2012. *From Learning Outcomes to Life Outcomes: What Can You Do and Who Can You Be? A Case Study in Girls' Education in India.* Working Paper 4. Washington: Brookings Institution.

Lloyd, Cynthia B. 2013. "Education for Girls: Alternative Pathways to Girls' Empowerment." Integrated Approaches to Improving the Lives of Adolescent Girls Issue Paper Series. GirlEffect.org.

Teachers Demonstrate and Teach Gender Equality

As pointed out in chapter 4, how a teacher teaches is key. Too few teachers are trained in ways of reaching girls effectively or in ways of helping children think beyond gender stereotypes. The result is that girls are often portrayed only in highly restricted roles, teachers themselves expect less of girls, and girls are given less chance to participate and learn. Whether teachers think that mathematics is important for girls and whether boys and girls feel they receive equal treatment in the classroom substantially affects girls' probability of learning, feeling empowered, and staying in school. Moreover, if teachers think girls are less able, girls tend to underperform, whereas boys are less affected by teachers' views. Studies in Kenya and Nigeria, for example, found that boys are given more opportunities to ask and answer questions, to use learning materials, and to lead groups; girls are given less time on task than boys in science and receive less encouraging feedback. Such findings have also been the case in many countries in South Asia (Lloyd, Mensch, and Clark 1998; Ngware et al. 2012; UNICEF 2001, 2002).

In 2001, a report from UNICEF on its African Girls' Initiative identified efforts in Angola, Benin, Cameroon, Eritrea, and Malawi that tried such gender-sensitive teacher training and found that effective approaches include encouraging respect for girls and boys equally, making sure that girls can participate in class equally with boys, encouraging girls to study subjects such as mathematics and science where fewer girls than boys have done so, expressing similar expectations for boys and girls in learning performance, and suggesting nontraditional occupations for girls (King and Hill 1993; UNICEF 2001). Studies in India and Mali demonstrate further the impact of not only teachers' non-discriminatory and gender egalitarian attitudes on student performance, but also the importance of teachers engaging students in questioning gender discriminatory practices and attitudes on education's potential to help girls break out of cycles of oppression (Santhya et al. 2015; Fuhriman et al. 2006).

Sistema de Aprendizaje Tutorial in Central America

The Sistema de Aprendizaje Tutorial (SAT) was designed in the early 1980s by the Fundación para la Aplicación y Enseñanza de las Ciencias (FUNDAEC), a Colombian NGO, through a process of action research. SAT operates in several Central American countries, including Honduras, Guatemala, and Costa Rica. SAT began in Honduras in 1996, and is currently being implemented in thirty communities, with a plan to expand nationally by the end of the decade. SAT offers a nontraditional secondary school experience for both adolescent boys and girls (as well as adults), and its interdisciplinary curriculum sets it apart as a unique model of gender-responsive design and pedagogy. Rather than following traditional academic disciplines, SAT's curriculum is organized into five "capabilities": technology, mathematics, science, language and communication, and community service. Students get personal copies of textbooks, which are continuously revised through a process of consultation with communities.

In 2004, Erin Murphy-Graham conducted an in-depth longitudinal qualitative evaluation of the SAT program in Honduras in three villages where SAT had been in place for five years or more, and also in one village where SAT operated for 3 months before being canceled unexpectedly and that thus served as a comparison. She found that adolescent girls and women who completed their secondary education through SAT had gained specific knowledge, such as oral and written Spanish and chicken-raising, as well as a critical understanding that enabled them to identify problems in their communities and to identify and propose solutions. More important, SAT had strengthened their relational resources—not just their material resources—in ways that helped them fulfill the empowering potential of their education to transform unjust relationships and values. For example, women learned productive ways of communicating with their partners, like using change-directed negotiating skills to encourage partners to share household responsibilities more equitably (Murphy-Graham 2010, 329).

SAT presents a strong case for the consideration of content and process to promote a high-quality education for gender equality. Specific features of SAT that make it a good example of gender-responsive schooling include an emphasis on understanding rather than memorization; valuing dialogue and communication skills; engagement in practical activities that enable participants to apply their academic knowledge in relevant settings, such as agriculture, microenterprises, and community health; and mainstreaming gender issues into the curriculum rather than reserving them as separate topics. Together, these components raise girls' content knowledge, practical skills, and awareness of gender equity—all key ingredients to tapping into the empowering potential of education.

Murphy-Graham, Erin. 2008. "Opening the Black Box: Women's Empowerment and Innovative Secondary Education in Honduras." *Gender and Education* 20, no. 1: 31–50.

Murphy-Graham, Erin. 2010. "And When She Comes Home? Education and Women' Empowerment in Intimate Relationships." *International Journal of Educational Development* 30, no. 2010: 320–31.

and Population Activities, the program included (1) group-based learning opportunities that provided girls with a safe place to meet and interact regularly as well as to develop their peer networks; (2) life skills education focused on developing girls' agency, raising awareness about health matters like sexual and reproductive health and rights, and fostering more egalitarian gender role attitudes; and (3) livelihood skills training.

Acharya, Rajib, Shveta Kalyanwala, and Shireen J. Jejeebhoy. 2009. *Broadening Girls' Horizons: Effects of a Life Skills Education Program in Rural Uttar Pradesh.* New Delhi: Population Council.

Give All Girls the Skills to Work

To be empowered *within* with knowledge and skills is not enough for marginalized girls to enable them to be empowered to make choices, to influence others, or to change existing gender hierarchies (Rowlands 1997). In addition to strategies that aim to empower girls with life skills—such as goal setting, decision-making, and negotiation—girls also need a course of action to cultivate their "power to" change existing circumstances. This means going beyond putting the responsibility for change on girls by removing the structural barriers—the glass ceilings and glass doors—that continue to hold them back:

- **India's Better Life Options program**: Researchers who studied the Better Life Options program in India described above found that girls equipped with vocational skills did not necessarily use these skills to generate income, which demonstrates the need to build in measures that will enable girls to "bridge the schism between successful completion of the training program and independent use of the skill, and to link them with potential market and small business opportunities through existing channels, such as self-help groups."

  Acharya, Rajib, Shveta Kalyanwala, and Shireen J. Jejeebhoy. 2009. *Broadening Girls' Horizons: Effects of a Life Skills Education Program in Rural Uttar Pradesh.* New Delhi: Population Council, xi.

- **Combining life skills and vocational skills in the ELA program in Uganda:** Emerging research demonstrates that twin-pronged programs combining life skills education and vocational training can be especially effective in not only reducing risky behavior but also empowering girls with information and skills to help them reduce their exposure to economic, social, and sexual activities that could hurt their life outcomes.

The Empowerment and Livelihood for Adolescents (ELA) program in Uganda, operated by the NGO named BRAC, provides a promising example of how sustaining the long-term impact and efficacy of providing adolescent girls with empowering information about health is reinforced by program components that simultaneously work to empower girls to lead economically independent lives. By tracking nearly 4,800 adolescent girls (both those enrolled in school and those who had dropped out) for two years, researchers found that the girls in the treatment communities that hosted the ELA program were 7 percentage points more likely to engage in income-generating activities compared with girls in control communities. This 72 percent increase in such activities from baseline measurements was almost entirely driven by girls engaging in additional self-employment activities.

Meeting five afternoons per week in designated adolescent development clubs (rather than schools), under the leadership of a female mentor from within the community, the girls in the treatment communities who had dropped out of school were 8 percentage points more likely to want to reenroll in school. Moreover, no reduction in enrollment was observed among those girls who were enrolled in school and were participating in the program. The ELA program also significantly improved adolescent girls' control over their bodies, reducing the rates of early childbearing by 26 percent, reducing the rates of marriage/cohabitation by 58 percent, and increasing self-reported condom usage by 28 percent. The clearest marker that combining life skills and vocational training can be empowering is shown in the quality of adolescent girls' relationships with men; the proportion of girls who reported having had sex unwillingly was 6 percentage points lower in the treatment communities than in the control communities, starting from a baseline level of 14 percent. Finally, the ELA program offers potential for catalyzing intergenerational processes and beliefs that delay age at marriage and childbearing; among unmarried adolescent girls in the treatment communities, the preferred age at marriage increased, as did their expectations about their own daughter's age at marriage, and the desired fertility dropped by 7 percent.

Bandiera, Oriana, Niklas Buehren, Robin Burgess, Markus Goldstein, Selim Gulesci, Imran Rasul, and Munshi Sulaiman. 2014. "Women's Empowerment in Action: Evidence from a Randomized Control Trial in Africa (No. 50)." Suntory and Toyota International Centres for Economics and Related Disciplines, London School of Economics and Political Science. http://www.ucl.ac.uk/~uctpimr/research/ELA.pdf.

Provide Avenues for Developing Girls' Leadership Skills

An important aspect of empowering marginalized girls and women is strengthening their capacity to influence or have power over their circumstances (Rowlands 1997). An emerging body of literature shows that developing women's leadership skills increases girls' and women's status and presence in their communities, especially in decisionmaking circles and civic associations. And the literature also shows that once they have this presence, they are able to influence policy outcomes and budgetary allocations that are more favorable for girls and women:

- **Education increases political participation**: In a UNESCO study, a review of data from more than 100 countries found that the emergence of democracy followed increases in primary school enrollment, particularly when girls' enrollment caught up to the levels of boys' enrollment. The study argues that these findings confirm the hypothesis that "expanded educational opportunities for females goes along with a social structure that is generally more participatory and, hence, more receptive to democracy." Likewise, a Bangladesh study found that educated women were three times more likely to participate in political meetings than illiterate women.

  UNESCO. 2000. *Women and Girls: Education, Not Discrimination.* Paris: UNESCO.

- **An example from India**: In India, a 1993 constitutional amendment required that each state randomly reserve one-third of village council head positions for female *pradhan* (chiefs). Those village councils headed by women invested more in water and infrastructure—when their female constituents complained about these goods—than did those village councils not headed by women but that also received complaints about drinking water and infrastructure like roads.

  Chattopadhyay, Raghabendra, and Esther Duflo. 2004. "Women as Policy Makers: Evidence from a Randomized Policy Experiment in India." *Econometrica* 72, no. 5: 1409–43.

- **An example from Bangladesh:** In Bangladesh, members of the women's rights organization Nagorik Uddyog had more of a presence in traditional, male-dominated community mediations, known as *shalish.* These mediations issued more favorable decisions for women in property and marriage disputes.

Higgitt, R. 2011. "Women's Leadership Building as Poverty Reduction Strategy: Lessons from Bangladesh." *Journal of South Asian Development* 6, no. 1: 93–119.

But can more girls be empowered to take leadership roles? As with other life skills, researchers are beginning to understand how leadership opportunities (e.g., civic clubs, school clubs, being a peer mentor) and extracurricular activities (e.g., sports, performing arts, music) offered at an early age are essential for creating pathways that foster leadership later in life when girls become women (O'Neil, Plank, and Domingo 2015).

Empower Girls through Sports and Extracurricular Activities

Although more research is needed to understand the exact impact of sports and extracurricular activities on the development of girls' leadership skills, recent evaluations of CARE's Innovation through Sport: Promoting Leaders, Empowering Youth (ITSPLEY) project and DFID's Women Win: Building Young Women's Leadership through Sport program provide some insight on the potential outcomes:

- **CARE and ITSPLEY: The girls who participated in ITSPLEY activities scored higher on multiple dimensions of leadership than the girls who did not participate.** While being implemented for three years in Bangladesh, Egypt, Kenya, and Tanzania, ITSPLEY provided girls with the opportunity to develop and practice leadership skills through sports-based activities. According to an external evaluation, ITSPLEY Bangladesh appeared to positively affect the way girls see themselves in relation to others. The girls who participated in ITSPLEY activities scored 3.11, on average, on the Girls' Leadership Index (GLI), compared with 2.88, on average, for the girls who did not participate. CARE's GLI measures self-reported changes in the girls' leadership competencies and their perceptions of themselves as leaders. For example, 75 percent of the girls in the active group indicated that they recognized themselves as leaders, compared with 31 percent of the girls in the comparison group. And a total of 81 percent of the girls in the active group reported not hesitating to provide their opinion, compared with 61 percent in the comparison group; and 71 percent of the girls in the active group indicated not hesitating to speak, especially with adults, compared with 52 percent of the girls in the comparison group. Before making decisions, 88 percent of the girls in the active group reported trying to consider things from different perspectives, whereas only 71 percent of the girls in the comparison group did so. And finally, 56 percent of the girls in the active group reported making decisions that influenced others, compared with 31 percent in the comparison group. And though girls in both groups reported difficulty taking action against wrongdoings, the girls in the active group reported a greater sense of self-efficacy.

Eschenbacher, Heidi. 2011. *CARE Bangladesh Girls' Education and Leadership Evaluation Innovation through Sport: Promoting Leaders, Empowering Youth.* Final evaluation report. Saint Paul: Miske Witt.

- **DFID and Women Win:** After one year of Women Win, internal reviews of DFID's sport program demonstrated that its participants experienced increased confidence and self-esteem. Nine out of 11 participants reported new personal leadership skills, and 75 percent of girls reported increased adolescent life skills related to sexual and reproductive health and rights, gender-based violence, and economic empowerment.

O'Neil, T., G. Plank, and P. Domingo. 2015. *Support to Women and Girls' Leadership: A Rapid Review of the Evidence.* London: Overseas Development Institute.

CARE's Power to Lead Alliance

The Power to Lead Alliance (PTLA) was a three-year (2008–11) project implemented by CARE and funded by USAID in six countries: Honduras, Yemen, India, Malawi, Tanzania, and Egypt. One of its primary objectives was to promote leadership skills development among young adolescent girls (ages ten to fourteen) from vulnerable communities by providing them with multiple and diverse opportunities to practice their leadership skills. PTLA incorporated extracurricular activities, social networks, and civic action into its programming, offering twelve primary activities: sports, health, arts and drama, debate, music, youth councils and boards, life skills groups, academic clubs, scouts, awareness campaigns, environmental work, and classroom support. Although the project was targeted at girls, 30 percent of its participants were young adolescent boys, which allowed the project implementers to pilot activities aimed at changing gender norms and attitudes. Although evaluations revealed discrepancies between boys' attitudes and behaviors toward gender equality, the overall findings illustrate that community attitudes toward girls changed as a result of PTLA programming.

As assessed using the GLI, evaluations demonstrate that the provision of extracurricular activities for girls is an essential component of their leadership development.

All countries involved in PTLA achieved or were at least close to achieving the 70 percent target of girls possessing leadership skills and competencies. All countries, except Malawi, showed statistically significant differences in leadership skills development between girls in the active and comparison groups. Moreover, all countries except Honduras met the 70 percent target of girls taking leadership action, and all countries met or were close to meeting the 50 percent target of improving girls' self-confidence. Although the 70 percent target for girls displaying leadership action in homes, schools, and communities was not met, at least 50 percent of girls in all the participating countries improved in these areas.

Baric, Stephanie. 2013. "Where the Boys Are: Engaging Young Adolescent Boys in Support of Girls' Education and Leadership." *Gender and Development* 21, no. 1: 147–60.

Miske Witt and Associates. 2011. *The Power to Lead Alliance (PTLA): Empowering Girls to Learn and Lead*. Final evaluation report for CARE USA. Saint Paul: Miske Witt and Associates.

BIBLIOGRAPHY

Abner, Allison, et al. 2013. *Child Sex Trafficking in the United States, Identifying Gaps and Research Priorities from a Public Health Perspective.* Baltimore: Johns Hopkins Bloomberg School of Public Health.

Abu Jaber, Mayyada. 2014. *Breaking Through Glass Doors: A Gender Analysis of Womenomics in the Jordanian National Curriculum.* Working Papers from the 2014 Echidna Global Scholars. Washington: Brookings Institution.

Abu-Ghaida, Dina, and Stephan Klasen. 2004. "The Economic and Human Development Costs of Missing the Millennium Development Goal on Gender Equity." *World Development* 32, no. 7:1075–1107.

Abuya, Benta A., James Ciera, and Elizabeth Kimani-Murage. 2012. "Effect of Mother's Education on Child's Nutritional Status in the Slums of Nairobi." *BMC Pediatrics* 12: 80.

Acharya, Rajib, Shveta Kalyanwala, and Shireen J. Jejeebhoy. 2009. *Broadening Girls' Horizons: Effects of a Life Skills Education Program in Rural Uttar Pradesh.* New Delhi: Population Council.

Ackerman, Xanthe. 2015. *Innovation and Action in Funding Girls' Education.* Working Paper 84. Washington: Brookings Institution.

Adoho, Franck, Shubha Chakravarty, Dala T. Korkoya, Mattias Lundberg, and Afia Tasneem. 2014. *Impact of an Adolescent Girls' Employment Program: The EPAG Project in Liberia.* Washington: World Bank Africa Region Poverty Reduction and Economic Management Unit.

Adukia, Anjali. 2014. "Sanitation and Education." http://scholar.harvard.edu/files/adukia/files/adukia_sanitation_and_education.pdf.

Ahmed, Akhter U., and Mary Arends-Kuenning. 2003. *Do Crowded Classrooms Crowd Out Learning? Evidence from the Food for Education Program in Bangladesh.* Washington: International Food Policy Research Institute.

Aikman, Sheila, and Nitya Rao. 2010. "Quality Education for Gender Equality." Background paper for the Quality Education Stream E4 Conference, UN Girls' Education Initiative, New York.

———. 2012. ""Gender Equality and Girls' Education: Investigating Frameworks, Disjunctures and Meanings of Quality Education." *Theory and Research in Education* 10, no. 3: 211–28.

Aikman, Sheila, and Elaine Unterhalter. 2007. *Practising Gender Equality in Education.* Oxford: Oxfam Great Britain.

———. Aikman, Sheila, and Elaine Unterhalter. 2012. Gender Equality, Capabilities and the Terrain of Quality Education. In *Education Quality and Social Justice in the Global South: Challenges for Policy, Practice, and Research*, edited by L. Tikly, A. M. Barrett, S. Aikman, and E. Unterhalter. New York: Routledge / Taylor & Francis.

Aikman, Sheila, Elaine Unterhalter, and Chloe Challender. 2005. "The Education MDGs: Achieving Gender Equality through Curriculum and Pedagogy Change. *Gender and Development* 13, no. 1: 44-55.

Akresh, Richard, Damien de Walque, and Harounan Kazianga. 2013. *Cash Transfers and Child Schooling: Evidence from a Randomized Evaluation of the Role of Conditionality.* Policy Research Working Paper 6340. Washington: World Bank.

Alam, Andaleeb, Javier E. Baez, and Ximena V. Del Carpio. 2011. *Does Cash for School Influence Young Women's Behavior in the Longer Term? Evidence from Pakistan.* Policy Research Working Paper 5669. Washington: World Bank.

Alderman, Harold, and Elizabeth M. King. 1998. "Gender Differences in Parental Investment in Education." *Structural Change and Economic Dynamics* 9, no. 4: 453–68.

Alexander, Robin. 2015. "Teaching and Learning for All? The Quality Imperative Revisited." *International Journal of Educational Development* 40, 250-58.

American Institutes for Research. 2015. *Are Latin American Children's Reading Skills Improving? Highlights from the Second and Third Regional Comparative and Explanatory Studies (SERCE and TERCE).* Washington: American Institutes of Research.

Ames, Patricia. 2012. "Constructing New Identities? The Role of Gender and Education in Rural Girls' Life Aspirations in Peru." *Gender and Educations* 25, no. 3.

Andrabi, Tahir, Jishnu Das, and Asim Ijaz Khwaja. 2011. *Students Today, Teachers Tomorrow: Identifying Constraints on the Provision of Education.* Policy Research Working Paper 5674. Washington: World Bank.

Angrist, Joshua, Eric Bettinger, Erik Bloom, Elizabeth King, and Michael Kremer. 2002. "Vouchers for Private Schooling in Colombia: Evidence from a Randomized Natural Experiment." *American Economic Review* 92, no. 5: 1535–58.

Arnold, Catherine, Tim Conway, and Matthew Greenslade. 2011. *Cash Transfers: Evidence Paper.* London: UK Department for International Development.

Arnot, Madelein. 2006. "Gender Equality, Pedagogy and Citizenship: Affirmative and Transformative Approaches in the UK." *Theory and Research in Education* 4, no. 2: 131-50.

ASER (Annual Status of Education Report) Centre. 2015. *Annual Status of Education Report (Rural) 2014.* Provisional, January 13. http://img.asercentre.org.

Ashraf, Nava, Corinee Low, and Kathleen McGinn. 2013. *Negotiating a Better Future: The Impact of Teaching Negotiation Skills on Girls' Education and Health Outcomes.* Final Pilot Report. Lusaka: Innovations for Poverty Action.

Aslam, Monazza. 2013. *Empowering Women: Education and the Pathways of Change.* Background paper for *EFA Global Monitoring Report 2013/4.* Paris: UNESCO.

Aslam, Monazza, Faisal Bari, and Geeta Kingdon. 2012. "Returns to Schooling, Ability and Cognitive Skills in Pakistan." *Education Economics* 20, no. 2:139–73.

Aslam, Monazza, and Geeta Kingdon. 2012. "Can Education Be a Path to Gender Equality in the Labour Market? An Update on Pakistan." *Comparative Education* 48, no. 2: 211–29.

Aslam, Monazza, Geeta Kingdon, Anuradha De, and Rajeev Kumar. 2010. *Economic Returns to Schooling and Skills: An Analysis of India and Pakistan.* RECOUP Working Paper 38. London: UK Department for International Development.

Aslam, Monazza and Shenila Rawal. 2013. "Preparing Women of Substance? Education, Training, and Labor Market Outcomes for Women in Pakistan." *Lahore Journal of Economics* 93.

Aslan, Marcella, and David Cutler. 2013. "Girls' Education and HIV Risk: Evidence from Uganda." *Journal of Health Economics* 32, no. 5: 863–72.

Assaad, Ragui, Deborah Levison, and Nadia Zibani. 2010. "The Effect of Domestic Work on Girls' Schooling: Evidence from Egypt." *Feminist Economics* 16, no. 1: 79–128.

Attanasio, Orazio, Adriana Kugler, and Costas Meghir. 2011. "Subsidizing Vocational Training for Disadvantaged Youth in Colombia: Evidence from a Randomized Trial." *American Economic Journal: Applied Economics* 3: 188–220.

Babson College. 2014. "Investing in the Power of Women: Progress Report on the Goldman Sachs 10,000 Women Initiative." http://www.goldmansachs. com/citizenship/10000women/news-and-events/10kw-progress-report/progress-report-full.pdf.

Baird, Sarah, Ephraim Chirwa, Craig McIntosh, and Berk Ozler. 2015. *What Happens Once the Intervention Ends? The Medium-Term Impacts of a Cash Transfer Program in Malawi.* 3ie Grantee Final Report. New Delhi: International Initiative for Impact Evaluation.

Baird, Sarah, Francisco H. G. Ferreira, Berk Ozler, and Michael Woolcock. 2013. "Relative Effectiveness of Conditional and Unconditional Cash Transfers for Schooling Outcomes in Developing Countries: A Systematic Review." *Campbell Systematic Reviews* 8.

Baird, Sarah, Richard Garfein, C. McIntosh, and Berk Ozler. 2012. "Effect of a Cash Transfer Programme for Schooling on Prevalence of HIV and Herpes Simplex Type 2 in Malawi: A Cluster Randomised Trial." *The Lancet* 379, no. 9823: 1320–29.

Baird, Sarah, Craig McIntosh, and Berk Ozler. 2011. "Cash or Condition? Evidence from a Cash Transfer Experiment." *Quarterly Journal of Economics* 126, no. 4: 1709–53.

Baldwin, Wendy. 2011. *Creating "Safe Space" for Adolescent Girls: Promoting Healthy, Safe, and Productive Transitions to Adulthood.* Brief 39. Washington: Population Council.

Bandiera, Oriana, Niklas Buehren, Robin Burgess, Markus Goldstein, Selim Gulesci, Imran Rasul, and Munshi Sulaiman. 2014. "Women's Empowerment in Action: Evidence from a Randomized Control Trial in Africa (No. 50)." Suntory and Toyota International Centres for Economics and Related Disciplines, London School of Economics and Political Science. http://www.ucl. ac.uk/~uctpimr/research/ELA.pdf.

Banerjee, Abhijit V., Shawn Cole, Esther Duflo, and Leigh Linden. 2007. "Remedying Education: Evidence from Two Randomized Experiments in India." *Quarterly Journal of Economics* 122, no. 3: 1235–64.

Banerjee, Rukmini. 2015. "The Gap Years." In *Annual Status of Education Report (Rural) 2014: Provisional.* New Delhi: ASER Centre.

Baric, Stephanie. 2013. "Where the Boys Are: Engaging Young Adolescent Boys in Support of Girls' Education and Leadership." *Gender and Development* 21, no. 1: 147–60.

Barker, Gary. 2003. "How Do We Know If Men Have Changed? Promoting and Measuring Attitude Change with Young Men: Lessons from Program H in Latin America." In *Expert Group Meeting on the Role of Men and Boys in Achieving Gender Equality.* Brasília: United Nations. http://www. un.org/womenwatch/daw/egm/men-boys2003/OP2-Barker.pdf.

———. 2006. "Engaging Boys and Men to Empower Girls: Reflections from Practice and Evidence of Impact." Document EGM/DVGC/2006/EP3, United Nations, New York. http:// www.un.org/womenwatch/daw/egm/ elim-disc-viol-girlchild/ExpertPapers/ EP.3%20%20%20Barker.pdf.

Barker, Gary, Christine Ricardo, and Marcos Nascimento. 2007. *Engaging Men and Boys in Changing Gender-Based Inequity in Health Evidence from Programme Interventions.* Geneva: World Health Organization.

Barker, Gary, Ravi Verma, John Crownover, Marcio Segundo, Vanessa Fonseca,

Juan M. Contreras, Brian Heilman, and Peter Pawlak. 2012. "Boys and Education in the Global South: Emerging Vulnerabilities and New Opportunities for Promoting Changes in Gender Norms." *Thymos* 6, nos. 1–2: 137–50.

Barrera-Osorio, Felipe, Marianna Bertrand, Leigh L. Linden, and Francisco Perez-Calle. 2011. "Improving the Design of Conditional Transfer Programs: Evidence from a Randomized Education Experiment in Colombia." *American Economic Journal: Applied Economics* 3: 167–95.

Barrera-Osorio, Felipe, and Leigh L. Linden. 2009. "The Use and Misuse of Computers in Education: Evidence from a Randomized Controlled Trial of a Language Arts Program." http://www.povertyactionlab.org/publication/use-and-misuse-computers-education-evidence-randomized-controlled-trial-language-arts-pr.

Barrett, Angeline M. 2007. "Beyond the Polarization of Pedagogy: Models of Classroom Practice in Tanzanian Primary Schools." *Comparative Education* 43, no. 2: 273–94.

Barro, Robert J. 1991. "Economic Growth in a Cross Section of Countries." *Quarterly Journal of Economics* 106, no. 2: 407–43. doi:10.1016/0167-2231(94)90002-7.

Barro, Robert J., and Jong-Wha Lee. 1994. "Sources of Economic Growth." *Carnegie-Rochester Series on Public Policy* 40: 1–46.

———. 2013. "A New Data Set of Educational Attainment in the World, 1950–2010." *Journal of Development Economics* 104: 184–98.

———. 2014. "Updated Data Set (Version 2.0) for 'A New Data Set of Educational Attainment in the World, 1950–2010' [R. J. Barro and J. W. Lee, 2013]." *Journal of Development Economics* 104: 184–98.

Basu, Ananya, and Elizabeth M. King. 2001. *Does Education Promote Growth and Democracy? Some Evidence from East Asia and Latin America.* Washington: World Bank.

Baulch, Bob. 2010. *The Medium-Term Impact of the Primary Education Stipend in Rural Bangladesh.* IFPRI Discussion Paper 00976. Washington: International Food Policy Research Institute.

Beaman, Lori, Esther Duflo, Rohindi Pande, and Petra Topalova. 2012. "Female Leadership Raises Aspirations and Educational Attainment for Girls: A Policy Experiment in India." *Science* 335, no. 6068: 582–86.

Beasley, Elizabeth, and Elise Huillery. 2014. "Willing but Unable: Short-Term Experimental Evidence on Parent Empowerment and School Quality." Working paper. http://www.povertyactionlab.org/publication/willing-unable-short-term-experimental-evidence-parent-empowerment-and-school-quality-0.

Behrman, Jere, Andrew D. Foster, Mark R. Rosenzweig, and Prem Vashishtha. 1999. "Women's Schooling, Home Teaching, and Economic Growth." *Journal of Political Economy* 107, no. 4: 682–714.

Behrman, Jere R., Piyali Sengupta, and Petra Todd. 2005. "Progressing through PROGRESA: An Impact Assessment of a School Subsidy Experiment in Rural Mexico." *Economic Development and Cultural Change* 54, no. 1: 237–75.

Beltramo, Theresa, and David Levine. 2012. *Do SMS Text Messaging and SMS Community Forums Improve Outcomes of Adult and Adolescent Literacy Programs? Evidence from the Jokko Initiative in Senegal.* CEGA Working Paper 15. Berkeley: Center for Effective Global Action at University of California.

Bennett, Joshua, Maro Chermayeff, Michelle Ferrari, Meg Ryan, Diane Lane, Gabrielle Union, Eva Mendes, America Ferrera, Olivia Wilde, Nicholas

D. Kristof, Sheryl WuDunn, Nico Abondolo, and Wolfgang Held. 2012. *Half the Sky: Turning Oppression into Opportunity for Women Worldwide.* New York: Docurama Films.

Benveniste, L., and P. J. McEwan. 2000. "Constraints to Implementing Educational Innovations: The Case of Multi-Grade Schools." *International Review of Education* 46, nos. 1–2: 31–48.

Bhalotra, Sonia, and Damian Clarke. 2013. *Educational Attainment and Maternal Mortality.* Paper commissioned for *EFA Global Monitoring Report 2013/4.* Paris: UNESCO.

Bhalotra, Sonia, Irma Clots-Figueras, and Lakshmi Iyer. 2013. *Women's Political Participation and the Female–Male Literacy Differential in India.* Background paper commissioned for *EFA Global Monitoring Report 2013/4.* Paris: UNESCO.

Bhalotra, Sonia, Kenneth Harttgen, and Stephan Klasen. 2013. *The Impact of School Fees on the Intergenerational Transmission of Education.* Background paper commissioned for *EFA Global Monitoring Report 2013/4.* Paris: UNESCO.

Bhatla, Nandita, Pranita Achyut, Nizamuddin Khan, Sunayana Walia, and Alessandra Tranquilli. 2015. *Promoting Equality and Safety in Schools: Are Schools Safe and Equal Places for Girls and Boys in Asia? Research Findings On School-Related Gender-Based Violence.* Bangkok: Plan International.

Biraimah, Karen Coffyn. 1980. "Different Knowledge for Different Folks: Knowledge Distribution in a Togolese Secondary School." In *Comparative Education,* ed. Philip G. Altbock, Robert F. Arnove, and Gail P. Kelly. New York: Macmillan.

Birdthistle, Isolde, Kelly Dickson, Matthew Freeman, and Leila Javidi. 2011. *What Impacts Does the Provision of Separate Toilets for Girls at Schools Have on Their Primary and Secondary School Enrolment, Attendance and Completion? A Systematic Review of the Evidence.* London: EPPI-Centre, Social Science Research Unit, Institute of Education, University of London.

Black, R. E., L. H. Allen, Z. A. Bhutta, L. E. Caulfield, M. De Onis, M. Ezzati, C. Mathers, and J. Rivera. 2008. "Maternal and Child Undernutrition: Global and Regional Exposures and Health Consequences." *The Lancet* 371, no. 9608: 243–60.

Blankespoor, Brian, Susmita Dasgupta, Benoit Laplante, and David Wheeler. 2010. *Adaptation to Climate Extremes in Developing Countries: The Role of Education.* Policy Research Working Paper 5342. Washington: World Bank.

Blumberg, Rae. 2007. *Gender Bias in Textbooks: A Hidden Obstacle On the Road to Gender Equality in Education.* Background paper for *EFA Global Monitoring Report 2008.* Paris: UNESCO.

———. 2015. *Eliminating Gender Bias in Textbooks: Pushing for Policy Reforms That Promote Gender Equity in Education.* Background paper for *EFA Global Monitoring Report 2015.* Paris: UNESCO.

Bobonis, Gustavo, Edward Miguel, and Charu Sharma. 2002. *Iron Supplementation and Early Childhood Development: A Randomized Evaluation in India.* Berkeley: University of California.

Boyden, J. 2003. "Children under Fire: Challenging Assumptions About Children's Resilience." *Children, Youth and Environments* 13, no. 1:1–29.

Brooks, Mohamad, Malcolm Bryant, Mary Shann, Paul Bukuluki, Denis Muhangi, Joe Lugalla, and Gideon Kwesigabo. 2013. "Gender Analysis of Educational Support Programs for OVC in Uganda and Tanzania: Are They Helping Girls in Secondary School?" *Vulnerable Children and Youth Studies,* November, 1–14.

Browne, Angela W., and Hazel R. Barrett. 1991. "Female Education in

Sub-Saharan Africa: the Key to Development?" *Comparative Education* 27, no. 3: 275–85.

Bruns, Barbara, Alain Mingar, and Ramahatra Rakotomalala. 2003. *Achieving Universal Primary Education by 2015: A Chance for Every Child.* Washington: World Bank.

Buckland, P. 2005. *Reshaping the Future: Education and Post-Conflict Reconstruction.* Washington: World Bank.

Burde, Dana, and Leigh L. Linden. 2013. "Bringing Education to Afghan Girls: A Randomized Controlled Trial of Village-Based Schools." *American Economic Journal: Applied Economics* 5, no. 3: 27–40.

Buscher, Dale. 2005. *Masculinities: Male Roles and Male Involvement in the Promotion of Gender Equality. A Resource Packet.* New York: Women's Commission for Refugee Women and Children.

Calves, Anne-Emmanuele. 2002. "Abortion Risk and Decision-Making Among Young People in Urban Cameroon. *Studies in Family Planning* 33, no. 3: 249–60.

Camfed (Campaign for Female Education). 2010a. *Impact Report: A Power Sharing Model for Systemic Change.* San Francisco: Camfed.

———. 2010b. "Prioritizing Education in the Midst of Crisis: Assessing the Resilience and Responsiveness of Camfed Partner Structures in Zimbabwe, 2009." Harare: Camfed.

———. 2011. *Cambridge Consortium Report: Progress and Achievements of the Goldman Sachs 10,000 Women Certificate Programme in Young Women's Leadership and Enterprise.* San Francisco: Camfed.

———. 2012. *What Works in Girls' Education in Ghana: A Critical Review of the Ghanaian and International Literature.* Accra: Camfed Ghana.

———. 2014a. "The Learner Guide Program: A Scalable Model for Transforming Young People's Prospects." https://camfed.org/what-we-do/learner-guide-program/.

———. 2014b. *A New Equilibrium for Girls: Tanzania and Zimbabwe Baseline Report for the Girls' Education Challenge.* London: Camfed.

CARE. 2014. *Addressing the Intergenerational Transmission of Gender-Based Violence: Focus on Educational Settings.* Geneva: CARE.

Caton, Carolyn, Josh Chaffin, Mendy Marsh, and Sophie Read-Hamilton. 2014. *Empowered and Safe: Economic Strengthening for Girls in Emergencies.* Report from Child Protection in Crisis Network, Women's Refugee Commission, and United Nations Children's Fund. https://womensrefugeecommission.org/programs/youth/research-and-resources/download/1151.

Center for Universal Education at Brookings. 2015. "Learning Metrics Task Force 2.0." http://www.brookings.edu/about/centers/universal-education/learning-metrics-task-force-2.

Chapman, David W., and Sarah Mushlin, 2008. "Do Girls' Scholarship Programs Work? Evidence from Two Countries." *International Journal of Educational Development* 28: 460–72.

Chapman, David W., John Weidman, Marc Cohen, and Malcolm Mercer. 2005. "The Search for Quality: A Five Country Study of National Strategies To Improve Educational Quality in Central Asia." *International Journal of Educational Development* 25, no. 5: 514–30.

Chattopadhyay, Raghabendra, and Esther Duflo. 2004. "Women as Policy Makers: Evidence from a Randomized Policy Experiment in India." *Econometrica* 72, no. 5: 1409–43.

Chaudhury, N., and D. Parajuli. 2008. "Conditional Cash Transfers and Female Schooling: The Impact of the Female School Stipend Program on Public School Enrollments in

Punjab, Pakistan." *Journal of Applied Economics.*

Chepleting, S., A. Chepkemei, K. L. Yano, and L. L. Chebet. 2013. "Factors Influencing Girls' Participation in Free Primary Education: A Survey of Schools in Kapenguria Division–West Pokot District, Kenya." *International Journal of Business and Commerce* 2, no. 6: 20–35.

Chilisa, Bagele. 2002. "National Policies on Pregnancy in Education Systems in Sub-Saharan Africa: The Case of Botswana. *Gender and Education* 14, no. 1: 21–35.

Chin, Aimee. 2004. "Can Redistributing Teachers Across Schools Raise Attainment? Evidence from Operation Blackboard in India." *Journal of Development Economics* 78 2005: 384–405.

Cho, Yoonyoung, Davie Kalomba, Ahmed M. Mobarak, and Victor Orozco. 2013. *Gender Differences in the Effects of Vocational Training: Constraints on Women and Drop-Out Behavior.* Discussion Paper 7408. Bonn: IZA–Institute for the Study of Labor.

Chudgar, Amita, and Sankar, Vyjayanthi. 2008. The Relationship Between Teacher Gender and Student Achievement: Evidence from Five Indian States. *Compare* 38, no. 5: 627–42.

Clinton Foundation, Bill & Melinda Gates Foundation, Economist Intelligence Unit, and WORLD Policy Analysis Center. 2015. *The Full Participation Report: No Ceilings.* Full Participation Project. New York: Clinton Foundation.

Coalition for Health and Education Rights. 2002. *User Fees: The Right to Education and Health Denied.* Policy Brief. New York: Coalition for Health and Education Rights.

Coffey International Development. 2015. *Baseline Report: Innovation Window—Evaluation Manager Girls' Education Challenge Fund.* London: UK Department for International Development.

Colclough, C., G. Kingdon, and H. A. Patrinos. 2009. *The Pattern of Returns to Education and Its Implications.* Policy Brief 4. Cambridge: Research Consortium on Educational Outcomes and Poverty.

Conn, K. 2014. "Identifying Effective Education Interventions in Sub-Saharan Africa: A Meta-Analysis of Rigorous Impact Evaluations." Unpublished manuscript, Columbia University, New York.

Connolly, Susan, and Marni Sommer. 2013. "Cambodian Girls' Recommendations for Facilitating Menstrual Hygiene Management in School." *Journal of Water, Sanitation and Hygiene for Development* 3, no. 4: 612–22.

CPWG (Child Protection Working Group). 2012. *Minimum Standards for Child Protection in Humanitarian Response.* Geneva: CPWG.

Creighton, Mathew, and Park, Hyunjoon. 2010. "Closing the Gender Gap: Six Decades of Reform in Mexican Education." *Comparative Education Review* 54, no. 4: 513–37.

Crouch, L., and A. Gove. 2011. "Leaps Ahead or One Step At a Time? Skirting or Helping Engage the Debate." In *Policy Debates in Comparative, International and Development Education*, edited by J. N. Hawkins and W. J. Jacob. New York: Palgrave Macmillan.

Cummings, Clare. & O'Neil, Tam. (2015). Do digital information and communication technologies increase the voice and influence of women and girls? A rapid review of the evidence. Overseas Development Institute.

Das, Jinshu, and S. Das. 2003. "Trust, Learning and Vaccination: A Case Study of a North Indian Village." *Social Science Medicine* 57: 97–112.

Das, J., P. Pandey, and T. Zajonc. 2006. *Learning Levels and Gaps in Pakistan.*

Policy Research Working Paper 4067. Washington: World Bank.

Davis, Anthony, Claire Postles, and Giorgiana Rosa. 2013. *A Girl's Right to Say No to Marriage: Working to End Child Marriage and Keep Girls In School.* Woking, UK: Plan International.

Davis, Kristin, Ephraim Nkonya, Edward Kato, Daniel Ayalew Mekonnen, Martins Odendo, Richard Miiro, and Jackson Nkuba. 2012. "Impact of Farmer Field Schools on Agricultural Productivity and Poverty in East Africa." *World Development* 40, no. 2: 402–13.

De Walque, Damien. 2004. *How Does Educational Attainment Affect the Risk of Being Infected by HIV/AIDS? Evidence from a General Population Cohort in Rural Uganda.* World Bank Development Research Group Working Paper. Washington: World Bank.

Deininger, Klaus. 2003. "Does the Cost of Schooling Affect Enrollment by the Poor? Universal Primary Education in Uganda." *Economics of Education Review* 22, no. 3: 291–305.

Desai, Sonalde, and Soumya Alva. 1998. "Maternal Education and Child Health: Is There a Strong Causal Relationship?" *Demography* 35, no. 1: 71–81.

DeStefano, Joseph, Audrey-marie Schuh Moore, David Balwanz, and Ash Hartwell. 2007. *Reaching the Underserved: Complementary Models of Effective Schooling.* USAID and Equip2.

Diallo, Yacouba, Alex Etienne, and Farhad Mehran. 2013. *Global Child Labour Trends, 2008 to 2012.* Geneva: International Labor Organization.

Dolan, Catherine S., Caitlin R. Ryus, Sue Dopson, Paul Montgomery, and Linda Scott. 2014. "A Blind Spot in Girls' Education: Menarche and Its Webs of Exclusion in Ghana." *Journal of International Development* 26: 643–57.

Dollar, David, and Roberta Gatti. 1999. *Gender Inequality, Income, and Growth: Are Good Times Good for Women?* Working Paper 1 for *Policy Research Report on Gender and Development.* Washington: World Bank.

Dryden-Peterson, Sarah. 2011. *Refugee Education: A Global Review.* Geneva: UNHCR.

Duflo, Esther. 2001. "Schooling and Labor Market Consequences of School Construction in Indonesia: Evidence from an Unusual Policy Experiment." *American Economic Review* 92, no. 4: 795–813.

Duflo, Esther, Pascaline Dupas, and Michael Kremer. 2011. "Peer Effects, Teacher Incentives, and the Impact of Tracking: Evidence from a Randomized Evaluation in Kenya." *American Economic Review* 101, no. 5: 1739–74.

———. 2014. *Education, HIV, and Early Fertility: Experimental Evidence from Kenya.* NBER Working Paper 20784. Cambridge, Mass.: National Bureau of Economic Research. http://www.nber.org/papers/w20784.pdf.

Duflo, Esther, Rema Hanna, and Stephen P. Ryan. 2012. "Incentives Work: Getting Teachers to Come to School." *American Economic Review* 102, no. 4: 1241–78.

Dunifon, Rachel, and Greg J. Duncan. 1998. "Long-Run Effects of Motivation on Labor-Market Success." *Social Psychology Quarterly* 61, no. 1: 33–48.

Edmonds, Eric, and Norbert Schady. 2010. *Poverty Alleviation and Child Labor.* Hanover: Department of Economics, Dartmouth College.

Education for Change. 2013. *Thematic Study on Education and Gender Equality.* Oslo: Norwegian Agency for Development Cooperation.

EMERGE. 2015. "Engendering Men: Evidence on Routes to Gender Equality." http://menandboys.ids.ac.uk/.

Engel, Jakob. 2012. *Review of Policies to Strengthen Skills—Employment Linkages for Marginalised Young People.* Background paper for *EFA Global Monitoring Report 2012.* Paris: UNESCO.

Erden, F. T. 2009. "A Course on Gender Equity in Education: Does It Affect Gender Role Attitudes of Preservice Teachers?" *Teaching and Teacher Education* 25, no. 3: 409–14.

Erulkar, A., A. Ferede, W. Girma, and W. Ambelu. 2013. "Valuation of 'Biruh Tesfa' (Bright Future) HIV Prevention Program for Vulnerable Girls in Ethiopia." *Vulnerable Child and Youth Studies* 8, no. 2: 182–92.

Erulkar, Annabel, and Girmay Medhin. 2014. *Evaluation of Health and Education Impacts of a Girls' Safe Spaces Program in Addis Ababa, Ethiopia*. Addis Ababa: Population Council.

Eschenbacher, Heidi. 2011. *CARE Bangladesh Girls' Education and Leadership Evaluation Innovation through Sport: Promoting Leaders, Empowering Youth*. Final evaluation report. Saint Paul: Miske Witt.

Esiobu, G. O. 2011. "Achieving Gender Equity in science class: Shift from Competition to Cooperative Learning." *Multicultural Education and Technology Journal* 5, no. 4: 244–57.

Ethiopian Ministry of Education. 1980. *Gender Analysis of Primary School Textbooks*. Addis Ababa: Ethiopian Ministry of Education.

Evans, David, Michael Kremer, and Muthoni Ngatia. 2008. "The Impact of Distributing School Uniforms on Children's Education in Kenya." Poverty Action Lab. http://www.povertyactionlab.org/publication/impact-distributing-school-uniforms-childrens-education-kenya.

FAWE (Forum for African Women Educationalists). 2001. "Girls' Education and Poverty Eradication: FAWE's Response." Presentation to the Third United Nations Conference on the Least Developed Countries, Brussels, May 10–20.

———..FAWE. (2009). "Centres of Excellence." http://fawe.org/activities/interventions/COEs/index.php.

Ferre, Celine. 2009. *Age at First Child: Does Education Delay Fertility Timing? The Case of Kenya*. Policy Research Working Paper 4833. Washington: World Bank.

Fewer, Sarah, Josie Ramos, and Denise Dunning. 2013. "Economic Empowerment Strategies for Adolescent Girls: A Research Study Conducted for the Adolescent Girls' Advocacy and Leadership Initiative," Adolescent Girls' Advocacy and Leadership Initiative, Oakland.

FHI360. 2013. "Demand-Side Barriers to Girls' Secondary Education in Madhya Pradesh, India." FHI360, Durham, N.C. https://www.gov.uk/government/uploads/system/uploads/attachment_data/file/249722/W0704_Demand-Side-Barriers-Girls-Secondary-Education.pdf.

Filmer, Deon. 1999. *The Structure of Social Disparities in education: Gender and Wealth*. Policy Research Report, Gender and Development Working Paper 5. Washington: World Bank.

———. 2000. *The Structure of Social Disparities in Education: Gender and Wealth*. Policy Research Working Paper 2268. Washington: World Bank.

Filmer, Deon, and Norbert Schady. 2008. "Getting Girls into School: Evidence from a Scholarship Program in Cambodia." *Economic Development and Cultural Change* 56, no. 3: 581–617.

———. 2011. "Does More Cash in Conditional Cash Transfer Programs Always Lead to Larger Impacts on School Attendance?" *Journal of Development Economics* 96: 150–57.

Fleming, Paul J., Gary Barker, Jennifer McCleary-Sills, and Matthew Morton. 2013. *Engaging Men and Boys in Advancing Women's Agency: Where We Stand and New Directions*. Women's Voice, Agency, and Participation Research Series 2013, No. 1. Washington: World Bank.

Freeman, Matthew C., Leslie E. Greene, Robert Dreibelbis, Shadi Saboori, Richard

Muga, Babette Brumback, and Richard Rheingans. 2012. "Assessing the Impacts of a School-Based Water Treatment, Hygiene and Sanitation Programme on Pupil Absence in Nyanza Province, Kenya: A Cluster-Randomized Trial." *Tropical Medicine and International Health* 17, no. 3: 380–91.

Friedman, Willa, Michael Kremer, Edward Miguel, and Rebecca Thornton. 2011. *Education as Liberation?* NBER Working Paper 16939. Cambridge, Mass.: National Bureau of Economic Research. http://www.nber.org/papers/w16939.

Fuhriman, Addie, Bonnie Ballif-Spanvill, Carol Ward, Yodi Solomon, and Kacey Widdison-Jones. 2006. "Meaningful learning? Gendered experiences with an NGO-sponsored literacy program in rural Mali." *Ethnography and Education* 1, no. 1: 103-24.

Gachukia, E., W. M. Kabira, and M. Masinjila. 1992. *Meeting the Basic Learning Needs of Adolescent Mothers in Kenya: A Situation Analysis.* Nairobi: International Childhood Development Centre and UNICEF KCO.

Gajigo, Ousman. 2012. *Closing the Education Gender Gap: Estimating the Impact of Girls' Scholarship Program in the Gambia.* Working Paper 164. Abidjan: African Development Bank Group.

Gakidou, Emmanuela. 2013. *Education, Literacy, and Health Outcomes Findings.* Background paper commissioned for *EFA Global Monitoring Report 2013/4.* Paris: UNESCO.

Gakidou, Emmanuela, Krycia Cowling, Rafael Lozano, and Christopher J. L. Murray. 2010. "Increased Educational Attainment and Its Effect on Child Mortality in 175 Countries Between 1970 and 2009: A Systematic Analysis." *The Lancet* 376, no. 9745: 959–74.

GCE (Global Campaign for Education) and RESULTS Educational Fund. 2010. *Make It Right: Ending the Crisis in Girls' Education.* Johannesburg and Washington: GCE and RESULTS Education Fund.

GCPEA (Global Coalition to Protect Education from Attack). 2014a. *Draft Lucens Guidelines for Protecting Schools and Universities from Military Use during Armed Conflict.* New York: GCPEA. http://protectingeducation.org/sites/default/files/documents/guidelines_en.pdf.

———. 2014b. *Education Under Attack 2014.* New York: GCPEA.

———. 2015. *Lessons in War 2015: Military Use of Schools and Universities during Armed Conflict.* New York: GCPEA.

———. N.d. "Questions and Answers: On the Guidelines for Protecting Schools and Universities from Military Use." GCPEA, New York.

Gee, Kevin A. 2015. "Achieving Gender Equality in Learning Outcomes: Evidence from a Non-Formal Education Program in Bangladesh." *International Journal of Educational Development* 40: 207–16.

Gelli, Aulo, Ute Meir, and Francisco Espejo. 2007. "Does Provision of Food in School Increase Girls' Enrollment? Evidence from Schools in Sub-Saharan Africa." *Food and Nutrition Bulletin* 28, no. 2: 149–55.

Gertler, Paul, and Paul Glewwe. 1992. "The Willingness to Pay for Education for Daughters in Contrast to Sons: Evidence from Rural Peru." *World Bank Economic Review* 6, no. 1: 171–88.

Gertler, Paul, James Heckman, Rodrigo Pinto, Arianna Zanollini, Christel Vermeersch, Susan Walker, Susan M. Chang, and Sally Grantham-McGregor. 2014. "Labor Market Returns to an Early Childhood Stimulation Intervention in Jamaica." *Science* 344, no. 6187: 998–1001.

Gilmore, Julianne. 1997. *Phoenix Rising.* USAID Technical Paper 76. Washington: USAID.

Glewwe, Paul, Eric Hanushek, Sarah Humpage, and Renato Ravina. 2011.

School Resources and Educational
Outcomes in Developing Countries: A
Review of the Literature from 1990 to
2010. NBER Working Paper 17554.
Cambridge, Mass.: National Bureau of
Economic Research.

Glewwe, Paul, Nauman Ilia, and Michael
Kremer. 2003. Teacher Incentives.
NBER Working Paper 9671.
Cambridge, Mass.: National Bureau of
Economic Research. http://www.nber.
org/papers/w9671.

Glewwe, Paul, Michael Kremer, and Sylvie
Moulin. 2009. "Many Children Left
Behind? Textbooks and Test Scores in
Kenya." American Economic Journal:
Applied Economics 1, no. 1: 112–35.

Glewwe, Paul, Michael Kremer, Sylvie
Moulin, and Eric Zitzewitz. 2004.
"Retrospective vs. Prospective
Analyses of School Inputs: The Case
of Flip Charts in Kenya." Journal of
Development Economics 74: 251–68.

Glick, Peter. 2008. "What Policies Will
Reduce Gender Schooling Gaps in
Developing Countries: Evidence and
Interpretation." World Development 36,
no. 9: 1623–46.

Global Campaign for Education. 2010. Back
to School: The Worst Places in the
World to Be a School Child in 2010.
Saxonwold, South Africa: Global
Campaign for Education.

Gonsalves, Gregg S., Edward H. Kaplan,
and A. David Paltiel. 2015. "Reducing
Sexual Violence by Increasing the
Supply of Toilets in Khayelitsha, South
Africa: A Mathematical Model." PLoS
One 10, no. 4.

GPE (Global Partnership for Education).
2014. Cash Transfer Programs for
Gender Equality in Girls' Secondary
Education. Discussion paper. New
York: UNICEF.

———. 2015. Results for Learning Report
2014/2015: Basic Education at Risk.
Washington: GPE.

Grant, Monica J., and Frank F. Furstenburg
Jr. 2007. "Changes in the Transition

to Adulthood in Less Developed
Countries." European Journal of
Population 23: 415–28.

Grant, Monica J., and Kelly K. Hallman. 2008.
"Pregnancy-Related School Dropout
and Prior School Performance in
KwaZulu-Natal, South Africa. Studies
in Family Planning 39, no. 4: 369-82.

Grant, Monica, Cynthia Lloyd, and Barbara
Mensch. 2013. "Menstruation and
School Absenteeism: Evidence from
Rural Malawi. Comparative Education
Review 57, no. 2: 260-84.

Greene, Margaret Eleanor, O. Robles, K.
Stout, and T. Suvilaakso. 2013. A Girl's
Right to Learn without Fear: Working to
End Gender-Based Violence at School.
Woking: Plan International.

Groh, Matthew, Nandini Krishnam, David
McKenzie, and Tara Vishwanath. 2012.
"Soft Skills or Hard Cash? The Impact
of Training and Wage Subsidy on
Female Youth Employment in Jordan."
Development Research Group, World
Bank, Washington.

Groneman, Christine. 2011. Study on Field-
Based Programmatic Measures to
Protect Education from Attack. New
York: Global Coalition to Protect
Education from Attack.

Gyimah, Stephen Obeng. 2009. "Cohort
Differences in Women's Educational
Attainment and the Transition to
First Marriage in Ghana." Population
Research Policy Review 28: 455–71.

Haberland, Nicole A. 2015. "The Case of
Addressing Gender and Power in Sexuality
and HIV Education: A Comprehensive
Review of Evaluation Studies." International
Perspectives on Sexual and Reproductive
Health 41, no. 1: 31-42.

Haberland, Nicole, and Deborah Rogow, eds.
2009. It's All One Curriculum—Volume
1: Guidelines for a Unified Approach
to Sexuality, Gender, HIV, and
Human Rights Education. New York:
Population Council.

Hallman, Kelly, Marie Stoner, Michelle Chau,
and A. J. Melnikas. 2013. "A Review

of Control-Comparison Interventions on Girls and Health in Low- and Middle-Income Countries." Paper commissioned by Girl Hub, London.

Halperin, Daniel, Owen Mugurungi, Timothy B. Hallett, Backson Muchini, Bruce Campbell, Tapuwa Magure, Clemens Benedikt, and Simon Gregson. 2011. "A Surprising Prevention Success: Why Did the HIV Epidemic Decline in Zimbabwe?" *Plos Medicine* 8, no. 2: e1000414.

Hanushek, Eric A., Steven G. Rivkin. 2010. "Generalizations about Using Value-Added Measures of Teacher Quality." *The American Economic Review* 100, no. 2: 267-71.

Hanushek, Eric A., Guido Schwerdt, Simon Widerhold, and Ludger Woessmann. 2015. "Returns to Skills Around the World: Evidence from PIAAC." *European Economic Review* 73: 103–30.

Hanushek, Eric A., and Ludgar Woessman. 2008. "The Role of Cognitive Skills in Development." *Journal of Economic Literature* 46, no. 3: 607–68.

Hardman, Frank, Jan Abd-Kadir, Catherine Agg, James Migwi, Jacinta Ndambuku, and Fay Smith. 2009. "Changing Pedagogical Practices in Kenyan Primary Schools: The Impact of School-Based Training." *Comparative Education* 45, no. 1: 65–86.

Heady, Derek D. 2013. "Developmental Drivers of Nutritional Change: A Cross-Country Analysis." *World Development* 42: 76–88. doi:10.1016/j.worlddev.2012.07.002.

Heath, Rachel, and Mushfiq Mobarak. 2012. *Supply and Demand Constraints on Educational Investment: Evidence from Garment Sector Jobs and the Female Stipend Program in Bangladesh.* Working Paper 2(4). New Haven, Conn.: Yale School of Management.

Heckman, James; Seong Hyeok Moon, Rodrigo Pinto, Peter A. Savalyev, and Adam Yavitz. 2010. "The Rate of Return to the HighScope Perry Preschool Program." *Journal of Public Economics* 94: 114–28.

Heckman, James J., Jora Stixrud, and Sergio Urzua. 2006. *The Effects of Cognitive and Noncognitive Abilities on Labor Market Outcomes and Social Behavior.* NBER Working Paper 12006. Cambridge, Mass.: National Bureau of Economic Research.

Heise, Lori, Mary Elsberg, and Megan Gottemoeller. 1999. *Ending Violence against Women.* Population Report L11, Population Information Program. Baltimore: Johns Hopkins University School of Public Health.

Herz, Barbara. 2002. *Universal Basic Education: What Works.* Paper prepared for Coalition for Basic Education. Washington: Academy for Educational Development.

Herz, Barbara, and Gene B. Sperling. 2004. *What Works in Girls' Education: Evidence and Policies from the Developing World.* New York: Council on Foreign Relations.

Herz, Barbara, K. Subbarao, Masooma Habib, and Laura Raney. 1991. *Letting Girls Learn: Promising Approaches in Primary and Secondary Education.* World Bank Discussion Paper 133. Washington: World Bank.

Higgitt, R. 2011. "Women's Leadership Building as Poverty Reduction Strategy: Lessons from Bangladesh." *Journal of South Asian Development* 6, no. 1: 93–119.

Hill, M. Anne, and Elizabeth King. 1995. "Women's Education and Economic Well-Being." *Feminist Economics* 1, no. 2: 21–46. doi: 10.1080/714042230.

Hirsh-Pasek, Kathy, and Roberta Golinkoff. N.d. "Skills: The 6 Cs: Developing 21st-Century Skills." http://www.ultimateblockparty.com/download/the_6_Cs.pdf.

Hossain, M. A., and Rohani A. Tarmizi. 2012. "Gender-Related Effects of Group Learning on Mathematics Achievement among the Rural Secondary Students."

Eurasian Journal of Educational Research 47: 1–22.

House, Sarah, Thérèse Mahon, and Sue Cavill. 2012. *Menstrual Hygiene Matters: A Resource for Improving Menstrual Hygiene Around the World.* London: WaterAid.

ICF International. 2012. *STATcompiler: Building Tables with DHS Data.* Calverton, Md.: ICF International. Available at www.statcompiler.com.

ICRW (International Center for Research on Women). 2006. *Too Young to Wed: Education and Action toward Ending Child Marriage, Brief on Child Marriage and Domestic Violence.* Washington: ICRW.

———. 2014. *"I Wanted to Study with All My Heart": Unpacking Reasons for Girls' School Drop-Out in West Nile, Uganda.* Washington: ICRW.

———. 2015. *Are Schools Safe and Equal Places for Girls and Boys in Asia?* New York: Plan International.

IEG (Independent Evaluation Group). 2012. *World Bank and IFC Support for Youth Employment Programs.* Washington: World Bank.

IFPRI (International Food Policy Research Institute). 2005. *Women: Still the Key to Food and Nutrition Security.* Washington: IFPRI.

ILO (International Labor Organization). 2009. *Give Girls a Chance: Tackling Child Labour, a Key to the Future.* Geneva: ILO.

———. 2012. *Global Employment Trends for Women.* Geneva: ILO.

———. 2013. *Global Employment Trends for Youth.* Geneva: ILO.

———. 2014. *Promoting Equality and Addressing Discrimination.* ILO Policy Brief. Geneva: ILO.

———. 2015. "What Is Child Labour?" http:// www.ilo.org/ipec/facts/lang--en/index. htm.

ILO-IPEC (International Program on the Elimination of Child Labor). 2013. *Making Progress Against Child Labor:* *Global Estimates and Trends 2000-2012.* Geneva: ILO.

INEE (Inter-Agency Network for Education in Emergencies). 2010. *Minimum Standards for Education: Preparedness, Response, Recovery.* New York: INEE Coordinator for Minimum Standards and Network Tools.

———. 2015. *EiE Crisis Spotlight: Ebola—West Africa.* http://www.ineesite.org/en/ crisisspotlights/ebola-west-africa.

Inter-Agency Standing Committee. 2007. *IASC Guidelines on Mental Health and Psychosocial Support in Emergencies.* Geneva: Inter-Agency Standing Committee.

International Youth Foundation. N.d. "Gender Framework: Youth: Work Leader with Associates Award," unpublished document, International Youth Foundation, Baltimore.

IPEC (International Program on the Elimination of Child Labor). 2009. *Combating Child Labour through Education: A Resource Kit For Policy-Makers and Practitioners.* Geneva: International Labor Organization.

Irish Consortium on Gender-Based Violence. 2013. *Addressing School-Related Gender-Based Violence: Learning from Practice.* Learning Brief 10. Dublin: Irish Consortium on Gender-Based Violence.

Islam, Asadul, and Chongwoo Choe. 2009. *Child Labour and Schooling Responses to Access to Microcredit in Rural Bangladesh.* MPRA Paper 16842. Munich: Munich Personal RePEc Archive. http://mpra.ub.uni-muenchen.de/16842/.

Jafarey, Saqib, and Dibyendu Maiti. 2015. "Glass Slippers and Glass Ceilings: An Analysis of Marital Anticipation and Female Education." *Journal of Development Economics* 115: 45–61.

Jalan, Jyotsna, and Martin Ravallion. 2003. "Does Piped Water Reduce Diarrhea for Children in Rural India?" *Journal of Econometrics* 112, no. 1: 153–73.

Jalbout, Maysa. 2015. *Reaching All Children with Education in Lebanon: Opportunities for Action.* London: Their World.

Jameel, Abdul L. 2012. *Raising Female Leaders.* Policy Brief. Cambridge, Mass.: Abdul Latif Jameel Poverty Action Lab.

Jejeebhoy, Shireen J. 1998. "Wife-Beating in Rural India: A Husband's Right? Evidence from Survey Data." *Economic and Political Weekly* 23, no. 15: 855–62.

Jensen, Robert T. 2010. *Economic Opportunities and Gender Differences in Human Capital: Experimental Evidence for India.* NBER Working Paper 16021. Cambridge, Mass.: National Bureau of Economic Research.

———. 2012. "Do Labor Market Opportunities Affect Young Women's Work and Family Decisions? Experimental Evidence from India." *Quarterly Journal of Economics* 127, no. 2: 753–92.

Jewitt, Sarah, and Harriet Ryley. 2014. "It's a Girl Thing: Menstruation, School Attendance, Spatial Mobility, and Wider Gender Inequalities in Kenya." *Geoforum* 56: 137–47.

Jewkes, R., J. Levin, N. Mbananga, and D. Bradshaw. 2002. "Rape of Girls in South Africa." *The Lancet* 359, no. 9303: 319–20.

Johnson-Hanks, Jennifer. 2004. "Uncertainty and the Second Space: Modern Birth Timing and the Dilemma of Education." *European Journal of Population* 20: 351–73.

Jones, Amir, and Ruth Naylor. 2014. "The Quantitative Impact of Armed Conflict on Education: Counting the Human and Financial Cost." Protect Education in Insecurity and Conflict Project of CfBT Education Trust, Reading, UK. http://cdn.cfbt.com/~/media/cfbtcorporate/files/research/2014/r-armed-conflict-2014.pdf.

Kagitcibasi, Cigdem. 1992. "A Model of Multipurpose Nonformal Education: The Case of the Turkish Early Enrichment Project." Proceedings from the First International Council on Education for Women.

Kagitcibasi, Cigdem, Diane Sunar, Sevda Bekman, Nazli Baydar, and Zeynep Cemalcilar. 2009. "Continuing Effects of Early Enrichment in Adult Life: The Turkish Early Enrichment Project 22 Years Later." *Journal of Applied Development Psychology* 30, no. 6: 764-79.

Kang, N. H., and M. Hong. 2008. "Achieving Excellence in Teacher Workforce and Equity in Learning Opportunities in South Korea. *Educational Researcher* 37, no. 4: 200–207.

Karcher, Michael. J. 2008. "The Study of Mentoring in the Learning Environment (SMILE): A Randomized Evaluation of the Effectiveness of School-Based Mentoring." *Prevention Science* 9, no. 2: 99–113.

Karlsen, Saffron, Lale Say, João-Paulo Souza, Carol J. Hogue, Dinorah L. Calles, A. Metin Gülmezoglu, and Rosalind Raine. 2011. "The Relationship Between Maternal Education and Mortality Among Women Giving Birth in Health Care Institutions: Analysis of the Cross-Sectional WHO Global Survey on Maternal and Perinatal Health." *BMC Public Health* 11: 606.

Kautz, Tim, James J. Heckman, Ron Diris, Bas ter Weel, and Lex Borghans. 2014. *Fostering and Measuring Skills: Improving Cognitive and Noncognitive Skills to Promote Lifetime Success.* NBER Working Paper 20749. Cambridge, Mass.: National Bureau of Economic Research.

Kazianga, Harounan, Damien de Walque, and Harold Alderman. 2012. "Education and Child Labour Impacts of Two Food-for-Education Schemes: Evidence from a Randomised Trial in Rural Burkina Faso." *Journal of African Economies* 21, no. 5: 723–60.

Kazianga, Harounan, Dan Levy, Leigh L. Linden, and Matt Sloan. 2013. "The Effects of 'Girl-Friendly' Schools: Evidence from the BRIGHT School Construction Program in Burkina Faso." *American Economic Journal: Applied Economics* 5, no. 3: 41–62.

Kea, Pamela. 2007. "Girl Farm Labour and Double-Shift Schooling in the Gambia: The Paradox of Development Intervention." *Canadian Journal of African Studies* 41, no. 2: 258–88.

Khandkher, Shahidur. 1996. *Education Achievements and School Efficiency in Rural Bangladesh*. World Bank Discussion Paper 319. Washington: World Bank.

Khandker, Shahidur R., Mark M. Pitt, and Nobuhiko Fuwa. 2003. *Subsidy to Promote Girls' Secondary Education: The Female Stipend Program in Bangladesh*. MPRA Paper 23688. Munich: Munich Personal RePEc Archive. http://mpra.ub.uni-muenchen.de/23688/.

Kim, Booyuel. 2014. "The Impact of Girls' Education Support Program on Human Capital Development: Evidence from a Randomized Evaluation of Malawian Secondary Schools." Princeton University, Princeton, N.J. http://paa2015.princeton.edu/uploads/153404.

Kim, Jooseop, Harold Alderman, and Peter Orazem. 1998. *Can Cultural Barriers Be Overcome in Girls' Schooling? The Community Support Program in Rural Balochistan*. Working Paper on Impact Evaluation of Education Reforms 10. Washington: World Bank.

Kim, Julia, Giulia Ferrari, Tanya Abramsky, Charlotte Watts, James Hargreaves, Linda Morison, Godfrey Phetla, John Porter, and Paul Pronyk. 2009. "Assessing the Incremental Effects of Combining Economic and Health Interventions: The IMAGE Study in South Africa." *Bulletin of the World Health Organization* 87: 824–32.

King, Elizabeth, and Rosemary Bellew. 1991. "Gains in the Education of Peruvian Women, 1940–1980." In *Women's Work, Education, and Family Welfare in Peru*, edited by Barbara Herz and Shahidur Khandkher. World Bank Discussion Paper 116. Washington: World Bank.

King, Elizabeth M., and M. Anne Hill, eds. 1993. *Women's Education in Developing Countries*. Baltimore: Johns Hopkins University Press.

King, Elizabeth M. and Lee A. Lillard. 1987. "Education Policy and Schooling: Attainment in Malaysia and the Philippines." *Economics of Education Review* 6, no. 2: 167–81.

King, Elizabeth M., Peter Orazem, and Darin Wohlgemuth. 1999. "Central Mandates and Local Incentives: The Colombia Education Voucher Program." *World Bank Economic Review* 13, no. 3: 467–91.

King, Elizabeth, and Rebecca Winthrop. 2015. *Today's Challenges for Girls' Education*. Washington: Brookings Institution.

Kingdon, Geeta, and Mans Soderbom. 2008. *Education, Skills and Labor Market Outcomes: Evidence from Ghana*. Education Working Paper 12. Washington: World Bank.

Kirk, Jackie. 2004. "Promoting a Gender-Just Peace: The Roles of Women Teachers in Peacebuilding and Reconstruction." *Gender and Development* 12, no. 3: 50–59.

———. 2006. *The Impact of Women Teachers on Girls' Education: Advocacy Brief*. Bangkok: UNESCO.

———. 2009. *Certification Counts: Recognizing the Learning Attainments of Displaced and Refugee Students*. Paris: International Institute for Educational Planning.

Kirk, Jackie, and Rebecca Winthrop. 2005. *Changing the Gendered Dynamics of Refugee Classrooms in West Africa: Introducing Female Classroom Assistants*. New York: International Rescue Committee.

Klasen, Stephan, and Francesca Lamanna. 2009. "The Impact of Gender Inequality in Education and Employment on Economic Growth: New Evidence for a Panel of Countries." *Feminist Economics* 15, no. 3: 91–132.

Klugman, Jeni, Lucia Hanmer, Sarah Twigg, Tazeen Hasan, Jennifer McCleary-Sills, and Julieth Santamaria. 2014. *Voice and Agency: Empowering Women and Girls for Shared Prosperity*. Washington: World Bank.

Kluve, Jochen. 2010. "The Effectiveness of European Active Labor Market Programs." *Labour Economics* 17: 904–18.

Knight, John, Sharada Weir, and Tassew Woldehanna. 2003. "The Role of Education in Facilitating Risk-Taking and Innovation in Agriculture." *Journal of Development Studies* 39, no. 6: 1–22.

Koch, Elard, John Thorp, Miguel Bravo, Sebastián Gatica, Camila X. Romero, Hernán Aguilera, and Ivonne Ahlers. 2012. "Women's Education Level, Maternal Health Facilities, Abortion Legislation and Maternal Deaths: A Natural Experiment in Chile from 1957 to 2007." *PLoS One* 7, no. 5: e36613.

Kolev, Alexandre, and Nicolas Sirven. 2010. "Gender Disparities in Africa's Labor Market: A Cross-Country Comparison Using Standardized Survey Data." In *Gender Disparities in Africa's Labor Market*, edited by Jorge Saba Arbache, Alexandre Kolev, and Ewa Filipiak. Washington: World Bank.

Kondylis, Florence, and Marco Manacorda. 2012. "School Proximity and Child Labor: Evidence from Rural Tanzania." *Journal of Human Resources* 47, no. 1: 32–63.

Kostelny, Kathleen. 2008. *Starting Up Child-Centered Spaces in Emergencies: A Field Manual*. Richmond: ChildFund International.

Kothari, Brij. 2014. "Better Late Than Never." In *Education and Skills 2.0: New Targets and Innovative Approaches*, edited by World Economic Forum. Geneva: World Economic Forum.

Kothari, Brij, Avinash Pandey, and Amita R. Chudgar. 2004. "Reading Out of the "Idiot Box": Same-Language Subtitling on Television in India." *Information Technologies and International Development* 2, no. 1: 23–44.

Kothari, Brij, Joe Takeda, Ashok Joshi, and Avinash Pandey. 2002. *Same Language Subtitling: A Butterfly for Literacy?* Working Paper 2001-07-02. Ahmedabad: Indian Institute of Management.

Kremer, Michael, Conner Brannen, and Rachel Glennerster. 2013. "The Challenge of Education and Learning in the Developing World." *Science* 340: 297–300.

Kremer, Michael, Nazmul Chaudhury, F. Halsey Rogers, Karthik Muralidharan, and Jeffrey Hammer. 2005. "Teacher Absence in India: A Snapshot." *Journal of the European Economic Association* 3, nos. 2–3: 658–67.

Kremer, Michael, Edward Miguel, and Rebecca Thornton. 2009. "Incentives to Learn." *Review of Economics and Statistics* 91, no. 3: 437–56.

Kremer, Michael, Sylvie Moulin, and Robert Namunyu. 2002. *Unbalanced Decentralization: Results of a Randomized School Supplies Provision Program in Kenya*. Cambridge, Mass.: Harvard University.

Krishnaratne, Shari, Howard White, and Ella Carpenter. 2013. *Quality Education for All Children? What Works in Education in Developing Countries*. 3ie Working Paper 20. New Delhi: International Initiative for Impact Evaluation (3ie)

Kristof, Nicholas D., and Sheryl WuDunn. 2009a. Half the Sky: Turning Oppression into Opportunity for Women Worldwide. New York: Alfred A. Knopf.

———. 2009b. "The Women's Crusade." New York Times. August 17.

Lacey, Mark. 2003. "Primary Schools in Kenya, Fees Abolished, Are Filled to Overflowing." *New York Times*. January 7.

Laugharn, Peter. 2007. *Negotiating "Education for Many": Enrolment, Dropout and Persistence in the Community Schools of Kolondieba, Mali*. Create Pathways to Access Research Monograph 14. Brighton: Consortium for Research on Educational Access, Transitions, and Equity.

Lavy, Victor. 1996. "School Supply Constraints and Children's Educational Outcomes in Rural Ghana." *Journal of Development Economics* 51, no. 2: 291–314.

Lawn, Joy, Hannah Blencowe, Shefali Oza, Danzhen You, Anne C. C. Lee, Peter Waiswa, Marek Lalli, Zulfiqar Bhutta, Aluisio J. D. Barros, Parul Christian, Colin Mathers, and Simon N. Cousens. 2014. "Every Newborn: Progress, Priorities, and Potential beyond Survival." *The Lancet* 384, no. 9938: 189–205.

Lazear, Edward P. 2003. "Teacher Incentives." *Swedish Economic Policy Review* 10: 179–214.

Leach, Fiona, Máiréad Dunne, and Francesca Salvi. 2014. "School-Related Gender-Based Violence: A Global Review of Current Issues and Approaches in Policy, Programming, and Implementation Responses to SRGBV for the Education Sector." Background research paper prepared for UNESCO, New York. http://www.ungei.org/resources/files/SRGBV_UNESCO_Global_Review_Jan_2014.pdf.

Leach, F., V. Fiscian, E. Kadzamira, E. Lemani, and P. Machakanja. 2003. *An Investigative Study into the Abuse of Girls in African Schools*. London: UK Department for International Development.

Learning Metrics Task Force. 2013. *Toward Universal Learning: What Every Child Should Learn*. Montreal and Washington: UNESCO Institute of Statistics and Brookings Institution.

Lehman, Douglas. 2013. *Bringing the School to the Children: Shortening the Path to EFA*. Education Notes. Washington: World Bank.

Leon, Gianmarco, and Martin Valdivia. 2015. "Inequality in School Resources and Academic Achievement: Evidence from Peru." *International Journal of Educational Development* 40: 71–84.

LeVine, Robert A., Sarah E. LeVine, and Beatrice Schnell. 2001. "'Improve the Women': Mass Schooling, Female Literacy, and Worldwide Social Change." *Harvard Educational Review,* 71, no. 1: 1–50.

LeVine, Robert, and Meredith Rowe. 2009. "Maternal Literacy and Child Health in Less-Developed Countries: Evidence, Processes, and Limitations." *Journal of Development and Behavioral Pediatrics*. 30, no. 4: 340–49.

Lewin, Keith M., and Janet M. Stuart. 2003. "Insights into the Policy and Practice of Teacher Education in Low-Income Countries: The Multi-Site Teacher Education Research Project." *British Educational Research Journal* 29, no. 5: 691–707.

Lewis, Maureen, and Marlaine Lockheed. 2006. *Exclusion, Gender and Education*. Washington: Center for Global Development.

———.2008. *Social Exclusion and the Gender Gap in Education*. Policy Research Working Paper 4562. Washington: World Bank.

Lincove, Jane Arnold. 2009. "Determinants of Schooling for Boys and Girls in Nigeria under a Policy of Free Primary Education." *Economics of Education Review* 28: 474–84.

Lindelow, Magnus. 2008. "Health as a Family Matter: Do Intra-Household Education Externalities Matter for Maternal and Child Health?" *Journal of Development Studies* 44, no. 4: 562–85.

Lippman, Laura H., Renee Ryberg, Rachel Carney, and Kristin A. Moore. 2015. "Key 'Soft Skills' That Foster Youth Workforce Success: Toward a Consensus across Fields." Unpublished document, Child Trends Inc., Washington.

Liu, Li, Hope L. Johnson, Simon Cousens, Jamie Perin, Susana Scott, Joy E. Lawn, Igor Rudan, Harry Campbell, Richard Cibulskis, Mengying Li, Colin Mathers, and Robert E. Black. 2012. "Global, Regional, and National Causes of Child Mortality: An Updated Systematic Analysis for 2010 with Time Trends since 2000." *The Lancet* 379, no. 9832: 2151–61.

Lloyd, Cynthia B. 2013. "Education for Girls: Alternative Pathways to Girls' Empowerment." Integrated Approaches to Improving the Lives of Adolescent Girls Issue Paper Series. GirlEffect.org.

Lloyd, Cynthia B., and Barbara S. Mensch. 2008. "Marriage and Childbirth as Factors in Dropping Out from School: An Analysis of DHS Data from Sub-Saharan Africa." *Population Studies* 61, no. 1: 1–13.

Lloyd, Cynthia B., Barbara S. Mensch, and, Wesley H. Clark. 2000. "The Effects of Primary School Quality on School Dropout among Kenyan Girls and Boys." *Comparative Education Review,* 44, no. 2: 113–47.

Lloyd, C. B., and J. Young. 2009. *New Lessons: The Power of Educating Adolescent Girls—A Girls Count Report on Adolescent Girls.* New York: Population Council.

Lloyd, Cynthia B., Cem Mete, and Zeba A. Sathar. 2005. "The Effect of Gender Differences in Primary School Access, Type, and Quality on the Decision to Enroll in Rural Pakistan." *Economic Development and Cultural Change* 53, no. 3: 685–710.

Lloyd, Cynthia B., Sahar E. Tawila, Wesley H. Clark, and Barbara S. Mensch. 2003. "The Impact of Educational Quality on School Exit in Egypt." *Comparative Education Review* 47, no. 4: 444–67.

Lokshin, Michael, Elena Glinskaya, and Marito Garcia. 2000. *The Effect of Early Childhood Development Programs on Women's Labor Force Participation and Older Children's Schooling in Kenya.* Policy Research Report on Gender and Development Working Paper 15. Washington: World Bank.

Loughry, Maryanne, and Carola Eyber, eds. 2003. *Psychosocial Concepts in Humanitarian Work with Children: A Review of the Concepts and Related Literature.* Washington: National Research Council.

Loughry, Maryanne, Colin Macmullin, Carola Eyber, Behailu Abebe, Alastair Ager, Kathleen Kostelny, and Michael Wessells. 2005. *Assessing Afghan Children's Psychosocial Well-Being: A Multi-Modal Study of Intervention Outcomes.* Richmond: ChildFund International.

Lucas, Adrienne M., and Isaac M. Mbiti. 2012. "Does Free Primary Education Narrow Gender Differences in Schooling? Evidence from Kenya." *Journal of African Economies* 21, no. 5: 1–32.

Luschei, Thomas F., Amita Chudgar, and W. Joshua Rew. 2013. "Exploring Differences in the Distribution of Teacher Qualifications across Mexico and South Korea: Evidence from the Teaching and Learning International Survey." *Teachers College Record* 115, no. 5: 1–38.

Lutz, Wolfgang, and K. C. Samir. 2011. "Global Human Capital: Integrating Education and Population." *Science* 333, no. 6042: 587–92.

Madfis, Josh, Daryl Martyris, and Carl Triplehorn. 2010. "Emergency Safe Spaces in Haiti and the Solomon Islands." *Overseas Development Institute: Disasters* 34, no. 3: 845–64.

Madsen, Susan R. 2008a. *Developing Leadership: Learning from the Experiences of Women Governors.* Lanham, Md.: University Press of America.

————. 2008b. *On Becoming a Woman Leader: Learning from the Experiences of University Presidents*. San Francisco: Jossey-Bass.

————. 2010. "The Experiences of UAE Women Leaders in Developing Leadership Early in Life." *Feminist Formations* 22, no. 3: 75–95.

Makwati, Glory, Bernard Audinos, and Thierry Lairez. 2003. "The Role of Statistics in Improving the Quality of Basic Education in Sub-Saharan Africa." Paper presented at biennial meeting of Association for the Development of Education in Africa, Grande Baie, Mauritius, December 3–6.

Malhotra, Anju, Caren Grown, and Rohini Pande. 2003. *Impact of Investments in Female Education on Gender Inequality*. Washington: International Center for Research on Women.

Mansson, Alicia Borges, and Ulf Farnsveden. 2012. *Gender and Skills Development: A Review*. Background paper for the *EFA Global Monitoring Report 2012*. Working Paper 4. New York: UN Girls' Education Initiative.

Manzini-Henwood, Cebile, Nokwanda Dlamini, and Francis Obare. 2015. "School-Based Girls' Clubs as a Means of Addressing Sexual And Gender-Based Violence in Swaziland." *BMC Proceedings* 9 (supplement 4): A5–A7.

Martinez, Sebastian, Sophie Naudeau, and Victor Pereira. 2012. "The Promise of Preschool in Africa: A Randomized Impact Evaluation of Early Childhood Development in Rural Mozambique." Washington: The World Bank Group and Save the Children.

Martone, G. 2007. *Educating Children in Emergency Settings: An Unexpected Lifeline*. New York: International Rescue Committee.

Maswikwa, Belinda, Linda Richter, Jay Kaufman, and Arijit Nandi. 2015. "Minimum Marriage Age Laws and the Prevalence of Child Marriage and Adolescent Birth: Evidence from Sub-Saharan Africa." *International Perspectives on Sexual and Reproductive Health* 41, no. 2: 58–68.

May, Christina. N.d. *Evaluacion del proyecto "Hombres jovenes por la igualdad de genero": El Salvador, Guatemala, Republica Dominicana, Honduras y Alemania*. Washington: Plan International.

McAlister, Chryssa, and Thomas Baskett. 2006. "Female Education and Maternal Mortality: A Worldwide Survey." *Journal of Obstetrics and Gynaecology Canada* 28, no. 11:983–90.

Metzler, Janna, Robert Kaijuka, Marisa Vojta, Kevin Savage, Makiba Yamano, Alison Schafer, Gary Yu, George Ebulu, and Alastair Ager. 2013. *Evaluation of Child-Friendly Spaces: Uganda Field Study Summary Report*. London and New York: Save the Children, Columbia University, UNICEF, and World Vision.

Michaelowa, Katharina. 2001. "Primary Education Quality in Francophone Sub-Saharan Africa: Determinants of Learning Achievement and Efficiency Considerations." *World Development* 29, no. 10: 1699–1716.

Michau, Lori, Jessica Horn, Amy Bank, Malika Dutt, and Cathy Zimmerman. 2015. "Prevention of Violence Against Women and Girls: Lessons from Practice." *The Lancet* 385: 1672–84.

Michelo, Chris, Ingvild Sandoy, and Knut Fylkesnes. 2006. "Marked HIV Prevalence Declines in Higher Educated Young People: Evidence from Population-Based Surveys (1995–2003) in Zambia." *AIDS* 20: 1031–38.

Miguel, Edward, and Michael Kremer. 2004. "Worms: Identifying Impacts on Education and Health in the Present of Treatment Externalities." *Econometrica* 72, no. 1: 159–217.

Miller-Grandvaux, Yolande, and Karla Yoder. 2002. *A Literature Review of Community Schools in Africa*. Washington: USAID.

Miske, Shirley J. 2008. "Education Quality: Meanings and Measurement." Keynote speech at the CARE International Education Regional Advisory Committee Meeting, Johannesburg.

Miske, Shirley, and Joan DeJaeghere. 2013. "Measuring Gender and Educational Quality: The Need for Social Learning Outcomes." Paper presented at twelfth UKFIET International Conference on Education and Development, Oxford.

Miske, Shirley, Joan DeJaeghere, and Joyce Adolwa. 2012. "Equality at the Intersection of Gender and Poverty in Education: Conceptual and Methodological Considerations for Measurement." Background paper to the Global Thematic Consultation.

Miske Witt and Associates. 2007. *Transition to Post-Primary Education with a Special Focus on Girls: Medium-Term Strategies for Developing Post-Primary Education in Eastern and Southern Africa*. Nairobi: UNICEF.

———. 2011. *The Power to Lead Alliance (PTLA): Empowering Girls to Learn and Lead*. Final evaluation report for CARE USA. Saint Paul: Miske Witt and Associates.

Mlama, Penina, Marema Dioum, Herbert Makoye, Lornah Murage, Margaret Wagah, and Rose Washika. 2005. *Gender-Responsive Pedagogy: A Teacher's Handbook*. Nairobi: Forum for African Women Educationalists.

Mocan, Naci H., and Colin Cannonier. 2012. *Empowering Women through Education: Evidence from Sierra Leone*. NBER Working Paper w18016. Cambridge, Mass.: National Bureau of Economic Research. doi: 10.3386/w18016.

Moletsane, Relebohile. 2014. *The Need for Quality Sexual and Reproductive Health Education to Address Barriers to Girls' Educational Outcomes in South Africa*. Working Papers from the 2014 Echidna Global Scholars. Washington: Brookings Institution.

Moll, Amanda, Ginny Kintz, and Emily Janoch. 2015. "Empowering Girls Through Leadership Development: CARE's Model in Action. In *Educating Adolescent Girls Around the Globe: Challenges and Opportunities*, edited by Sandra L. Stacki and Supriya Baily, 118-38. New York: Routledge.

Montgomery, Paul, Caitlin R. Ryus, Catherine S. Dolan, Sue Dopson, and Linda M. Scott. 2012. "Sanitary Pad Interventions for Girls' Education in Ghana: A Pilot Study." *Plos One* 7, no. 1: e48274.

Morley, Steven, and David Coady. 2003. *From Social Assistance to Social Development: Targeted Education Subsidies in Developing Countries*. Washington: Center for Global Development and International Food Policy Research Institute.

Muralidharan, Karthik, and Nishith Prakash. 2013. *Cycling to School: Increasing Secondary School Enrollment for Girls in India*. IZA Discussion Paper 7585. Bonn: Institute for the Study of Labour.

Muralidharan, Karthik, and Ketki Sheth. 2014. *Bridging Education Gender Gaps in Developing Countries: The Role of Female Teachers*. NBER Working Paper 19341. Cambridge, Mass.: National Bureau of Economic Research. http://www.nber.org/papers/w19341.

Muralidharan, K., and Y. Zieleniak. 2014. "Cashing the Syllabus: Measuring Learning Trajectories in Developing Countries with Longitudinal Data and Item Response Theory." Working paper, University of California San Diego, San Diego.

Murnane, R. J., and A. J. Ganimian. 2014. *Improving Educational Outcomes in Developing Countries: Lessons from Rigorous Evaluations*. NBER Working Paper 20284. Cambridge, Mass.: National Bureau of Economic Research.

Murphy-Graham, Erin. 2008. "Opening the Black Box: Women's Empowerment and Innovative Secondary Education in

Honduras." *Gender and Education* 20, no. 1: 31–50.

———. 2010. "And When She Comes Home? Education and Women' Empowerment in Intimate Relationships." *International Journal of Educational Development* 30, no. 2010: 320–31.

Nafissatou, J. Diop, Amadou Moreau, and Helene Benga. 2008. *Evaluation of the Long-Term Impact of the TOSTAN Programme on the Abandonment of FGM/C and Early Marriage: Results from a Qualitative Study in Senegal.* Dakar: Population Council. http://www.popcouncil.org/uploads/pdfs/frontiers/FR_FinalReports/Senegal_TOSTAN_EarlyMarriage.pdf.

Nanda, Priya, Nitin Datta, and Priya Das. 2014. *Impact of Condition Cash Transfers on Girls' Education.* Washington: International Center for Research on Women.

Nascimento, Marcos. 2006. "Working with Young Men to Promote Gender Equality: An Experience in Brazil and Latin America." Eldis. http://www.eldis.org/fulltext/working-with-young-men-Jan2006.pdf.

Nguyen, Phuong-Mai, Cees Terlouw, and Albert Pilot. 2006. "Culturally Appropriate Pedagogy: The Case of Group Learning in a Confucian Heritage Culture Context." *Intercultural Education* 17, no. 1: 1–19.

Nguyen, Trang. 2008. "Information, Role Models and Perceived Returns to Education: Experimental Evidence from Madagascar." Abdul Latif Jameel Poverty Action Lab, Cambridge, Mass. http://www.povertyactionlab.org/doc/information-role-models-and-perceived-returns-education.

Ngware, Moses W., James Ciera, Benta A. Abuya, Moses Oketch, and Maurice Mutisya. 2012. "What Explains Gender Gaps in Maths Achievement in Primary Schools in Kenya?" *London Review of Education* 10, no. 1: 55-73.

Nicolai, Susan. 2004. *Learning Independence: Education in Emergency and Transition in Timor-Leste since 1999.* Paris: UNESCO International Institute for Educational Planning.

Nicolai, Susan, S. Hine, and J. Wales. 2015. *Education in Emergencies and Protracted Crises: Towards a Strengthened Response.* Background paper for the Oslo Summit on Education for Development. London: Overseas Development Institute.

Nicolai, Susan, and Carl Triplehorn. 2003. *The Role of Education in Protecting Children in Conflict.* HPN Network Paper 42. London: Overseas Development Institute.

Nkansa, Grace Akukwe, and David W. Chapman. 2006. "Sustaining Community Participation: What Remains After the Money Ends?" *International Review of Education* 52, no. 6: 509–32.

Obura, A. 1985. *The Image of Girls and Women in Primary Textbooks in Kenya.* Nairobi: University of Nairobi.

O'Donnell, Owen. 2007. "Access to Health Care in Developing Countries: Breaking Down Demand Side Barriers." *Cadernos de Saúde Pública* 23, no. 12: 2820–34. http://dx.doi.org/10.1590/S0102-311X2007001200003.

OECD (Organization for Economic Cooperation and Development). 2012. *Closing the Gender Gap: Act Now.* Paris: OECD.

———. 2013. *PISA 2012 Results: What Makes Schools Successful? Resources, Policies, and Practices (Volume IV).* Paris: OECD.

———. 2015a. *The ABCs of Gender Equality in Education: Aptitude, Behaviour, Confidence.* Paris: PISA and OECD. http://dx.doi.org/10.1787/9789264229945-en.

———. 2015b. *Skills for Social Progress: The Power of Social and Emotional Skills.* Paris: OECD. http://dx.doi.org/10.1787/9789264226159-en.

OHCHR (Office of the United Nations High Commissioner for Human Rights).

2015. "Background Paper on Attacks Against Girls Seeking to Access Education." http://www.ohchr.org/ Documents/HRBodies/CEDAW/ Report_attacks_on_girls_Feb2015.pdf.

Omoeva, Carina, Rachel Hatch, and Benjamin Sylla. 2014. *Teenage, Married, and Out Of School: Effects of Early Marriage and Childbirth on School Dropout*. Education Policy and Data Center Working Paper. Washington: FHI360.

O'Neil, T., G. Plank, and P. Domingo. 2015. *Support to Women and Girls' Leadership: A Rapid Review of the Evidence*. London: Overseas Development Institute.

ORC Macro International. 1995. *Demographic and Health Survey: Kenya*. Calverton, Md.: ORC Macro International.

Osili, Una Okonkwo, and Bridget Terry Long. 2008. "Does Female Schooling Reduce Fertility? Evidence from Nigeria." *Journal of Development Economics* 87, no. 1: 57–75.

Oster, Emily, and M. Bryce Millet. 2010. "Do IT Service Centers Promote School Enrollment? Evidence from India." *Journal of Development Economics* 104: 123–35.

Oster, Emily, and Rebecca Thornton. 2011. "Menstruation, Sanitary Products, and School Attendance: Evidence from a Randomized Evaluation." *American Economic Journal: Applied Economics* 3, no. 1: 91–100.

O'Sullivan, Margo. 2004. "The Reconceptualization of Learner-Centered Approaches: A Namibian Case Study." *International Journal of Educational Development* 24: 585–602.

Over, Mead. 1998. "The Effects of Societal Variables on Urban Rates of HIV Infection in Developing Countries: An Exploratory Analysis." In *Confronting AIDS: Evidence from the Developing World*, edited by Martha Ainsworth, Lieve Fransen, and Mead Over.

Brussels and Washington: European Commission and World Bank.

Oxfam. 2014. *Programming on the Right to be Heard: A Learning Companion*. Oxford: Oxfam.

Pande, Rohini, and A. Yazbeck. 2003. "What's in a Country Average? Wealth, Gender, and Regional Inequalities in Immunization in India." *Social Science Medicine* 57: 2075–88.

Pappas, G., A. Agha, G. Rafique, K. S. Khan, S. H. Badruddin, and H. Peermohamed. 2008. "Community-Based Approaches to Combating Malnutrition and Poor Education Among Girls in Resource-Poor Settings: Report of a Large-Scale Intervention in Pakistan." *Rural and Remote Health* 8, no. 3: 8–20.

Parkes, Jenny, and Jo Heslop. 2011. *Stop Violence Against Girls in School: A Cross-Country Analysis of Change in Ghana, Kenya and Mozambique*. Johannesburg: ActionAid International.

Parkes, Jenny, Jo Heslop, Samwel Oando, Susan Sbaa, Francisco Januario, and Asmara Figue. 2013. "Conceptualising Gender and Violence in Research: Insights from Studies in Schools and Communities in Kenya, Ghana and Mozambique." *International Journal of Educational Development* 33, no. 6: 546–56.

Partnership for 21st-Century Skills. 2011. *Framework for 21st Century Learning*. Washington: Partnership for 21st-Century Skills.

Patrinos, Harry A. 2008. "Returns to Education: The Gender Perspective." In *Girls' Education in the 21st Century: Gender Equality, Empowerment, and Economic Growth*, edited by Mercy Tembon and Lucia Fort. Washington: World Bank.

Patrinos, Harry, and Claudio E. Montenegro. 2014. *Comparable Estimates of Returns to Schooling Around the World*. World Bank Policy Research Working Paper 7020. Washington: World Bank.

Peacock, Dean, and Gary Barker. 2014. "Working with Men and Boys to Prevent Gender-Based Violence: Principles, Lessons Learned, and Ways Forward." *Men and Masculinities* 17, no. 5: 578–99.

Perlman Robinson, J. 2011. *The Global Compact on Learning: Taking Action on Education in Developing Countries.* Washington: Brookings Institution.

Pettifor, Audrey E., Brooke A. Levandowski, Catherine MacPhail, Nancy S. Padian, Myron S. Cohen, and Helen V. Rees. 2008. "Keep Them in School: The Importance of Education as a Protective Factor Against HIV Infection Among Young South African Women." *International Journal of Epidemiology* 37, no. 6: 1266–73.

Pettifor, Audrey, Eboni Taylor, David Nku, Sandra Duvall, Martine Tabala, Steve Meshnick, and Frieda Behets. 2008. "Bed Net Ownership, Use and Perceptions Among Women Seeking Antenatal Care in Kinshasa, Democratic Republic of the Congo (DRC): Opportunities for Improved Maternal and Child Health." *BMC Public Health* 8: 331.

Piper, Benjamin, and Medina Korda. 2010. *EGRA Plus: Liberia.* Program Evaluation Report. Research Triangle Park, NC: RTI International.

Plan International. 2008. *Paying the Price: The Economic Cost of Failing to Educate Girls.* Woking, UK: Plan International.

———. 2013a. *Girls' Learning: Investigating the Classroom Practices That Promote Girls' Learning.* Woking, UK: Plan International.

———. 2013b. *Include Us! A Study of Disability among Plan International's Sponsored Children.* Woking, UK: Plan International.

Planet Read. N.d. "Same-Language Subtitling (SLS) Project: Some Key Research Findings." Unpublished project document. http://www.planetread.org/pdf/Research%20Summary_SLS.

Population Council. 2012. *Female Disadvantage in the Egyptian Labor Market: A Youth Perspective.* SYPE Policy Brief 4. Cairo: Population Council.

Pradhan, Menno, Daniel Suryadarma, Amanda Beatty, Maisy Wong, Armida Alishjabana, Arya Gaduh, and Rima Prama Artha. 2014. "Improving Educational Quality through Enhancing Community Participation: Results from a Randomized Field Experiment in Indonesia." *American Economic Journal: Applied Economics* 6, no. 2: 105–26.

Prinsloo, S. 2006. "Sexual Harassment and Violence in South African Schools." *South African Journal of Education* 26, no. 2: 305–18.

Pritchett, Lant. 2014. *The Rebirth of Education: Schooling Ain't Learning.* Washington: Center for Global Development.

Pritchett, Lant, and Amanda Beatty. 2015. "Slow Down, You're Going Too Fast: Matching Curricula to Student Skill Levels." *International Journal of Educational Development* 40: 276–88.

Psacharopoulos, George, and Harry Anthony Patrinos. 2004. "Returns to Investment in Education: A Further Update." *Education Economics* 12, no. 2: 111–34.

Psaki, Stephanie. 2015. "Does Pregnancy Really Cause Girls to Drop Out of School?" Population Council. http://www.popcouncil.org/news/does-pregnancy-really-cause-girls-to-drop-out-of-school.

Psaki, Stephanie, Erica Soler-Hampejsek, Barbara Mensch, Christina A. Kelly, Monica Grant, and Paul C. Hewett. 2014. "The effect of gender-related aspects of school quality on schoolgirl pregnancy in rural Malawi. http://paa2014.princeton.edu/papers/142615.

Pulerwitz, Julie, Lindsay Hughes, Manisha Mehta, Akiliu Kidanu, Fablo Verani, and Samuel Tewolde. 2015. "Changing Gender Norms and Reducing Intimate

Partner Violence: Results from a Quasi-Experimental Intervention Study with Young Men in Ethiopia." *American Journal of Public Health* 105, no. 1: 132–37.

Queen, Emily Forsyth, Lorena Gonzalez, and Shannon Meehan. 2015. "Doorways: Preventing and Responding to School-Related, Gender-Based Violence in West Africa." In *Educating Adolescent Girls Around the Globe: Challenges and Opportunities*, edited by Sandra L. Stacki and Supriya Baily, 96-117. New York: Routledge.

Quisumbing, Agnes. 1996. "Male–Female Differences in Agricultural Productivity: Methodological Issues and Empirical Evidence." *World Development* 24, no. 10: 1579–95.

Quisumbing, Agnes R., Jere Behrman, Alexis Murphy, and Kathryn Yount. 2010. *Mothers' Human Capital and the Intergenerational Transmission of Poverty: The Impact of Mothers' Intellectual Human Capital and Long-Run Nutritional Status on Children's Human Capital in Guatemala*. Chronic Poverty Research Centre Working Paper 160 and IFPRI Discussion Paper 12-4. Washington: International Food Policy Research Institute. http://dx.doi.org/10.2139/ssrn.1719646.

Raftree, Linda. 2015. "Landscape Review: Mobiles for Youth Workforce Development." MasterCard Foundation. http://www.meducationalliance.org/sites/default/files/landscape_review_final.pdf.

Raj, Anita. 2010. "When the Mother Is a Child: The Impact of Child Marriage on Health and Human Rights of Girls." *Archives of Diseases in Childhood* 95: 931–35.

Raj, S. N. Rajesh; Kunal Sen, Vinod B. Annigeri, Arun K. Kulkarni, and D. R. Revankar. 2015. "Joyful Learning? The Effects of a School Intervention on Learning Outcomes in Karnataka." *International Journal of Educational Development* 40: 183–95.

Rankin, Bruce H., and Isik A. Aytac. 2006. "Gender Inequality in Schooling: The Case of Turkey." *Sociology of Education* 79, no. 1: 25–43.

Rawal, Shenila, and Geeta Kingdon. 2010. *Akin to My Teacher: Does Caste, Religious, or Gender Distance Between Student and Teacher Matter? Some Evidence from India*. Department of Quantitative Social Science Working Paper 10-18. London: Institute of Education of University of London.

Raynore, Janet, and Kate Wesson. 2006. "The Girls' Stipend Program in Bangladesh." *Journal of Education for International Development* 2, no. 2. http://www.equip123.net/JEID/articles/3/Girls'StipendPrograminBangladesh.pdf.

Reilly, A. 2014. "Adolescent Girls' Experiences of Violence in School in Sierra Leone and the Challenges to Sustainable Change." *Gender and Development* 22, no. 1: 13–29.

Results for Development Institute. 2015. *Bringing Learning to Light: The Role of Citizen-Led Assessments in Shifting the Education Agenda*. Washington: Results for Development Institute.

Reyes, J. 2013. *What Matters Most for Students in Contexts of Adversity: A Framework Paper*. Washington: World Bank.

Ricardo, Christine, Marcos Nascimento, Vanessa Fonseca, and Marcio Segundo. 2010. *Program H and Program M: Engaging Young Men and Empowering Young Women to Promote Gender Equality and Health*. PAHO / Best Practices in Gender and Health. Washington: Pan American Health Organization and Promundo. http://promundo.org.br/wp-content/uploads/2014/12/Program-H-and-Program-M-Evaluation.pdf.

Ridker, Ronald G., ed. 1997. *Determinants of Educational Achievement and Attainment in Africa: Findings from Nine Case Studies*. SD Publication Series, Technical Paper 62. Washington: USAID.

Romaine, Suzanne. 2013. "Keeping the Promise of the Millennium Development Goals: Why Language Matters." *Applied Linguistics Review* 4, no. 1: 1–21.

Room to Read. 2015. *School Libraries Cross-National Evaluation.* San Francisco: Room to Read.

Rowlands, J. 1997. *Questioning Empowerment: Working with Women in Honduras.* Oxford: Oxfam.

Rugh, Andrea. 2000. *Starting Now: Strategies for Helping Girls Complete Primary.* SAGE Project. Washington: Academy for Educational Development.

Rugh, Andrea, and Heather Bossert. 1998. *Involving Communities: Participation in the Delivery of Education Programs.* Washington: USAID.

Sabarwal, Shwetlena, David K. Evans, and Anastasia Marshak. 2014. *The Permanent Input Hypothesis: The Case of Textbooks and (No) Student Learning in Sierra Leone.* Policy Research Working Paper 7021. Washington: World Bank.

Sadker, David, and Karen Zittleman. 2007. "Gender Bias from Colonial America to Today's Classrooms." In *Multicultural Education: Issues and Perspectives*, edited by James A. Banks and Cherry A. McGee Banks. Hoboken, NJ: John Wiley and Sons.

Sahni, Urvashi. 2012. *From Learning Outcomes to Life Outcomes: What Can You Do and Who Can You Be? A Case Study in Girls' Education in India.* Working Paper 4. Washington: Brookings Institution.

Saito, Katrine, Hailu Mekonnen, and Daphne Spurling, 1994. *Raising the Productivity of Women Farmers in Sub-Saharan Africa.* World Bank Discussion Paper 230. Washington: World Bank.

Santhya, K. G., A. J. Francis Zavier, and Shireen J. Jejeebhoy. 2015. "School Quality and Its Association with Agency and Academic Achievements in Girls and Boys in Secondary Schools: Evidence from Bihar, India." *International Journal of Educational Development* 41: 35–46.

Santos, Indira, Iffath Sharif, Hossain Zilur Rahman, and Hassan Zaman. 2011. *How Do the Poor Cope with Shocks in Bangladesh? Evidence from Survey Data.* Policy Research Working Paper 1810. Washington: World Bank.

Save the Children. 2000. *What's the Difference? The Impact of Early Childhood Development Programs.* Kathmandu: Save the Children.

Scales, Peter C., Peter L. Benson, Kathlee Fraher, Amy K. Syvertsen, Larry Desrhem, Raphael Makonnen, Shahana Nazneen, and Sarah Titus. 2013. "Building Developmental Assets to Empower Adolescent Girls in Rural Bangladesh: Evaluation of Project Kishoree Kontha." *Journal of Research on Adolescence* 23, no. 1: 171–84.

Scheuermann, A. K. 2013. *Equity in Education in Nepal: Spotlight on Access, Attainment and Retention.* Kathmandu: UNICEF Nepal Country Office.

Schuelka, Matthew, and Christopher J. Johnstone. 2011. "Global Trends in Meeting the Educational Rights of Children with Disabilities: From International Institutions to Local Responses." *Reconsidering Development* 2, no. 2. http://reconsideringdevelopment. org/issues/iii/global-trends-in-meeting-the-educational-rights-of-children-with-disabilities/.

Schultz, T. Paul. 1992. "Investments in Schooling and Health of Women and Men: Quantities and Returns." Paper prepared for Conference on Women's Human Capital and Development, May, Bellagio, Italy.

———. 1993. "Returns to Women's Schooling." In *Women's Education in Developing Countries: Barriers, Benefits, and Policy*, edited by Elizabeth King and M. Anne Hill. Baltimore: Johns Hopkins University Press.

———. 1995. *Investment in Women's Human Capital.* Chicago: University of Chicago Press.

———. 2002. "Why Governments Should Invest More to Educate Girls." *World Development* 30, no. 2: 207–25.

———. 2004. "School Subsidies for the Poor: Evaluating the Mexican PROGRESA Poverty Program." *Journal of Development Economics* 74: 199–250.

Schurmann, Anna T. 2009. "Review of the Bangladesh Female Secondary School Stipend Project Using a Social Exclusion Framework." *Journal of Health, Population and Nutrition* 27, no. 4: 505–17.

Schweisfurth, Michele. 2011. "Learner-Centred Education in Developing Country Contexts: From Solution to Problem?" *International Journal of Educational Development* 31, no. 5: 425–32.

Seged, A., A. Beyenne, T. Dubale, B. Fuller, S. Holloway, and E. King. 1991. "What Factors Shape Girls' School Performance? Evidence from Ethiopia." *International Journal of Educational Development* 11, no. 2: 107–18.

Sen, Amartya. 2000. *Development as Freedom.* New York: Anchor Books.

Sen, Purna. 1999. "Enhancing Women's Choices in Responding to Domestic Violence in Calcutta: A Comparison of Employment and Education." *European Journal of Development Research* 11, no. 2: 65–86.

Serbessa, Derebssa Dufera. 2006. "Tension between Traditional And Modern Teaching-Learning Approaches in Ethiopian primary Schools." *Journal of International Cooperation in Education* 9, no. 1: 123–40.

Sigsgaard, Morten. 2012. *Conflict-Sensitive Education Policy: A Preliminary Review.* Doha: Education Above All. http://protectingeducation.org/sites/default/files/documents/eaa_conflict_sensitive_education_policy.pdf.

Simmonds, Shan. 2014. "Curriculum-Making in South Africa: Promoting Gender Equality and Empowering Women (?)." *Gender and Education* 26, no. 6: 636–52.

Sipahimanlani, Vandana. 1999. *Education in the Rural Indian Household: The Impact of Household and School Characteristics on Gender Differences.* Working Paper 68. New Delhi: National Council of Applied Economic Research.

Siri, Jose G. 2014. "Independent Associations of Maternal Education and Household Wealth with Malaria Risk in Children." *Ecology and Society* 19, no. 1: 33.

Slavin, Robert. E. 2010. "Can Financial Incentives Enhance Educational Outcomes? Evidence from International Experiments." *Educational Research Review* 5, no. 1: 68–80.

Smith, A., and T. Vaux. 2003. *Education, Conflict and International Development.* London: UK Department for International Development.

Smith, Lisa C., and Lawrence Haddad. 1999. *Explaining Child Malnutrition in Developing Countries: A Cross-Country Analysis.* IFPRI Food Consumption and Nutrition Division Discussion Paper 60. Washington: International Food Policy Research Institute.

Sommer, Marni. 2009. "Where the Education System and Women's Bodies Collide: The Social and Health Impact of Girls' Experiences of Menstruation and Schooling in Tanzania." *Journal of Adolescence* 33, no. 4: 521–29.

———. 2011. "An Early Window of Opportunity for Promoting Girls' Health: Policy Implications of the Girls' Puberty Book Project in Tanzania." *International Electronic Journal of Health Education* 14: 77–92.

Sommer, Marni, and Nana Mokoah Ackatia-Armah. 2012. "The Gendered Nature of Schooling in Ghana: Hurdles to Girls' Menstrual Management in School." *JENdA: A Journal of Culture and African Women Studies* 20: 63–79.

Sommer, Marni, and Mura Sahin. 2013. "Overcoming the Taboo: Advancing The Global Agenda for Menstrual Hygiene Management for Schoolgirls." *American Journal of Public Health* 103, no. 9: e1–e4.

Spencer-Smith, Garth, and Nicky Roberts. 2014. "Mobile Education for Numeracy: Evidence from Interventions in Low-Income Countries." GIZ. http://www.meducationalliance.org/sites/default/files/giz_landscape_review_long_version_final_1.pdf.

Sperandio, Jill. 2011. "Context and the Gendered Status of Teachers: Women's Empowerment Through Leadership of Non-Formal Schooling in Rural Bangladesh." *Gender and Education* 23, no. 2: 121–35.

Sperling, Gene. 2001a. "Educating the World." *The New York Times.* November 22, 2001.

———. 2001b. "Toward Universal Education: Making a Promise and Keeping It." *Foreign Affairs* 80, no. 5: 7-13.

———. 2006a. "Closing Trust Gaps: Unlocking Financing for Education in Fragile States." Paper Presented at the 4ᵗʰ FTI Partnership Meeting, Cairo, November 2006.

———. 2006b. "The Way Forward for Universal Education." In *Educating All Children: A Global Agenda*, edited by Joel E. Cohen, David E. Bloom, and Martin B. Malin. Cambridge: The American Academy of Arts and Sciences.

———. 2008. *A Global Education Fund: Toward a True Global Compact on Universal Education.* Working Paper. New York: Council on Foreign Relations.

Streissnig, Erich, Wolfgang Lutz, and Anthony Patt. 2013. *Effects of Educational Attainment on Climate Risk Vulnerability Ecology and Society* 18, no. 1: 16. http://dx.doi.org/10.5751/ES-05252-180116.

Stromquist, Nelly P., Molly Lee, and Birgit Brock-Utne. 1998. "The Explicit and the Hidden School Curriculum." In *Women in the Third World: An Encyclopedia of Contemporary Issues*, edited by Nelly Stromquist and Karen Monkman. New York: Garland.

Subbarao, K., and Laura Raney. 1995. "Social Gains from Female Education." *Economic Development and Cultural Change* 44, no. 1: 105–28.

Suleeman, Julia and I. G. A. A. Jackie Viemilawati. 2015. "Empowering Indonesian Street Girls: Processes and Possibilities." In *Educating Adolescent Girls Around the Globe: Challenges and Opportunities*, edited by Sandra L. Stacki and Supriya Baily, 159-77. New York: Routledge.

Summers, Lawrence H. 1994. *Investing in All the People: Educating Women in Developing Countries.* Washington: World Bank.

Sutherland-Addy, Esi. 2008. *Gender Equity in Junior and Senior Secondary Education in Sub-Saharan Africa.* Washington: World Bank.

Swarup, Anita, Irene Dankelman, Kanwal Ahluwalia, and Kelly Hawrylyshyn. 2011. *Weathering the Storm: Adolescent Girls and Climate Change.* London: Plan International.

Tadros, Mariz. 2014. "Engaging Politically: Rethinking Women's Pathways to Power." In *Women in Politics: Gender, Power and Development*, edited by Mariz Tadros. London: Zed Books.

Tayfur, Meltem Dayioglu, Murat G. Kirdar, and Ismet Koc. 2011. *The Effect of Compulsory Schooling Laws on Teenage Marriage and Births in Turkey.* IZA Discussion Paper 5887. Bonn: Institute for the Study of Labor. http://ftp.iza.org/dp5887.pdf.

Taylor, Bruce, Nan Stein, and Frances Burden. 2010. "The Effects of Gender Violence / Harassment Prevention Programming in Middle Schools: A Randomized Experimental Evaluation." *Violence and Victims* 25, no. 2: 202–23.

Thompson, Hannah. 2014. *The Role of Communities in Protecting Education from Attack*. New York: Global Coalition to Protect Education from Attack.

3ie (International Initiative for Impact Evaluation). 2010. *Conditional Cash Transfer Programmes: A Magic Bullet to Improve People's Health and Education?* Impact Evaluation 01. New Delhi: 3ie.

Tietjen, Karen. 1999. *Community Schools in Mali: A Comparative Cost Study*. SD Publication Series Technical Paper 97. Washington: USAID.

Tomasevski, Katarina. 2003. *Education Denied: Costs and Remedies*. New York: Zed Books.

Toya, Hideki, and Mark Sidmore. 2007. "Economic Development and the Impacts of Natural Disasters." *Economics Letters* 94, no. 1: 20–25.

Ullah, Hazir, and Christine Skelton. 2013. "Gender Representation in the Public Sector Schools Textbooks of Pakistan." *Educational Studies* 39, no. 2: 183–94.

———. 2014. *Discussion Paper: Cash Transfers and HIV Prevention*. New York: UNDP.

UNESCO Institute for Statistics. (2012). International Standard Classification of Education: ISCED 2011. Montreal: UNESCO.

———. UIS StatCentre. Education Statistics. Retrieved July 21, 2015.

UNESCO. 2000. *Women and Girls: Education, Not Discrimination*. Paris: UNESCO.

———. 2005. *Guidelines for Inclusion: Ensuring Access to Education for All*. Paris: UNESCO.

———. 2007. *Education for All by 2015: Will We Make It? Global Monitoring Report 2008*. Paris: UNESCO.

———. 2011. *The Hidden Crisis: Armed Conflict and Education: EFA Global Monitoring Report 2011*. Paris: UNESCO.

———. 2012a. *Reaching Out-of-School Children Is Crucial for Development: UIS Fact Sheet No. 18*. Paris: UNESCO.

———. 2012b. *Youth and Skills: Putting Education to Work—EFA Global Monitoring Report 2012*. Paris: UNESCO.

———. 2014a. *Gender Summary: Teaching and Learning—Achieving Quality for All—EFA Global Monitoring Report 2013/4*. Paris: UNESCO.

———. 2014b. *School-Related Gender-Based Violence in the Asia-Pacific Region*. Bangkok: UNESCO.

———. 2014c. *Teaching and Learning: Achieving Quality for All—EFA Global Monitoring Report 2013/4*. Paris: UNESCO.

———. 2015a. *Education for All 2000–2015: Achievements and Challenges—Education for All Global Monitoring Report 2015*. Paris: UNESCO.

———. 2015b. "World Inequality Database on Education." http://www.education-inequalities.org/.

UNFPA (United Nations Population Fund). 2012. *Marrying Too Young: End Child Marriage*. New York: UNFPA.

UNGEI (United Nations Girls' Education Initiative), UNESCO, and EFA (Education for All). 2015. *School-Related Gender-Based Violence Is Preventing the Achievement of Quality Education for All*. Policy Paper 17. Paris: UNESCO.

UNHCR (United Nations High Commissioner for Refugees). 2014. *World At War: Global Trends, Forced Displacement in 2014*. Geneva: UNHCR. http://www.unhcr.org/556725e69.html.

UNICEF (United Nations Children's Fund). 2001. *Fourth Consolidated Report to the Government of Norway on the UNICEF African Girls' Education Initiative*. New York: UNICEF.

———. 2002. *Case Studies in Girls' Education*. New York: UNICEF.

———. 2003. *State of the World's Children 2004*. New York: UNICEF.

———. 2005. *State of the World's Children 2006*. New York: UNICEF.

———. 2008. *South Sudan: Progress Report for UNICEF's Education in Emergencies and Post-Crisis Transition Programme.* Juba: UNICEF South Sudan.

———. 2010. *Progress for Children: Achieving the MDGs with Equity.* New York: UNICEF.

———. 2011. *Guidelines for Child-Friendly Spaces in Emergencies.* New York: UNICEF.

———. 2013. *Children and Young People with Disabilities Fact Sheet.* New York: UNICEF. http://www.unicef.org/disabilities/files/Factsheet_A5_Web_NEW.pdf.

———. 2014a. *Levels and Trends in Child Mortality Report 2014: Estimates Developed by the UN Interagency Group for Child Mortality Estimation.* New York: UNICEF.

———. 2014b. *Philippines Humanitarian Situation Report.* Manila: UNICEF Philippines.

———. 2014c. *State of the World's Children 2015: Reimagine the Future— Innovation for Every Child.* New York: UNICEF.

———. 2015. "Nepal Earthquake: New Appeal for Children Amid Growing Need." United Nations Children's Fund. http://www.unicef.org/infobycountry/media_81729.html.

UNICEF Jordan Country Office. 2014. *A Study on Early Marriage in Jordan.* New York: UNICEF.

UNIGME (United Nations Interagency Group for Child Mortality Estimation). 2014. *Levels and Trends in Child Mortality Report 2014: Estimates Developed by the UNIGME.* New York: UNICEF.

UNPD (United Nations Population Division). 2011. *World Population Prospects: The 2010 Revision.* New York: UNPD. http://esa.un.org/wpp/Documentation/WPP%202010%20publications.htm.

United Nations. 2000. *The World's Women 2000: Trends and Statistics.* New York: United Nations.

———. 2014. *Millennium Development Goals Report 2014.* New York: United Nations.

United Nations Statistics Division. 2015. "Millennium Development Goals Indicators Database." http://mdgs.un.org/unsd/mdg/.

UNDP (United Nations Development Program). 2010. *Millennium Development Goals Report.* New York: UNDP.

Unterhalter, Elaine. 2012. "A Convenient Myth." In *Because I Am a Girl: State of the World's Girls 2012—Learning for Life,* edited by Plan International. London: Plan International.

Unterhalter, Elaine, and Jo Heslop. 2012. *Transforming Education for Girls in Nigeria and Tanzania: A Cross-Country Analysis of Endline Research Studies.* Washington: ActionAid.

Unterhalter, Elaine, Amy North, Madeleine Arnot, Cynthia Lloyd, Lebo Moletsane, Erin Murphy-Graham, Jenny Parkes, and Mioko Saito. 2014. "Interventions to Enhance Girls' Education and Gender Equality." Education rigorous literature review, UK Department for International Development, London. http://r4d.dfid.gov.uk/pdf/outputs/HumanDev_evidence/Girls_Education_Literature_Review_2014_Unterhalter.pdf.

USAID (US Agency for International Development). 2008a. *Are Schools Safe Havens for Children? Examining School-Related Gender-Based Violence.* Washington: USAID.

———. 2008b. *Safe Schools Program: Final Report.* Washington: USAID.

Uwezo East Africa at Twaweza. 2014. *Are Our Children Learning? Literacy and Numeracy Across East Africa, 2013.* Nairobi: Hivos/Twaweza.

Van der Gaag, Nikki. 2011. *Because I Am a Girl: The State of the World's Girls 2011—So, What about Boys?* London: Plan International.

———. 2013. *Because I Am a Girl: The State of the World's Girls 2013—In Double Jeopardy: Adolescent Girls and*

Disasters. London: Plan International.

Vandemoortele, Jan, and Enrique Delamonica. 2000. "Education 'Vaccine' against HIV/AIDS." *Current Issues in Comparative Education* 3, no. 1.

Vavrus, Frances. 2009. "The Cultural Politics of Constructivist Pedagogies: Teacher Education Reform in the United Republic of Tanzania." *International Journal of Educational Development* 29: 303–11.

Vavrus, Frances, Matthew Thomas, and Lesley Bartlett. 2011. *Ensuring Quality by Attending to Inquiry: Learner-Centered Pedagogy in Sub-Saharan Africa*. Fundamentals of Teacher Education Development 4. Addis Ababa: UNESCO International Institute for Capacity Building in Africa.

Vermeersch, Christel. 2003. "School Meals, Educational Achievement, and School Competition: Evidence from a Randomized Experiment." University of Oxford, Oxford. http://www.nuff.ox.ac.uk/users/vermeersch/schoolmeals.pdf.

Vikram, Kriti, Reeve Vanneman, and Sonalde Desai. 2012. "Linkages between Maternal Education and Childhood Immunization in India." *Social Science and Medicine* 75, no. 2: 331–39.

Wagner, Daniel A. 2014. "Mobiles for Reading: A Landscape Research Review." Washington: USAID. http://www.meducationalliance.org/sites/default/files/usaid_wagner_report_finalforweb_14jun25_1.pdf.

Walker, Jo. 2013. *Equal Right, Equal Opportunity: Inclusive Education for Children with Disabilities*. Global Campaign for Education and Handicap International.

Wamani, Henry, Thorkild Tylleskär, Anne Nordrehaug Åstrøm, James K. Tumwine, and Stefan Peterson. 2004. "Mothers' Education but Not Fathers' Education, Household Assets or Land Ownership Is the Best Predictor of Child Health Inequalities in Rural Uganda." *International Journal for Equity in Health* 3: 9.

Warwick, Donald P., and Haroona Jatoi. 1994. "Teacher Gender and Student Achievement in Pakistan." *Comparative Education Review* 38, no. 3: 377–99.

Warwick, Donald, and Fernando Reimers. 1995. *Hope or Despair? Learning in Pakistan's Primary Schools*. Westport, Conn.: Praeger.

Watanabe, Koichiro, Rafael Flores, Junko Fujiwara, and Lien Thi Huong Tran. 2005. "Early Childhood Development Interventions and Cognitive Development of Young Children in Rural Vietnam." *Journal of Nutrition* 135, no. 8: 1918-25.

Weinberger, Catherine J. 2014. "The Increasing Complementarity Between Cognitive and Social Skills." *Review of Economics and Statistics* 96, no. 5: 849–61.

Weir, Sharada. 1999. *The Effects of Education on Farmer Productivity in Rural Ethiopia*. Working Paper 99-7. Oxford: Centre for the Study of the African Economies.

Wells, Ryan. 2009. "Gender and Age-Appropriate Enrolment in Uganda." *International Journal of Educational Research* 48: 40–50.

Westbrook, Jo, Naureen Durrani, Rhona Brown, David Orr, John Pryor, Janet Boddy, and Francesca Salvi. 2013. "Pedagogy, Curriculum, Teaching Practices, and Teacher Education in Developing Countries: Education Rigorous Literature Review." UK Department for International Development, London.

Wheeler, David, and Dan Hammer. 2010. *The Economics of Population Policy for Carbon Emissions Reduction in Developing Countries*. Working Paper 229. Washington: Center for Global Development. http://ssrn.com/abstract=1824442.

WHO (World Health Organization). 1998. *Female Genital Mutilation*. Geneva:

World Health Organization.
———. 2011. *World Report on Disability.* Geneva: World Health Organization.

Winthrop, Rebecca. December 12, 2014. "Mobilizing Children's Rights, Supporting Local Leaders and Improving Girls' Education." PowerPoint presentation. Center for Universal Education, The Brookings Institution.

Winthrop, Rebecca, and Elena Matsui. 2013. *A New Agenda for Education in Fragile States.* Washington: Brookings Institution.

Winthrop, Rebecca, and Eileen McGivney. 2014a. *Raising the Global Ambition for Girls' Education.* Policy Paper 2014-05. Washington: Brookings Institution.

———. 2014b. "Top 10 List You Don't Want to Be One: Dangerous Places for Girls' Education," blog post, Center for Universal Education, Brookings Institution. http://www.brookings.edu/ blogs/education-plus-development/ posts/2014/09/23-dangerous-places- girls-education-winthrop-mcgivney.

———. 2015. *Why Wait 100 Years? Bridging the Gap in Global Education.* Washington: Brookings Institution.

Winthrop, Rebecca, and Marshall S. Smith. 2012. *A New Face of Education: Bringing Technology into the Classroom in the Developing World.* Brooke Shearer Working Paper Series. Washington: Brookings Institution.

Wodon, Quentin. Forthcoming. *Child Marriage and Education.* Washington: World Bank.

World Bank. 1996. *Improving Basic Education in Pakistan.* Report 14960-PAK. Washington: World Bank.

———. 1997. *Pakistan: New Approaches to Education—The Northern Areas Community School Program.* Washington: World Bank.

———. 2001. *Engendering Development through Gender Equality in Rights, Resources, and Voice.* World Bank Policy Research Report. New York: Oxford University Press.

———. 2011. *Learning for All: Investing in People's Knowledge and Skills to Promote Development—World Bank Group Education Strategy 2020.* Washington: World Bank.

———. 2012. *World Development Report 2012: Gender Equality and Development.* Washington: World Bank.

———. 2013. *Nepal Human Development Note: Access, Equity, and Quality in the Education, Health and Social Protection Sectors.* Report from Human Development Unit of South Asia Region. Washington: World Bank.

World Bank and International Finance Corporation. 2013. *Women, Business, and the Law 2014: Removing Restrictions to Enhance Gender Equality.* London: Bloomsbury.

WORLD Policy Analysis Center. 2015. "Facilitating Girls' Access to Quality Education: Global Findings on Tuition-Free and Compulsory Education." WORLD Education Database. http:// www.worldpolicyforum.org.

World Vision. N.d. "Harnessing Opportunities for Productive Education for the Girl Child." World Vision, Federal Way, Wash.

Yuki, Takako, Keiko Mizuno, Keiichi Ogawa, and Sakai Mihoko. 2013. "Promoting Gender Parity in Basic Education: Lessons from a Technical Cooperation Project in Yemen." *International Review of Education* 59: 47–66.

Zelezny-Green, Ronda. 2014. "She Called, She Googled, She Knew: Girls' Secondary Education, Interrupted School Attendance, and Educational Use of Mobile Phones in Nairobi." *Gender and Development* 22, no. 1: 63–74.

INDEX

absenteeism
    deworming and, 131
    menstruation-related, 133–35, 137–38
    student, 117, 131, 134–35, 137–38
    teacher, 129, 162
    See also menstruation; teacher incentives
accelerated learning programs, 234
    See also remedial learning
access
    and girls with disabilities, 233–34
    and marginalized girls, 231–35
    and/to quality education, 8, 9–10, 19, 109, 160,
        192–93, 196–200
    child care and, 149–50
    child marriage and, 126–27
    child-friendly spaces and, 182–85
    community schools and, 141–45
    flexible school schedules and, 146–47
    girl-friendly schools and, 147–50;
    hiring teachers and, 161
    in emergencies, 176–78, 179, 180–88
    preschool and, 149–50
    reducing direct, indirect, and opportunity costs
        and, 94, 107–11
    reducing time and distance to school, 138–40
    technology and, 238–41
    to credit, 24, 261
    to early childhood development, 150
    to health services, 34, 39, 42, 54, 58, 224
    to learning, 195–200, 205–11
    to power, 55, 56
    to primary education, 38, 145
    to secondary education, 103
    to water and sanitation, 130, 135
    universal, 9, 191
    See also cash transfers; child marriage; child-
        friendly spaces (general); community
        schools; costs of schooling: reducing; credit;
        distance to school; education in emergencies;
        employment: access to; empowerment: and
        education; girl-friendly schools; health:
        outcomes; inclusive education; nonformal
        education; quality learning; school fees:
        school fee abolition; technology and
        education
ActionAid
    Stop Violence Against Girls in School, 154, 157,
        158, 159
    Transforming Education for Girls in Nigeria and
        Tanzania (TEGINT), 154, 164, 228–29

active learning. *See* pedagogy
activity-based learning. *See* pedagogy
adolescent girls
    and secondary education, 11, 194–95, 225–30
    life skills training for, 262–64, 267–68
    technical training for, 246–47
    strategies for reaching marginalized, 11, 231–41
    unique needs of, 108, 130, 133–34, 136, 137
    See also absenteeism: menstruation-related;
        attendance: menstruation and; dropout:
        and adolescent girls; life skills training;
        menstruation; nonformal education; puberty
        education; return-to-school policies;
        secondary education; sexual and reproductive
        health education; technology and education;
        training; water, sanitation, and hygiene
        (WASH)
Adolescent Girls Empowerment Program (AGEP),
    158
    See also Department for International
        Development; Population Council; Zambia
Adolescent Girls' Voices. *See* Kishoree Kontha
Afghanistan, 3, 78, 83, 88, 89, 140, 181, 184, 185,
    215, 216, 249,
    See also Child-Centered Spaces program;
        community schools; Goldman Sachs 10,000
        Women Initiative; hot spots
Africa
    East, 97, 210, 236 (*see also* Tostan; Uwezo)
    North, 21, 53, 95, 96 (*see also* Middle East and
        North Africa)
    studies in/of, 24, 33–34, 47–48, 51, 138, 144,
        162–63, 164, 171–72
    Sub-Saharan, 24, 26, 27, 30, 31, 33, 35, 36, 44,
        45, 46, 48, 49, 50, 67, 69, 71, 72, 73, 74, 75,
        76, 78, 84, 86, 128, 132, 133, 161, 199, 205,
        224, 233 (*see also* Program H; World Food
        Program)
    West, 74, 188, 236 (*see also* Tostan)
    See also specific countries
African Girls' Initiative, 257
    See also UNICEF
agency, 52–53, 224, 262–63
agricultural productivity, 4, 17, 19, 22–24
Al-Abdullah, Rania, 225
al-Shabaab, 217
Ambassadors' Girls' Scholarship Program, 125
    See also Djibouti; Sierra Leone; USAID
Angola, 37, 78, 257
    See also African Girls' Initiative; hot spots

Bright Futures. *See* Biruh Tesfa
BRIGHT School, 147–49
    See also Burkina Faso; Millennium Challenge
      Corporation; USAID
Brighter Futures Program, 232
    See also Nepal; World Education
Brookings Institution, The
    Center for Universal Education (CUE), 5, 9–10,
      176, 193, 196, 203
    Echidna Global Scholars Program, 98, 176
    Global Compact on Learning, 9–10, 193, 196
    Learning Metrics Task Force, 203
Brown, Gordon, 97
    A World At School, 97
Brown, Sarah, 97
    A World At School, 97
Building Skills for Life project, 154–55
    See also Plan International; Sierra Leone
Building Young Women's Leadership through
    Sport, 266–67
    See also Department for International
      Development (DFID); Women Win
Burkina Faso, 30, 78, 88, 90, 123, 132–33, 147–49,
    156
    See also BRIGHT School; Centers of Excellence;
      hot spots
Business Process Outsourcing, 243, 249–50
    See also job recruiting services; India

Cabinet of the Government of Nepal
    Zones of Peace, 220
CAMA Network, 260–61
    See also Camfed
Cambodia, 78, 112, 116, 124, 133, 136
    See also Cambodia Education Sector Support
      Project Scholarship Program; *Girl's Puberty
      Book, The*; hot spots; Japan Fund for Poverty
      Reduction Scholarship Program
Cambodia Education Sector Support Project
    Scholarship Program, 112, 124
    See also Cambodia
Cameron, David, 99
    See also Department for International
      Development (DFID); Girls' Education
      Challenge
Cameroon, 48, 53, 78, 128, 257
    See also African Girls' Initiative; hot spots
Camfed, 141, 260–61
    CAMA Network, 260–61
    Learner Guide Program, 261
    See also Murimirwa, Angeline
Canada, 198
CARE
    Innovation through Sport: Promoting Leaders,
      Empowering Youth (ITSPLEY), 266–67
    Power to Lead Alliance, 267–68

cash transfers
    and delaying childbirth, 117
    and delaying early marriage, 126–29
    and reducing costs of schooling, 105, 108, 111–30
    and reducing HIV risk, 46
    conditional, 8, 112–16, 118–19, 120–28, 246–47
    design of, 112–13, 118–30
    in-kind, 113, 117, 118
    linked to behaviors, 112, 119–20
    unconditional, 119, 120–23, 126–27, 128–29
    unintended consequences of, 112–13
    what we know about, 119
    See also attendance; costs of schooling;
      enrollment: effect of reducing indirect and
      opportunity costs on; health: outcomes;
      scholarships; stipends; *and specific programs*
cell phones. *See* mobile phones
Center for Development and Population Activities
    Better Life Options, 262–63
    Choose a Future! Curriculum, 262–63
Center for Global Development, 61
Center for Universal Education (CUE). *See*
    Brookings Institution, The
Centers of Excellence, 149
    See also Burkina Faso; Chad; Forum for African
      Women Educationalists (FAWE);; Gambia,
      The; Guinea; Kenya; Madagascar; Rwanda;
      Tanzania; Uganda; Zambia
Central America, 257–58
    See also Sistema de Aprendizaje Tutorial (SAT);
      and specific countries
Chad, 72, 74, 78, 149, 180
    See also Centers of Excellence; hot spots
Champions of Change, 223
    See also El Salvador; Guatemala; Honduras;
      Latin America; Plan International
Chief Minister's Bicycle Program, The, 112, 118
    See also India
child care
    as barrier, 107, 129, 246, 250
    as solution, 105, 149–50, 211–12, 246
    See also costs of schooling: opportunity; early
      childhood development; preschool
Child Fund Afghanistan
    Child-Centered Spaces program, 185
child labor
    and schooling, 132, 231–32
    violence of, xix, 5, 191, 231–32
    See also International Labor Organization (ILO);
      marginalization: marginalized girls
child marriage
    and cash transfers, 126–28
    banning, 176
    effect of education on reducing, 4, 17, 18, 48–52,
      53, 212, 237
    impact on education completion, 51

Inter-Agency Network on Education in
Emergencies, The (INEE)
INEE Minimum Standards for Education, 179
Inter-Agency Standing Committee
IASC Guidelines on Mental Health and
Psychosocial Support in Emergencies, 178
International Center for Research on Women (ICRW)
Apni Beti Apna Dhan (ABAD), 126, 128
International Finance Corporation, 249
See also Goldman Sachs 10,000 Women Initiative
International Food Policy Research Institute
(IFPRI), 22, 43
International Labor Organization (ILO), 27
International Program for the Elimination of
Child Labor (IPEC), 231–32
International Training Center, 232
SCREAM Stop Child Labor Pack, 232
International Rescue Committee (IRC), 184
International Youth Foundation, 250–51
Iraq, 51, 72, 79, 81, 89
See also hot spots
Israel, 217
It's All One Curriculum, 136
See also Population Council

Jamaica, 79, 151
See also hot spots
Japan Fund for Poverty Reduction Scholarship
Program, 112, 116
See also Cambodia
job recruiting services, 243, 249–50
Jokko Initiative, 239–40
See also Tostan
Jordan, 51, 81, 225, 255
See also Al-Abdullah, Rania
Jóvenes en Acción (Youth in Action), 246–47, 249
See also Colombia

Karen Teachers Working Group, 218
See also Myanmar
Kenya, 22, 32, 24, 38, 43, 46, 78, 110, 112, 117, 127,
129, 131, 132, 134–35, 149, 158–59, 170, 200,
207–08, 209, 210, 238–39, 257, 266–67,
See also Centers of Excellence; Girls' Scholarship
Program (Kenya); Child Sponsorship
Program; hot spots; Innovation through
Sport: Promoting Leaders, Empowering
Youth (ITSPLEY); Stop Violence against Girls
in School (program); Uwezo
Kishoree Kontha, 212
See also Bangladesh; Save the Children
Kristof, Nicholas, 97–98
See also Half the Sky Movement

labor market. *See* employment
Laos, 79, 136
See also Girl's Puberty Book, The; hot spots

Latin America, 28, 33, 36, 47–48, 73, 76, 96, 143,
223, 224
See also Champions of Change; Escuela Nueva;
Program H; *specific countries*
latrines. *See* water, sanitation, and hygiene (WASH)
leadership
and sustainability of community participation,
175–76
development of, 56, 251, 254, 260–61, 263–64,
265–68
effect of women's leadership, 57, 58
political, 18, 54–58
teaching, 12
See also extracurricular activities; role models;
soft skills
leadership skills. *See* leadership
Learner Guide Program, 260–61
See also Camfed; Ghana; Tanzania; Zimbabwe
learning crisis, 75–77, 195, 196, 198, 210
See also learning outcomes
Learning Metrics Task Force, 203
See also Brookings Institution, The; UNESCO
Institute of Statistics
learning outcomes
as definition of quality education, 253
effect of community engagement on, 173–74
gender equality as a, 251–52
gender of teachers and student, 165
in mathematics, reading, and science, 75–76,
110, 198–200
numeracy, 236, 240, 253
teacher gender attitudes and, 171–72, 257
teacher training and, 170
test scores as measures of, 22
See also community schools: effect on learning;
hard skills; learning crisis; quality learning;
social learning outcomes; soft skills
Lebanon, xviii, 81
legal reforms
compulsory schooling, 128–29, 229
minimum marriage age, 128
military use of schools, against, 219–20
Let Girls Learn, 99
See also Obama, Michelle; USAID
Liberia, 79, 81, 169, 247
See also Economic Empowerment of Adolescent
Girls and Young Women (EPAG); EGRA
Plus; hot spots
life expectancy, 20, 60
life skills training, 144–45, 235–36, 247, 260–61,
262–64, 267
See also training
literacy
and empowerment, 50, 56–57, 238
and reduction of child marriage, 50
as pathway, 252–53
in everyday life, 238–41

Murimirwa, Angeline, 141
   See also Camfed
My Better World Curriculum, 261
   See also Camfed
Myanmar, 79, 218
   See also hot spots; Karen Teachers Working Group

Nagorik Uddyog (Bangladesh), 265–66
Nali Kali Program, 170–71
   See also India
natural disasters, 10, 79–80, 81, 105, 183, 187
   See also humanitarian crisis
Negotiating a Better Future, 262
   See also Zambia
Nepal, 50–51, 58, 81, 136, 137, 138, 150, 152, 217,
      220, 232
   See also Brighter Futures Program; *Girl's Puberty
      Book, The*; Zones of Peace
net enrollment ratio. *See* enrollment
New Zealand, 198
Nicaragua, 79, 124
   See also hot spots; Red de Protección Social
Niger, 79, 88, 172–73
   See also hot spots
Nigeria, xvii, 3, 10, 24, 36–37, 38, 67, 79, 82, 83, 89,
      90, 154, 164, 171, 193, 213, 215, 228–29, 257
   See also Boko Haram; hot spots; Transforming
      Education for Girls in Nigeria and Tanzania
      (TEGINT)
Nike Foundation, The
   The Girl Effect, 98, 99
noncognitive skills. *See* soft skills
nonformal education
   and development of soft skills, 212, 235
   examples of, 145, 162, 185, 235–37, 240–41
   features of, 234–35
   pathway to formal education, 142–43
   second chance schooling, 234–35
   See also child-friendly spaces (general);
      community schools; education in
      emergencies; flexible school schedules;
      refugee education
North Africa. *See* Africa
Norway, 55
   See also Solberg, Erna
numeracy
   and empowerment, 52, 238
   levels, 90, 198
   returns to, 26
   See also hard skills; learning outcomes

Obama, Michelle, 99
   See also Let Girls Learn
Occupied Palestinian Territories, 122, 217
Operation Blackboard, 165, 206
   See also India

Oportunidades, 112, 124
   See also Mexico
Organization for Economic Cooperation and
      Development (OECD)
   Education for Social Progress project, 204–05
   Program for International Student Assessment
      (PISA), 22, 228
   studies of OECD countries, 20, 26, 92, 205
out-of-school children
   numbers of, 66, 67, 69, 70–71, 80–81, 83, 85,
      86–87, 88, 94,
   reaching, 122, 231, 233, 235–36, 244, 260
   See also dropout
Overseas Development Institute, 79–81

Pacific. *See* Asia: Pacific
Pakistan, xvii, 3, 26, 27, 28, 37, 43–44, 46, 54, 67,
      72, 76, 79, 82–83, 112, 115–16, 127, 131, 142,
      146, 162–63, 165, 168–69, 176, 181–82, 200,
      207, 210, 215, 255, 260,
   See also Hussain, Khadim; hot spots; Project
      Hope; Punjab Female School Stipend
      Program; Yousafzai, Malala
Palestine. *See* Occupied Palestinian Territories
parateachers. *See* teachers
Partnership for 21st-Century Skills, 202
partnerships
   bilateral, 9–10
   from local to global, 210–11
   with communities, 172–76
pedagogy
   active learning, 143, 170
   activity-based learning, 256
   effective and engaging, 167
   gender-responsive pedagogy, 149, 171–72
   group-based learning, 263
   student-centered, 167–68
   teacher-centered, 167–68
perceived returns to education, 242–44
   See also returns to
Peru, 43, 87–88, 138
Philippines, The, 79, 187, 217
   See also Back-to-School Campaign; Bantay Cease-
      Fire Group; hot spots; Mindanao People's Caucus
Plan International
   Because I Am a Girl, 99, 223
   Building Skills for Life project, 154–55
   Champions of Change, 223
Planet Read, 240–41
   See also same language subtitling
political leadership. *See* leadership
Population Council
   Adolescent Girls Empowerment Program
      (AGEP), 158
   Better Life Options, 262, 263
   It's All One Curriculum, 136